The Battle for Hong Kong 1941–1945

Hostage to Fortune

Other books by Oliver Lindsay CBE FRHistS

The Lasting Honour: The Fall of Hong Kong 1941

At the Going Down of the Sun: Hong Kong and South-East Asia 1941–1945

A Guards General: The Memoirs of Major General Sir Allan Adair Bt (Editor)

Once a Grenadier: The Grenadier Guards 1945–1995

Whither Hong Kong: China's Shadow or Visionary Gleam? (with others)

THE BATTLE FOR HONG KONG 1941–1945

HOSTAGE TO FORTUNE

by

Oliver Lindsay

With the memories of John R Harris

SPELLMOUNT
Staplehurst

British Library Cataloguing in Publication Data:
A catalogue record for this book is available
from the British Library

ISBN 1-86227-315-4

First published in the UK in 2005 by
Spellmount Limited
The Village Centre
Staplehurst
Kent TN12 0BJ

Tel: 01580 893730
Fax: 01580 893731
E-mail: enquiries@spellmount.com
Website: www.spellmount.com

1 3 5 7 9 8 6 4 2

Printed in Great Britain by
Oaklands Book Services
Stonehouse, Gloucestershire GL10 3RQ

Contents

Acknowledgements x
List of Maps xi
Foreword xiii

Part 1: The Beat of Drums 1

1 The Beat of Drums 3

Part 2: When Time Was Young 11

2 When Time Was Young 13
3 The Outbreak of War in Europe 21
4 An Ocean of Change 29
5 Visions of Delight 35

Part 3: Remember Them with Pride 45

6 The Vulnerable Outpost 47
7 Battle Stations 59
8 Shingmun Redoubt: The Vital Ground 8th–10th December 1941 67
9 Nothing but Darkness Ahead 10th–13th December 1941 77
10 "Clay Pigeons in a Shooting Range" 13th–17th December 1941 85
11 Triumph or Disaster: The Japanese Landings 18th–19th December 1941 99
12 Hell's Destruction: 19th–20th December 1941 111

13 Slaughter and Manoeuvre: The Japanese Advance West and South 20th–24th December 1941 121
14 The Surrender of Hong Kong: Christmas Day 1941 135
15 Truth is the First Casualty in War 145

Part 4 Hostage to Fortune 155

16 Shamshuipo POW Camp and the Escapes 157
17 Argyle Street Officers' Camp 171
18 The Sinking of the *Lisbon Maru* 183
19 Operations Most Secret 189
20 The British Army Aid Group and Fresh Disasters 201
21 Sinister Developments: Stanley Internment Camp, the Japanese Occupation and the Privileged Nightmare 217
22 The Calm after Thunder: Returning Home 227
23 New Worlds to Find: An Architect At Last 235
24 Retribution 243
25 "Good and Gallant Leadership" 249

Bibliography 261
Despatches 263
War Diaries 263
Reports and Notes 263
Selected Articles 264
Diaries 264
Files 264
Websites 265
The Confusion of Events 265
Index 266

To all those Allies who fought and died in the Far East 1941–1945.

Each of them was a hostage to fortune.

"I submit that although I and my forces may have been a hostage to fortune, we were a detachment that deflected from more important objectives, such as the Philippines, Singapore, or perhaps even Australia, an enemy force that consisted of two first line divisions, one reserve division, corps artillery, about 80 aircraft, and a considerable naval blocking force. Strategically we gambled and lost, but it was a worthwhile gamble."

The post-war report of Major General Maltby CB MC
General Officer Commanding British Troops in Hong Kong in 1941

Acknowledgements

I am deeply grateful to John Harris for allowing me to edit his memoirs. I have known him for 25 years and have great admiration for him. His wife, Jill, gave me invaluable and astute guidance and support for this exciting project. I alone am responsible for any errors.

I must express my warmest thanks to Field Marshal Lord Bramall for writing the Foreword. I had the privilege of serving under him in Hong Kong in the mid 1970s. He has been a friend of John for many years too.

My scruffy, illegible drafts, covered by Tipp-Ex and confusing changes all stapled together, were turned into an immaculate format fit for the best of publishers. For this and more, I am greatly indebted to Marilyn Thompson, John's secretary.

Special thanks are due to my wife, Clare, for her love and patience, not only when I was researching and writing this book, but also over the last 40 years of our very happy life together.

I have been extremely fortunate in being able to interview over 100 veterans of the campaign and former civilian internees, largely in the late 1970s onwards. This book is their story. They faced bitter adversity. Nevertheless the story reflects some glorious deeds, great loyalty and proud endeavours. It has been a privilege to have the opportunity to write about them. I hope you enjoy the book.

Oliver Lindsay
Sherborne
August 2005

List of Maps

(Drawn by Denys Baker. For consistency, the spelling of place names has been kept to that of 1941)

1. Hong Kong and the Far East 5

2. Hong Kong and the New Territories 8th–12th December 1941 37

3. Hong Kong Island 90-1

4. Repulse Bay and Stanley Peninsula 126

Foreword

by Field Marshal The Lord Bramall KG, GCB, OBE, MC, JP

Volume I of the official history, *The War Against Japan* published back in 1957, devoted only 44 of its 568 pages to the defence of Hong Kong. This tended to obscure the fact that unlike some other defeats suffered, in those early years, by the Allies at the hands of the Japanese, no shame or disgrace whatsoever could be ascribed to the inexperienced, ill-equipped and often untrained British, Canadians, Indians and local Hong Kong garrison, when they heroically held up the overwhelming Japanese attack for nearly three weeks.

Now, to help put matters in their proper perspective and to coincide with the 60th anniversary of the liberation of Hong Kong, we have this new book by Oliver Lindsay. This is an authoritative, detailed and exciting account of the whole of the campaign using hitherto unpublished material.

In the 30 years that Oliver Lindsay has been studying the war as it affected Hong Kong and the events surrounding it, he has interviewed many of the survivors in Britain, Canada and in Hong Kong itself; he has been able to meet veterans in the Colony who could explain to him exactly what happened on the precise ground over which they fought. For many years he also ran battlefield tours for Servicemen in Hong Kong. All of this has given him a deep insight into the problems confronting the Canadian Brigade, the Royal Artillery, the Royal Engineers, the British and Indian Infantry Battalions, the Hong Kong Volunteers and some of the small Royal Navy and RNVR units, all of which had to face the ferocity of the Japanese attack as, later, did the nursing sisters who suffered appalling atrocities.

In the central part of the book Lindsay gives a graphic and revealing account of the 'nightmare' battle itself, leading to the surrender on Christmas Day 1941 of the first British Colony to fall to the enemy in the Second World War. All of which was indicative, he believes, of the fundamental weakness of democracies hoping above all things to avoid having to go to war, leading to deficiencies in force levels, equipment and training. But this informative book also contains the authentic, vivid and hitherto unpublished reminiscences of John Harris, a young architectural student who served in the Royal Engineers. He is the only survivor today of that small group of prisoners of war who smuggled secret information to and from the British intelligence organisation in China in 1943. They were operating with great gallantry under the very eyes of the inquisitive and brutal Japanese guards. The hardships and indignities of life in both the prisoner of war camps and the civilian internment camp were endured with fortitude and stubborn good humour despite the horrors of cholera, diphtheria and deficiency diseases. This throws new and heartrending light on the sacrifices made by those who defended Hong Kong.

Above all, this very readable book reflects supreme courage. I commanded the British forces in Hong Kong in 1970 and began to take a great interest in the battle that had been fought there 30 years before (pointing Oliver Lindsay in the direction of his subsequent research). I visited the military cemeteries there on a number of occasions and saw the graves of those who made the supreme sacrifice, including five recipients of the George Cross.

Those who read these chapters today can truly, I believe, remember those who fought and suffered in the defence of Hong Kong with considerable pride.

Dwin Bramall
Field Marshal

Part 1

THE BEAT OF DRUMS

by Oliver Lindsay

CHAPTER 1

The Beat of Drums

Hong Kong, Saturday 6th December 1941. The day of bright sunshine started no differently from any other relaxed weekend in the Colony's long history. Yet it turned out to be a day nobody there would ever forget.

The newly arrived Governor, Sir Mark Young, attended a fête at Christ Church in Waterloo Road. Happy Valley racecourse was crowded, as usual. The Middlesex Regiment played South China Athletic at football. In the evening at the massive Peninsula Hotel in Kowloon both ballrooms were packed for the 'Tin Hat Ball' which hoped to raise the last £160,000 to purchase a bomber squadron which the people of Hong Kong planned to present to Britain.

It could have been a typical weekend – but on that same day, following secret instructions from Tokyo, a large number of Japanese civilians left the Colony, most of them by boat to Macao and then on to Canton.

* * * * *

Some 3,700 miles to the east of Tokyo, Japanese midget submarines planned their approach to eight battleships of the American Pacific Fleet at anchor at Pearl Harbor. Beyond them lay another 86 American ships. The American aircraft nearby, and also in the Philippines southwest of Hong Kong, "were all tightly bunched together, wing tip to wing tip, for security against saboteurs," [1] despite orders to disperse them.

Some four weeks earlier, on 5th November 1941, Admiral Isoroku Yamamoto, the C-in-C Combined Fleet, was warned by Imperial Japanese Headquarters that war was feared to be unavoidable.

General Douglas MacArthur in Manila remained convinced that there would be no Japanese attack before the Spring of 1942. As the commander of the American and Filipino troops in the Philippines, and a man of immense prestige, few contradicted him.

The Japanese regarded the Philippines as a "pistol aimed at Japan's heart". An intercepted coded message from Emperor Hirohito's Foreign Office to the Japanese Embassy in Berlin referred to breaking "asunder this ever strengthening chain of encirclement which is being woven under the guidance of and with the participation of England and the United States, acting like a cunning dragon seemingly asleep". This was a surprising and rather silly claim because the Japanese had already seized every port on the Chinese coast except Hong Kong.

On 27th November the US Navy Department sent out a message which began most ominously. "This despatch is to be considered a war warning... an aggressive move by Japan is expected within the next few days... the number and equipment of Japanese troops and the organization of naval task forces indicates an amphibious expedition against either the Philippines, Thai or Kra Peninsula, or possibly Borneo."[2]

J C Grew, the US Ambassador in Tokyo, believed that the Japanese negotiations with the Americans in Washington were "a blind to conceal war preparations". He warned his Government that Japanese attacks might come with dramatic and dangerous suddenness. The Ambassador's estimate of the situation was confirmed by intercepted secret messages from Tokyo to Washington; they stressed the urgency of bringing the negotiations to a favourable conclusion by 29th November since "after that [date] things are automatically going to happen". Roosevelt gloomily concluded that America was likely to be attacked within a week.

On 29th November British, American and Dutch air reconnaissance was instituted over the China Sea; Malayan defences were brought to a higher state of readiness. The Japanese had earlier received intelligence of the arrival of the *Prince of Wales* and *Repulse* in the Far East.

All Japanese forces were notified on 1st December that the decision had been made to declare war on the United States, the British Empire and the Netherlands.

Four days later Admiral Sir Tom Phillips, the Commander in Chief of Britain's Eastern Fleet, flew back to Singapore from Manila after conferring with MacArthur and Admiral Tom Hart, MacArthur's naval counterpart. Phillips, who had four days to live, left empty-handed; the Americans could spare neither men nor weapons.

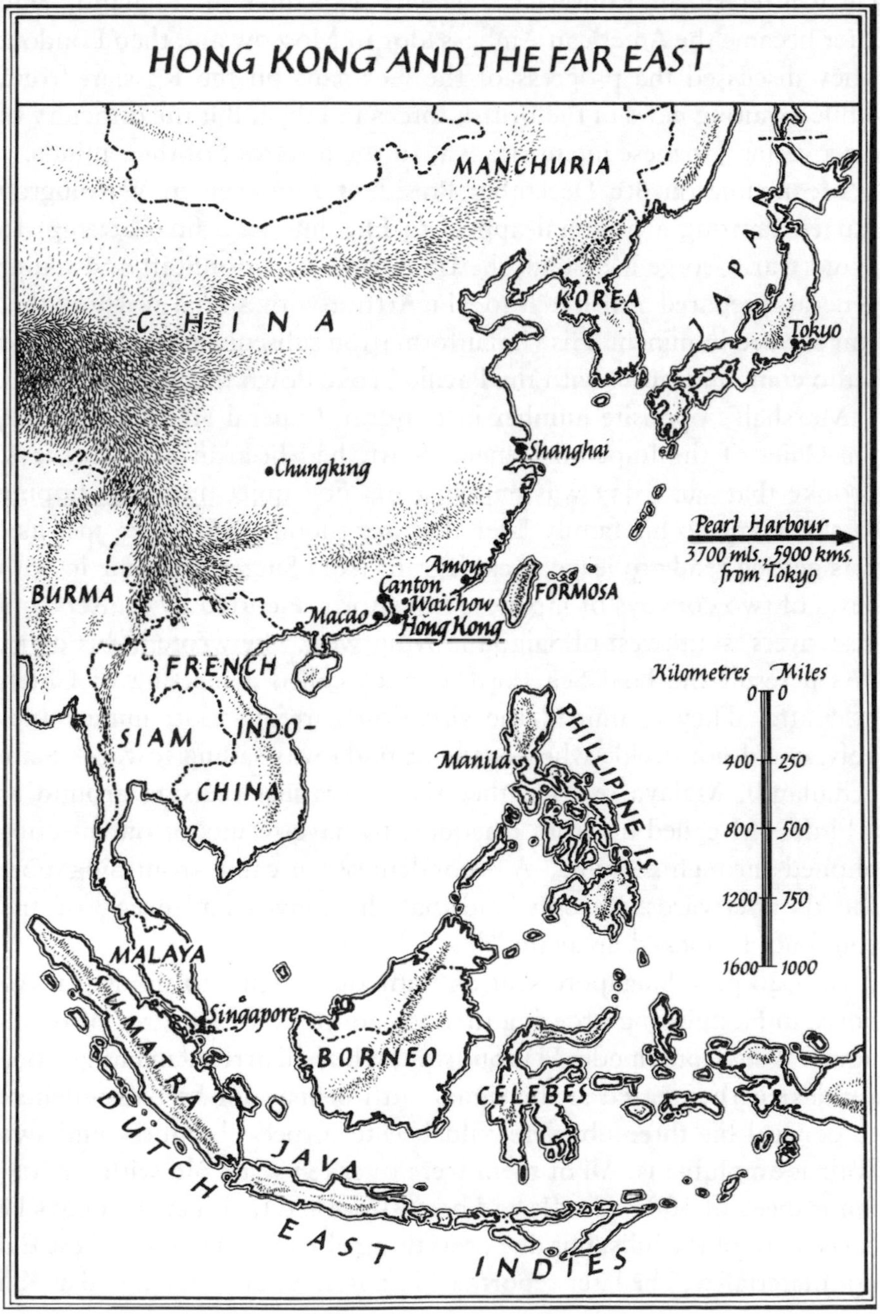

Hong Kong and the Far East

That weekend Churchill was at Chequers with Averell Harriman. He was President Roosevelt's 'defence expediter' in England, who later became the American Ambassador in Moscow and then London. They discussed the progress of the Germans on the Russian front, while awaiting news of the British forces in Libya. But the difficulty of discovering Japanese intentions was to the forefront of their minds.

Meanwhile on 6th December President Roosevelt in Washington started drafting a personal appeal to Hirohito in a final attempt to avoid war. George Marshall, the US Army's Chief of Staff and senior general, prepared a dispatch to MacArthur with a final warning that war seemed imminent. His vital information subsequently went astray; radio communication with the Pacific broke down the next day.

Marshall's opposite number in London, General Sir Alan Brooke, the Chief of the Imperial General Staff, had been in post six days. Brooke that same day was enjoying his first quiet morning, hoping to slip home to his family later that afternoon. "However, just as I was getting ready to leave, a cablegram from Singapore came in with news of two convoys of Japanese transports, escorted by cruisers and destroyers, southwest of Saigon moving west," he wrote in his diary. "As a result the First Sea Lord at once called a meeting of Chiefs of Staff." They examined the situation carefully but, understandably, could not decide whether the armada was sailing towards Siam (Thailand), Malaya or "whether they were just cruising around as a bluff. PM called up from Chequers to have results of our meeting phoned through to him." A second message came from Singapore shortly afterwards. "It only said that the convoy had been lost and could not be picked up again."[3]

At 7.20 p.m. Singapore sent an immediate signal to the Royal Air Force in Hong Kong ordering them to adopt "No. 1 degree of readiness". Wing Commander H G Sullivan, who had arrived in Hong Kong six days earlier, gazed at the signal with dismay for he had nowhere to conceal his three obsolete Vildebeeste torpedo bombers and two Walrus amphibians. All of them were over ten years old with a maximum speed of 100 mph. "It had been suggested that dispersal bays be carved out of the hills, but like everything else in Hong Kong these did not materialize," he later reported.[4] The RAF aircraft remained at Kai Tak airport.

That evening Major G E Grey 2/14 Punjabis, who was commanding the troops on Hong Kong's mainland frontier, "received a police message stating that three Japanese Divisions (38,000 men) had arrived at To Kat, eight miles from the frontier on the previous evening", recorded the second entry in Hong Kong's War Diary.[5]

Major General C M Maltby, the recently arrived General Officer Commanding British forces in the Colony, wondered whether the report was nonsense or if he should mobilise the Hong Kong Volunteer Defence Corps, order all his 12,000 troops to their battle stations and start activating the demolition plans. Should he ask the Governor, Sir Mark Young, to summon a meeting of the Defence Council for a lengthy discussion at Government House the following day?

The General's ADC, Captain Iain MacGregor, was about to be confronted by the Chairman of Hong Kong's largest and most distinguished bank, who was to arrive fuming at Flagstaff House demanding to see the General. "The Chairman paced the room, all the time telling me the whole thing was bloody nonsense, and that only two days before he had received a coded cable from one of his managers who had been dining the previous evening with the C-in-C of the Japanese Kwantung Army," MacGregor remembers. The C-in-C had assured the manager that under no circumstances would the Japanese ever attack their old ally, Great Britain. "'Good God, Iain,' said the Chairman, 'you're a civilian really, a Far East merchant. You know how these Army fellows flap. You know our intelligence is far better than theirs… '"[6]

General Maltby was not flapping. He was confident that the Royal Scots, Punjabis, Rajputs and Volunteers to the north of Kowloon could hold their defensive positions on the frontier and the Gin Drinkers' Line for seven days. This would allow sufficient time to complete demolitions of installations on the mainland of value to the enemy. The two newly arrived Canadian Battalions were at Shamshuipo Barracks but they had seen their battle positions, while in the musty, heavily camouflaged pill-boxes on Hong Kong Island, the machine-gun Battalion of the Middlesex Regiment was largely standing-to.

One topic of conversation on that last Saturday of peace in the Far East concerned Duff Cooper, who had been sent by Churchill on a special mission to establish whether the Government could do more about the situation. Cooper, accompanied by his wife, Lady Diana, had met MacArthur before visiting Burma, and then Australia where he met wives evacuated from Hong Kong. Most were demanding to rejoin their husbands in the Colony and he promised them that he would listen to their husbands' complaints. Fortunately it proved too late to reunite the families in Hong Kong.

One man who had no wish whatsoever to see his wife return from Australia was Major Charles Boxer The Lincolnshire Regiment, Maltby's senior Intelligence Officer. He infinitely preferred his mistress, Emily Hahn, an American writer who had once been the concubine, it was said, of Sinmay Zau, a frequently impecunious philosopher, publisher and father of a large family. Zau had introduced her to opium and for a time she had become a serious addict; she was also addicted to cigars. She had given birth to a daughter by Charles Boxer in October.

Hahn and Boxer hosted a cocktail party at his flat on that Saturday evening, 6th December. There were no Japanese present, naturally. But Boxer, who had served with the Japanese Army in the 1930s, was regarded by some as being too friendly with them. On the previous day he had enjoyed a lunch with a Japanese General beyond the frontier at which the General had casually asked Boxer whether he could obtain permission for him and his staff to attend a forthcoming race meeting at Happy Valley.[7]

Major Charles Boxer asked his guests where they would like to dine that night – a smart hotel perhaps, an exclusive restaurant or should they link up with friends at the 'Tin Hat Ball' in the prestigious Peninsula Hotel? Yet Boxer was visibly preoccupied; he knew that the massive Japanese armada had been spotted by British reconnaissance aircraft steaming along the coast of French Indo-China (now Vietnam) and that its destination was unknown. He planned to visit the frontier the following day to see what the Japanese were up to. Meanwhile, however, he accompanied Emily Hahn and their guests to a local restaurant for a buffet dinner.

It was just as well that they had not attended the Ball. Towards midnight the orchestra there had just started to play the current favourite, *The Best Things in Life are Free,* when suddenly the music stopped. T B Wilson, the local president of the American Steamships Line, appeared on a balcony above the dance floor. Urgently waving a megaphone for silence, he shouted, "Any men connected with any ships in the harbour – report aboard for duty." After a second's pause he added menacingly: "At once." The dance was forgotten. Men hurriedly said "Goodbye" before jumping into the waiting rickshaws.

Thirty miles to the north, the officers of Colonel Doi Teihichi's 228 Imperial Japanese Regiment studied markings in crimson ink upon their maps, while their men sharpened their bayonets and prepared for battle. Near Canton, 45 Japanese fighters equipped with machine guns examined air photographs of their targets, which were Kai Tak airport and Shamshuipo Barracks. Their objective was the British Crown Colony of Hong Kong.[8]

Notes

1. Manchester, William, *American Caesar*, New York: Dell, 1978, p. 224.
2. *Report of the Joint Committee on the Investigation of the Pearl Harbor Attack*, US 79th Congress, 2nd Session, Document No. 244.
3. Alanbrooke, FM, *War Diaries 1939–1945*, London: Weidenfeld & Nicolson, 2001, p. 208.
4. Letter, Sullivan to Oliver Lindsay (OL).
5. This Hong Kong War Diary is on Army Form C 2118 and is headed *Preliminary Summary*. It is undated and unsigned, and contains amplification in manuscript.
6. Interview MacGregor/OL.
7. Alden, Dauril, *Charles R Boxer: An Uncommon Life*, Lisbon: Fundação Oriente, 2001, p. 133.
8. Colonel Doi Teihichi's statements are in National Defence Headquarters (NDHQ), Ottawa.

Part 2

WHEN TIME WAS YOUNG

With memories by John R Harris
Edited by Oliver Lindsay

CHAPTER 2

When Time Was Young

John R Harris begins his memoirs

Luck has played a formidable part in my life. Looking back over the years – I'm now aged 86 – I count my blessings. How fortunate I was that I didn't suffer the same fate as my two closest friends in Hong Kong: they were killed in terrible circumstances by the Japanese in December 1941. Then, on 25th September 1942, I was among the prisoners of war who were assembled on the camp parade ground. The Japanese picked men on my immediate left and right to be sent to Japan on the *Lisbon Maru*. Why didn't they choose me? Some 1,816 men were incarcerated in the holds. The ship carried only two life rafts for the POWs. Of them, 842 were killed or drowned when the ship was torpedoed. I could so easily have been one of them. And later, dangerously ill with diphtheria, with little chance of survival when our Japanese guards were withholding vital drugs, how was it that, in a month when 41 Canadians died in Shamshuipo's primitive hospital, serum was given to me in the Argyle Street POW isolation hut, thereby saving my life?

Then I look at the post-war years. I rejoice at my marvellous good fortune in meeting Jill, a fellow architectural student who became my wife. I wouldn't have succeeded without her. The third big test we faced together in 1953 – an insurmountable challenge it seemed at the time – was an international open competition to be the architects to design and supervise the construction of the State Hospital Doha (Qatar). There were 74 entries from firms around the world. The assessors awarded us first prize. Thus we gained international recognition.

Of course there have also been years of turmoil, of traumatic change, of catastrophic events, particularly in the Far East, the repercussions of which I saw at first hand for five most dreadful years. But I should start at the beginning.

* * * * *

My father was born in Surrey during a snowstorm in 1888. Aged 17, he joined the 2nd Middlesex Royal Garrison Artillery Volunteers as a Territorial nine years before the First World War. Shortly after the beginning of the war, by which time he was a commissioned officer, he was billeted with a Mr and Mrs Alderson at Melrose in Hersham, Surrey; and in April 1916, when he was home from France on leave, he married their youngest daughter, Freda.

By 1915 he was in France fighting with the 36th (Ulster) Division in such fearsome battles as Neuve Chapelle, the Somme and Fleurs. Such was his gallantry that he was awarded the Distinguished Service Order and mentioned in Despatches in 1916 for his part in the first tank battle at Combles.

After more bitter fighting at Verdun, Vimy Ridge and the third battle of Ypres, fate caught up with him; he was badly wounded at Passchendaele. Threatened with a soulless hospital in the Midlands, he persuaded the authorities to send him instead to a private hospital near Bond Street in London where Freda could visit him. They had been married for scarcely a year. Back in France, he was dismayed at the lack of fitness of the men joining his battery. But good fortune smiled on him for he survived the war, commanding a brigade for several months before its end.

I was born in 1919 at Melrose near the railway bridge at Hersham, which still exists. The doctor came from Esher in a pony and trap. My first memory was watching, with my sister Rosina from a bedroom window, Father Christmas coming up the drive on Christmas Day. He carried a bulging sack and lantern. In the evening we all danced around the tree with Father Christmas before the excitement of opening our presents. Unfortunately, to our horror, Father Christmas's mask fell off – revealing our father. There was a scream and roars of laughter while he ran for the door!

My first school, Ovingdean, was behind Rodean girls' school. Glancing at our school photograph, I see there were 67 of us, wearing blazers and open neck shirts. A clergyman, with a large shaggy dog resting uncomfortably on his knees, sits alongside nine other adults.

What happened to them all, I have no idea. The pleasant buildings still exist. My parents had chosen Ovingdean because it had its own farm and should have been especially healthy. Paradoxically, the farm's cows nearly proved my undoing for I contracted tuberculosis. There was no easy cure in those days: there were no antibiotics. I was sent to a bungalow on the coast near Mundesley-on-Sea, Norfolk for the Summer so that I could attend a tuberculosis sanatorium nearby each day. Aged eight, I stayed there six months, doing little more at first than lying in the sun. My lungs were scarred for life. On the other hand, I won a 440 yards race before leaving Ovingdean, so I was not physically handicapped thereafter.

From the age of 11, I wanted to be an architect. I was admitted in 1933 to the bottom 4th form at Harrow, thanks to a dedicated master, Chris Carlisle, who interviewed me.

Over the years I have taken some pride and comfort in the fact that one of my predecessors had also been admitted into that same bottom form some 40 years earlier. "I found I was unable to answer a single question in the Latin paper. I wrote my name at the top of the page. I wrote down the number of the Question '1'. After much reflection I put a bracket round it thus '(1)'. But thereafter I could not think of anything connected with it that was either relevant or true," wrote my predecessor. "Incidentally there arrived from nowhere in particular a blot and several smudges. I gazed for two whole hours at this sad spectacle: and then merciful ushers collected up my piece of foolscap with all the others and carried it to the Headmaster's table. It was from these slender indications of scholarship that Mr Weldon drew the conclusion that I was worthy to pass into Harrow," recorded Winston Churchill in *My Early Life*.[1]

I suspect that Churchill was inclined to exaggerate his early ignorance so that in later years his brilliant success would be enhanced. We had to fag for older boys. Having entered at the bottom, it took me three years to work my way up to a respectable level when I would no longer have to clean the prefects' shoes, carry up their coal, deliver messages and so on. A pointer to my future career was the fact that I won the Henry Yates Thompson Art prize for the last two years.

I much enjoyed the art class excursions in the Summer and painting with watercolours. Maurice Clark, our art master, took us by train to Amersham and other pleasant places. True, many of the other boys only came for the opportunity to get away to smoke, which was strictly forbidden. One of the tasks Mr Clark gave me was to measure part of the school's war memorial, a building designed by Sir Herbert Barker. I was not to know that 12 years later I would become an architectural assistant in that firm.

Maurice Clark, whose paintings are still to be seen in books about Harrow, always exhibited in the Royal Academy. One day in 1935 the weekly art class was in progress. The rule was that all forms had an hour's art every week. Of course for many boys it was a bore. On this occasion the class had been arranged in a circle facing a bowl of fruit. (There was usually a bowl of fruit or a bust of Nero.) Every boy had a sheet of drawing paper, a pencil and a rubber.

Suddenly, sitting next to me, I O Liddell picked up his rubber and threw it at Maurice Clark. It hit him on the back of the neck. He swung round just in time to see Liddell's arm going down by his side. Maurice Clark leapt at Liddell, who ran out of the Arts School, down the steps and along the High Street. Maurice Clark pursued him, gown flowing behind; Liddell soon outpaced the master. By this time the art class were assembled on the terrace watching the dramatic chase.

On 3rd April 1945 Liddell, now a Captain in the Coldstream Guards, cut the wires of demolition charges while in full view of the Germans, thereby enabling his Company to capture the vital bridge on the Ems intact. He was subsequently wounded and died before he knew he had won the Victoria Cross.

When we left Harrow we gave our friends leaving photographs; in my case I was given 32. I checked recently and found that, within seven years of leaving the school, 14 out of those 32 friends were dead. They were all under the age of 25. Boys of my age group took the brunt of the Second World War.

In the General Strike my father drove a steam engine, with others, from Walton to Waterloo station – a schoolboy's dream. He became a very successful surveyor admired by the profession. Such was his success that in 1928, at the height of the slump, he purchased Brook Place at Chobham in Surrey. The house was a Grade II listed building dating back to 1656.

My father had started in practice in 1911 and joined a firm called Widnell and Trollope, whose first appointment had been as surveyor for the building of the Houses of Parliament. In 1928 he became the quantity surveyor for the new London Passenger Transport Board headquarter offices at St James's Park Station. His big professional breakthrough may have come when Dr Holden of Adams Holden and Pearson Architects and he appeared for an interview before the Senate Committee for the construction of London University's new buildings in Bloomsbury, including the tower behind the British Museum. The Chairman of the interview panel asked Dr Holden what he and my father would do if they were awarded the commission. "Our best," was Holden's reply. They were chosen, despite strong competition. By 1930 they were working for the London Transport Board on many stations as the system expanded, and also on Westminster Hospital's new buildings in Horseferry Road under Lionel Pearson and Sir Bernard Docker. Further successes followed.

There was little freedom at Harrow. Nevertheless we received a good all-round education and most of us learnt the importance of self-discipline. Above all, I met many people who became great friends later in life – the secret of a good school. Harrovians go out of their way to help each other. I was reminded of this in the desperate days in the prisoner of war camp in Hong Kong in 1942. Three of us Old Harrovians gave invaluable mutual support to aid our survival. (Incidentally Harrow Songs are unique: some of the chapter headings of this book are taken from them. Churchill used to visit Harrow to listen to Harrow Songs, sung by the whole school in Speech Room, during the darkest days of the war.)

Several hundred of us in the school's Officers Training Corps spent ten days in a training camp at Tidworth. I can't claim to have particularly enjoyed it. Boys from other schools were there too, but we had little opportunity to meet them.

Throughout my schooldays we were increasingly conscious of the growing threat from Germany. President von Hindenburg had handed over to Hitler in 1933. That same year Germany withdrew from the Disarmament Conference in Geneva and left the ineffective League of Nations. In March 1935 Hitler announced, in breach of the Versailles Treaty, the reintroduction of conscription and the building of an army of 550,000 men. The following year Hitler ordered the remilitarisation of the Rhineland in contravention of the Versailles and Locarno Treaties.

Jumping ahead almost 70 years to the early 21st century, we have seen how NATO troops, led by the Americans, moved into the war-torn former Yugoslavia to put a stop to ethnic cleansing and to arrest murderous war lords. Then, following the terrorists' attack on the

Twin Towers and the Pentagon in September 2001, we witnessed their deployment into Afghanistan to restore democracy and to bring to justice some of al-Qaeda, led by the notorious Osama bin Laden who is held responsible for much international terrorism. The US-led Coalition's controversial invasion of Iraq in the Spring of 2003 succeeded in removing Saddam Hussein, who had invaded Kuwait in 1990 and undoubtedly gassed tens of thousands of Kurds. Is one valid lesson of history that despicable, evil dictators, such as the potential Hitlers and Mussolinis of this world, should be sought out and brought to account before they wage war and commit crimes against humanity? Forty million people lost their lives in the Second World War.

Reverting back to the mid 1930s, we were simply in no position to act decisively. On the contrary, a very small minority of people in Britain looked at Hitler with admiration. "He was applauded, like Mussolini, for restoring order and national pride, bringing economic revival, and, not least, for suppressing the Left and forming a bulwark against the menace of Bolshevism," writes Ian Kershaw in the November 2004 *BBC History Magazine*. "Admiration was not confined to the fanatics who supported the British Union of Fascists. Hitler had also impressed others in high places, those among the social and political elite of the land."[2]

Britain's military weaknesses were due to our priority to put money into education, welfare and so on. We all wanted peace; the horrors of the First World War were fresh in our minds. Making friends with Hitler, or buying him off, seemed to offer the best prospect of avoiding another war – call it appeasement if you wish, but I didn't give much thought to such matters then.

On leaving Harrow in the Summer of 1937, I was accepted for the five-year course to become a student at the Architectural Association in Bedford Square. Run by architects for architects, it was one of the premier schools in the United Kingdom.

My architectural course consisted of a long sequence of different subjects. I enjoyed it immensely, often working late into the night (as my architect son, Mark, does to this day!). At weekends I used to bicycle a lot, sketching churches and other buildings around Surrey, with pencil and watercolours as at Harrow, but now for my diploma. In 1937 my father and I had watched from Park Lane the Coronation procession, seeing King George VI pass by.

Although I never considered myself cut out to be a soldier – far from it because I always wanted to be an architect – I volunteered to join the Territorial Army, which was growing fast. Many of my fellow students had chosen to do likewise. Naturally we preferred the Royal Engineers for we were familiar with construction and Sapper tasks. We started to take part once a week in exercises in London's Duke of York's Headquarters – now largely sold off to the private sector. In August 1939 we went to the TA camp on the cliffs above Dover and were taught how to dig trenches and make redoubts, using an outdated handbook published more than 20 years earlier. We could see naval convoys on the horizon going we knew not where, and wondered if one day we would be amidst them.

Time was marching on. The previous year, on 12th March 1938, German troops had entered Austria. The following day, Germany annexed the country. Western powers looked on with disapproval but did nothing. America's policy of isolation was scarcely a factor; we did not regard the Americans as 'sleeping giants' for they were set on non-intervention; their military capability, like ours, was, we now know, shockingly inadequate.

We feared that war was imminent.

Notes

1. Churchill, Randolph S, *Winston S Churchill: Vol I, Youth 1874–1900*, London: Heinemann, 1966, p. 106.
2. Kershaw, Ian, 'Making Friends with Hitler', *BBC History Magazine*, November 2004, pp. 13–16.

CHAPTER 3

The Outbreak of War in Europe

Czechoslovakia developed, during the years that followed its founding in 1918, into the most progressive, democratic, enlightened and prosperous state in Central Europe. But it was gripped by one domestic problem – its minorities of different nationalities, including 250,000 Sudeten Germans, although the Sudetens had never belonged to the German Reich. Hitler harangued his military leaders with the need to destroy the Czechoslovakian state and to grab its territory and inhabitants for the Third Reich. Despite what had happened in Austria, the leaders of Great Britain and France did not grasp this.[1] Appeasement was still paramount in unexpected quarters.

Rarely in the history of *The Times* has such abuse descended upon the newspaper as it did on 7th September 1938 when its leader advocated the handing over of the Sudetenland to Germany, with a hint that this policy "has found favour in some quarters" which led everyone to assume that the editor, Geoffrey Dawson, was relaying the British Government view. The Foreign Office disowned the leader in its communication with the Czech Government, but the damage had been done. The period of *The Times* being almost a great Department of State and its editor almost an honorary member of the Cabinet was over for good. Its influence declined accordingly.[2]

The Queen, the glossy magazine, was equally off-net. Persecution of the Jews was dismissed as unreal, and was claimed to be Germany's own domestic problem. There were attempts in the social journal to laugh it off as ridiculous or even humorous. A great joke was made of Hitler's decree that shops should only be allowed to sell dolls with Aryan features. *The Queen* estimated that in the matter of Mussolini's invasion of Abyssinia, his efforts were undoubtedly beneficial and there was nothing self-seeking about him. Mussolini was nominated in 1933 as one of the great personalities likely to become an immortal, along with the Prince of Wales, Charlie Chaplin and the Chief Scout.[3]

Having occupied Czechoslovakia with impunity in 1938, Hitler believed that the British and French would still not fight were he to further his territorial ambitions by invading Poland.

On the news of the German-Soviet pact signed on 22nd August 1939, the British Government at last took decisive steps: orders were issued for the immediate manning by key parties of the coast and anti-aircraft defences to protect vulnerable points. 30,000 reservists for the RAF, Air Auxiliary Force and overseas garrisons were called up. All leave was stopped throughout the fighting Services.[4]

On 25th August 1939 the British Government proclaimed a formal treaty with Poland. According to Goering's evidence at Nuremberg, Hitler immediately stopped the planned invasion of Poland to see if he could "eliminate British intervention". Accordingly, he postponed the invasion from 25th August to 1st September to enter into direct negotiation with Poland, as Prime Minister Chamberlain desired.

A year earlier, the journalist Leonard Mosley had an unexpected meeting with Hitler at Bayreuth. Hitler was initially in a good mood and told Mosley there would be no war over Poland. "Almost a year has passed since Munich was signed," Mosley replied. "Then Britain and France were unprepared. We had no troops, nor arms, nor planes. Now we have had almost a year to get ready..." Hitler turned on Mosley sarcastically, his pale face growing ruddy with passion, and his stubby forefinger with its bitten fingernail jabbing towards him. "A year to prepare! What foolishness is that!" growled Hitler. "The position of Britain and France is worse – far worse – than in September 1938. There will be no war, because you are less in a position to go to war than you were a year ago ..." Hitler proceeded to boast of the dramatic increases in Germany's ships, aircraft, tanks, guns and manpower. "I remember wondering who was supplying Hitler's information about our arms programme, and how near he was to the truth," concluded Mosley gloomily.[5]

Field Marshal Lord Alanbrooke (as he became) revealed in detail in his 1939–1945 War Diaries, published in 2001, Britain's lack of preparation for war. Our guarantees to Poland meant little to Hitler, just as the eleventh hour reinforcement of Hong Kong, to take place only weeks before the Japanese invasion of the British colony, had not the slightest deterrent effect on Japan's plans. Hitler had postponed his invasion of Poland not to reach agreement with that country, but instead to give the British Government every opportunity to escape from their guarantee. We can see how Hitler had miscalculated: any further appeasement from Chamberlain as the crisis intensified was unacceptable to the House of Commons following Germany's unprovoked attack on Poland on 1st September. "There was no doubt that the temper of the House was for war," wrote Churchill after the short but fierce debate.

* * * * *

Following my TA camp from the end of July to mid August with my Field Squadron of the Royal Engineers at Dover, I returned home. I had planned an architectural tour in my car around Italy before my TA unit was mobilized on about 27th August at the Duke of York's Barracks. On Sunday 3rd September I tuned the wireless to hear the Prime Minister's broadcast that we were at war with Germany.

Immediately the broadcast was over Londoners heard the prolonged, sinister, wailing air raid siren announcing, they assumed, the approach of German bombers. When they emerged from their shelters, they found that about 35 cylindrical silver-coloured balloons had been raised above London's roofs and spires to interfere with German bombing runs.

To my great disappointment, I had to stop my architectural course for the duration of the war. Now a Corporal, I was billeted at 21 Cadogan Square, which was my father's house. He had tried to let it, but couldn't because of the impending war. We had no furniture and were issued with two blankets and slept on the filthy floors. Fortunately, the food was excellent: it was delivered at regular intervals in a dirty demolition lorry from a top class Knightsbridge restaurant. Each morning we went for a run in Hyde Park, frightening the wild rabbits near the Serpentine.

I was foolish enough to believe, like some of my friends, that the war would be over in six months. Ignorant people like me thought that Germany was incapable of fighting another one and could not compete with our Royal Navy.

In October my Field Squadron paraded as usual – to be told that it would deploy imminently to join the British Expeditionary Force in France. About ten names were then read out indicating who were to be sent instead to the Royal Engineer Officer Cadet Training Unit at Malta Barracks, Aldershot. For better, or probably worse, my name was one of them. It never occurred to me for a second that I would end up fighting the Japanese rather than the Germans.

The six-month course was a good one. We were taught the necessary skills to support the combat formations – the infantry, the gunners and armoured units. Briefly, in defence, that meant the construction of field defences, laying anti-tank mines, and the improvement and construction of obstacles. In attack, we covered obstacle crossing, demolition of enemy defences such as bunkers, mine clearance, bridge or ferry construction. Other phases of war included withdrawal, which involved learning about blowing up or cratering roads, bridges, ammunition dumps and so on.

There was no time or inclination to teach us infantry work. I had no instruction therefore in such matters as ambushing enemy patrols, platoon skirmishes to capture an objective, or withdrawing from strategic positions under fire: all skills which I would need in Hong Kong.

The six months were not too intense; we certainly had good instructors. I was able to go home probably every other weekend. My father bought me a 90cc motorbike which was very economical on petrol; this was now rationed. The Colonel commanding us gave several dances in Aldershot. There was still no active fighting in France, virtually no bombing, and the food rationing scarcely affected us. We were certainly enjoying a good life compared to some others.

On 22nd March 1940 a photograph was taken of our course, Number 3 Class of 142nd OCTU. Forty-two of us are looking as confidently as possible at the cameraman. We thought we were a fairly professional lot. How many of us survived the war, I fear to think about.

In April 1940 we learnt our next appointment. Which theatre of war was I destined for? Students at the Staff College Camberley during most of the 20th century, or those at Quetta up to 1945, went to their 'pigeon holes' to collect the envelope containing the good news or bad; we newly commissioned Royal Engineer 2nd Lieutenants had ours read out to us. It was a moment of considerable tension.

Would the appointment be in a relatively peaceful location with a pleasant climate, a social life and none too taxing job? Or would one be destined for a challenging job, back to regimental duty in a theatre of war where fighting was imminent? Finally, much worse, would one be despatched at best possible speed, without leave, to replace a key officer who had been killed in action – so no hand-over, no prior knowledge of the local tactics, and no idea of the personalities under whom one had been sent to soldier? Inevitably, particularly in wartime, one might ask oneself if one was up to the job in question? Had the posting staff put a 'square peg in a round hole' – someone able, but quite unsuitable for the appointment, in a vital job?

Of course some of us, including me, would simply be told the theatre of war to which we would be sent. By the time we reached it, casualties, sickness, sackings or postings would create the vacancies into which we would be slotted. Others might go into reinforcement pools, well behind the front line, to be urgently moved forward to join, in all probability, a shattered unit following a particularly bloody battle and replace key men lost in action.

I and my close friends, Micky Holliday and Dickie Arundell, were to receive a considerable surprise when we Royal Engineers youngsters compared notes. "France, France, France," seemed to be on everyone's lips, with a trickle for Singapore. But for Micky, Dickie and me it was to be Hong Kong. Hurrah! I had no military ambitions, for I planned to be an architect. What could be better? The pleasant climate and social life for a year or so in the prosperous British colony would spare us from the fighting elsewhere and do us good. By then the formidable British Expeditionary Force (BEF) combined with the massive French forces, not forgetting the Canadians, Australians, Indians and New Zealanders who were rallying to support us, would have seen off Hitler and his henchmen. Japan was already heavily engaged in fighting the Chinese and was worried about her northern border with Russia, so posed no threat to us – or so we three 2nd Lieutenants convinced ourselves.

Naturally, therefore, I was delighted with the posting to Hong Kong. My parents were pleased; my other friends were envious. How lucky I was!

The German onslaught on 10th May 1940 came as a considerable shock even to Field Marshal Lord Gort, VC. "The tension which had been increasing during April," the commander of the BEF wrote in his official despatch, "had lessened somewhat during the early days of May.... It was not until the night of 9th/10th May that information was received of exceptional activity on the frontiers of Luxembourg, Belgium and Holland." At 8 a.m. on 10th May, front-line BEF battalion headquarters, listening to the BBC announcing the German invasion of the Low Countries, could see that German aircraft were already streaming above them, dropping a few bombs in their areas.[6]

I mention the above because it is indicative of the total failure of Allied intelligence to determine what the enemy was up to – both in Europe and, later, in even more traumatic circumstances, in the Far East when the Japanese launched their catastrophic invasion some 18 months later.

My Royal Engineer course had finished in April and I had been sent home to Chobham to await orders to sail to Hong Kong. Then came the German breakthrough, which led to lack of ships to take us to the Far East. It is quite possible, of course, that the posting authorities had simply forgotten about me. So what was I to do?

On 14th May, with families huddled as usual around their wireless sets after the BBC's nine o'clock news, Anthony Eden, the Secretary of State for War, announced that "the Government has received countless enquiries from all over the kingdom from men of all ages who wish to do something for the defence of their country. Well, now is your opportunity...." He went on to announce the formation of the Local Defence Volunteers, which was soon rechristened the Home Guard.[7]

My father became fairly senior in this unpaid force. I immediately joined to help him by undertaking night patrols, particularly in the Chobham Ridges area near Woking and south of London. The locality has excellent views over part of Surrey. We had good visibility on moonlit nights to see any enemy parachutists being dropped in our neighbourhood. I carried a shotgun with which I occasionally shot rabbits – it was all a bit ridiculous really. We stopped all traffic including buses to check the driver's identification card. If we saw lights, we promptly ordered that they be extinguished. Churchill seemed to be under the impression that there were some 25,000 organised Nazis in Britain when war was declared, and so keeping an eye out for saboteurs was important.

Despite being in Surrey, I heard very distinctly the rumble of gunfire during the evacuation of Dunkirk. I then witnessed some of the BEF survivors coming through Woking and Guildford. The Women's

Voluntary Service and other marvellous organisations served them hot drinks and sandwiches as the overloaded trains came through. My mother worked many hours there. The men's appearances and uniforms were dishevelled. Some were absolutely shattered and a few were never the same boisterous personalities again.

During all this time, I witnessed only one lone German aircraft. I was half a mile away working on an anti-tank ditch at Crondall when it dropped a single bomb, hitting a telephone box in Aldershot and killing the unfortunate man making a call. As the war intensified, nobody, however isolated, was entirely safe because German bomber crews, returning from raids and still carrying bombs, dropped them indiscriminately to lighten their loads and thereby endeavour to escape our fighters. For example, many of the leading schools were hit in 1940. Incendiary bombs caused some fires at Harrow, but the only significant damage was due to the Fire Service deluging the organ in Speech Room with too much water. In September, when the Battle of Britain was at its height, the sirens were constantly sounding throughout London and southeast England. There was a continual dash to the shelters. One German aircraft, annoyed by the anti-aircraft guns defending Windsor Castle, dropped two bombs on Eton out of sheer pique. One of them fell on the house of the master responsible for music, destroying his dining room, where he would have been killed had he not been elsewhere reading an article in *Punch*! The Headmaster of Wellington College was killed when visiting school houses during an air raid.

Waiting impatiently for a ship to Hong Kong, I tried to learn from Royal Engineer manuals what might be expected of me. But they seemed to relate more to the closing years of the First World War and what a sapper officer was supposed to do in 1918. Perhaps things hadn't changed much in the intervening years.

At last I received a cable telling me to report to Liverpool to board SS *Viceroy of India* bound for the Far East. The family gathered at Brook Place before I departed. They reminded me again how lucky I was to get away from Europe – to Hong Kong's wonderful lifestyle with no food rationing or blackout. My mother, in tears, said goodbye. My father accompanied me by train from Woking station to London, en route to Liverpool and the Far East at last. Little did I know that I was to return to Platform Two at Woking station five years later having circumnavigated the world.

Notes

1. Shirer, William L, *The Rise and Fall of the Third Reich*, London: Secker & Warburg, 1960, p. 360.
2. *The Times Past Present Future* (published to mark the newspaper's bicentenary), p. 30.
3. Crewe, Quentin, *The Frontiers of Privilege*, London: Collins, 1961, p. 196.
4. Churchill, Winston S, *The Second World War*, Vol. I, London: Cassell, 1949, p. 353.
5. Owen, James and Walters, Guy (eds), *The Voice of War*, London: Viking, 2004, p. 1.
6. Forbes, Patrick, *The Grenadier Guards in the War of 1939–1945*, Vol. I, Aldershot: Gale & Polden, 1949, p. 14.
7. Carroll, David, *The Home Guard*, Stroud: Sutton, 1999, p. 5.

CHAPTER 4

An Ocean of Change

Our ship was luxurious! SS *Viceroy of India* was the flagship of the P & O line. She proved to be the last civilian passenger ship of her type to go to Japan before hostilities. The civilian passengers on board were largely colonials with their families returning to India and Malaya. The Servicemen and women included Queen Alexandra's Military Imperial Nursing Service (known as QAs), TA Gunner officers and we three Royal Engineer 2nd Lieutenants – Dickie Arundell, Micky Holliday and me.

We sailed from Liverpool on 27th July 1940 bound for Gibraltar, Cape Verde, Cape Town, Mombasa, Bombay, Colombo, Singapore, and, for us, Hong Kong.

Almost precisely 64 years later I had a great friend, 'Bunny' Browne, to lunch in London who told me of his adventures when posted to Hong Kong, travelling on the *Empress of Australia*, which sailed from Southampton in mid September 1939. He is one of my very few Hong Kong contemporaries still alive. Horace Wilfred Browne, subsequently appointed CBE, was a civilian auditor working for the Army. His destination was meant to be secret and he was told to mark his baggage 'Q4'. At Waterloo station everyone seemed to know what 'Q4' indicated. "It's the Indian boat," the porters told him. The ship had a swimming pool; the food was excellent and all looked promising.

The *Empress of Australia* was accompanied by the *Franconia*, *Alcantara*, *Athlone Castle* and a Destroyer. After leaving Gibraltar, three of the ships were zigzagging in line abreast to avoid any enemy torpedoes when two of them inexplicably collided in broad daylight, crushing all the lifeboats hanging on one side of one ship and buckling the bows of another. At Bombay Bunny wisely insured his possessions. Most unexpectedly, the passengers were then told that their ship was returning to England and they would have to proceed across India by train. On reaching Calcutta, he was put on board the *Sedana*, a small cargo ship carrying some passengers. All went well, apart from a flood in his cabin which soaked all his possessions. He had accidentally left a tap on a little earlier when there was no water in the pipes.

On leaving Singapore on 13th November 1939, Bunny suddenly heard at 6.00 a.m. a big bang on the port side, followed by screaming. The *Sedana* had strayed into a British minefield, watched by a Gunner Battery on shore which did not have the authority to warn the ship. The minefield had apparently been marked in the wrong place on *Sedana*'s charts.

Bunny came up on deck, properly dressed, wearing his topee and life jacket, clutching two possessions which first came to hand – his new camera and an alarm clock. The ship was sinking fast and the crew useless. Lifeboats were capsizing as too many Indians, and the Chinese being deported from Singapore, crowded into them, standing on the lifeboats' oars. The one European woman bound for Hong Kong was thrown into a lifeboat while Bunny descended a ladder which suddenly flipped over leaving him hanging upside down ten feet above a heaving, tightly-packed lifeboat. Attempts to rescue the survivors were handicapped by the unwillingness of anyone to enter the minefield.

Bunny was met in Hong Kong by a violent typhoon, but he was a happy man: his insurance claim amounted to £100 which enabled him to buy his first yacht and a dress suit.

To revert to our own voyage, I was immediately struck by the luxury of SS *Viceroy of India*. Indian stewards served us cucumber sandwiches and marvellous cream cakes when we boarded her at teatime. There was a Palm Court orchestra to entertain us at tea and in the evening. I had a cabin to myself: all officers travelled first class. A Royal Artillery officer, the highly respected Lord Merthyr, was in charge of us. We were to become great friends in dire circumstances later.

Italy had entered the war on 10th June. Following the formation of the pro-Nazi Vichy Government, most of the French ships at Oran, their crews having refused to come over to the Allies, were sunk by Admiral Somerville after a bitter engagement.

Before the war it had been anticipated that, should Britain and France find themselves at war with both Germany and Japan, much of the British Mediterranean Fleet could be spared for the Far East. But now – with Italy's belligerence and no French Fleet to fight alongside us – the few Royal Navy ships at Singapore and Hong Kong would be largely on their own. Transferring the Eastern Mediterranean Fleet to the Indian Ocean, or to relieve Singapore, "would entail the complete loss of the Middle East, and all the prospects of beating Italy in the Mediterranean would be gone," Churchill told the Prime Ministers of Australia and New Zealand on 11th August 1940.[1] Naturally, I and my friends were quite unaware of this sinister warning or the repercussions for us in Hong Kong.

We reached Gibraltar and stayed at sea all night. On receiving the news of Oran, the Vichy Pétain Government ordered retaliation by bombing the harbour at Gibraltar from their African bases. Their bombing was spectacular as were the British warships' anti-aircraft guns, but both were equally ineffective. The following day we went ashore and met the apes, who seemed quite indifferent to having been under fire the previous night.

I must refer to one meeting of greater consequence. An architectural friend had been posted with the Royal Artillery to Gibraltar and was now in uniform. He told me quite categorically that, as everyone apart from me seemed to know, there was a major problem in both Singapore and Hong Kong: all the artillery – the great fortress guns – pointed out to sea to the south to safeguard against a seaborne attack, rather than to the northwest, north or northeast should the Japanese attack overland.

In 1991 the authoritative book, *The Guns and Gunners of Hong Kong*, was published: it addressed this point. The book shows quite conclusively that the above rumour was quite untrue as far as Hong Kong was concerned. The arcs of fire and range of the coast batteries at Stone Cutters, Mount Davis, Jubilee, Devil's Peak and Pakshawan between them could and would engage the enemy advancing upon Hong Kong.[2]

As far as Singapore is concerned, General Wavell told Churchill on 16th January 1942 that "the fortress cannon of heaviest nature have all-round traverse, but their flat trajectory makes them unsuitable for counter-battery work."[3] (It was true that there were no permanent fortifications covering the landward side of the naval base, but that was a different matter.) And so my architectural Royal Artillery friend's demoralising information was wrong on both counts.

The harbour at Cape Verde, where we stopped to refuel, provided a perfect setting for a dance on deck, with cheerful coloured lights instead of the usual blackout because the country was neutral.[4] There were a number of nice girls on board. It has been said and is undoubtedly true that the longer one is at sea, the more alluring and beautiful the girls seem to become, almost by the hour. One girl, educated at St Swithuns, whose father was a senior director of Dunlop, became a particular friend but there was no serious romance for me.

Ten days before reaching Cape Town, I went down with pneumonia. Lord Merthyr had a look at me and said, "You know, you're not really fit. I don't think we need you to carry on; we will unload you in Cape Town." Fortunately the ship had penicillin. After a week I was out of the ship's hospital and so not abandoned in Cape Town, swept into the 8th Army and possibly killed in the desert. A different fate awaited me.

When we reached Cape Town, we were told that we couldn't land because the Australian Army on the *Queen Mary* en route to England had earlier had a happy time creating havoc everywhere. In the end, as the passengers on the *Viceroy of India* were mainly civilians, the authorities relented and we had two very excellent, enjoyable days due to the overwhelming South African hospitality.

British Servicemen travelling to fight in North Africa who stopped at Durban had an equally memorable and marvellous time. This was just as well because so many of them were killed in the relentless battles in Egypt, Libya and Tunisia.[5]

Three days before we arrived at Cape Town we had come across the large, disabled *Ceramic* . She had been hit by another ship in the darkness; no ships carried navigation lights because of the threat of German submarines and raiders. The numerous women and children en route from Britain to Australia were transferred from the *Ceramic* to our ship. My beautiful cabin was surrendered to a woman with a band of children, leaving me to sleep with others on the ballroom's floor.

Our next stop was Mombassa where there was a swimming party one night at Port Reitz with the by now devastatingly beautiful QA nurses. At Bombay, on the other hand, we were berthed alongside a hospital ship which was unloading dead and wounded from Berbera – yet another timely reminder that we were in the corridors of war.

Colombo was worth a visit and then we reached Singapore with its legendary Raffles Hotel. Sadly, we were there for only one night but the beach club which I and my friends visited was truly splendid.

Six days later, on 11th September 1940, the *Viceroy of India* entered Hong Kong's fabulous harbour. My first exciting impressions were of the sheer beauty of the place – the bright green hills descending to the yellow sands of the picturesque bays. Even by the standards of the late 1930s, everything looked serene, beautiful and, yes, extraordinarily peaceful.

Notes

1. Churchill, W S, *The Second World War*, Vol. II, London: Cassell, 1949, p. 385.
2. Rollo, Denis, *The Guns and Gunners of Hong Kong*, The Gunners' Roll of Hong Kong, 1991, p. 123.
3. Churchill, op. cit., Vol. III, p. 42.
4. Wiseman, E P ('Bill'), *Hong Kong: Recollections of a British POW*, Ontario: Veterans Publications, 2001, p. 15.
5. Hawes, Sid, 'Durban 1942', in *The Guards Magazine*, 2004/5 Winter edition, p. 232.

CHAPTER 5

Visions of Delight

On arrival in Hong Kong on 11th September 1941, we were met by Major D C E Gross who commanded 22nd Company Royal Engineers. Being so junior, I was expecting to be put up in some dingy barracks, but instead Micky Holliday, Dickie Arundell and I were taken to the Hong Kong Club. It was on the waterfront of Hong Kong harbour and enjoyed the exclusive, dignified atmosphere of a 19th century London club; it had an historic air about it. The imposing premises overlooked the Cenotaph, an exact replica of Lutyens' Cenotaph in Whitehall. Membership was strictly controlled.

The Royal Engineers in Hong Kong amounted to two Field Companies and Royal Engineer Services, with a total strength of 465. There were also two Auxiliary Force Engineer units. In 1939 an Engineer Field Company in the Hong Kong Volunteer Defence Corps was formed to carry out when necessary certain initial demolitions. Then there were plans for a Hong Kong Engineer Corps to be formed to consist of over 1,500 Chinese.[1]

My appointment sounded very grand to me – Garrison Engineer West! I worked with half a dozen other Royal Engineer officers in Major W W Parsons' office in Victoria on building works such as repairs to military roads, constructing some pillboxes and preparing defences. To be more precise, I was in charge of hard working Chinese contractors whose responsibilities included constructing and maintaining the water supplies in the Colony. These reservoirs were of vital importance, as were the pumping stations. Without water, Hong Kong could not hold out for a week. So concrete pumping stations and drains became my business. This does not sound very exciting when it comes to war, but, as a fledgling architect, it suited me well as I knew something about it all. My two great friends, Holliday and Arundell, were sent to R.E. Field Companies.

I became familiar with the western part of Hong Kong Island which included the important Mount Davis gun position completed in 1912 and manned by 24th Coast Battery, 12th Coast Regiment Royal Artillery. It consisted of 115 Gunners and three massive 9.2 inch guns. They were well camouflaged and surrounded by barbed wire. Also there were the Headquarters of Western Fire Command, a Fire Control Position Finder, Fortress and Battery Observation Posts, Plotting Rooms and much else. I looked after the engineering part of the batteries, seeing that the mechanical equipment was working. I rebuilt some gun emplacements which needed attention. I also installed a water supply there, with some difficulty because it needed a special water pump. Three times the pump was ordered from the UK: the first ship bringing it out was sunk, as was the second one. Fortunately the third got through.

All the guns were able to fire at an enemy target at any one time. The targets might include Japanese ships approaching Victoria Harbour from the west where the sealane was 3,600 yards wide, or Japanese soldiers approaching from the northwest area of the Mainland.

After some 13 weeks of greatly enjoying life in the Hong Kong Club, Holliday, Arundell and I were lucky enough to be allocated a flat on May Road, which lay halfway up the exclusive Victoria Peak and about a mile from Mount Davis. We had our first Hong Kong Christmas there. The Peak is the highest point of Hong Kong Island and overlooks the capital, Victoria, which stretched in a narrow strip along the northern shore for about four miles. The Peak also overlooked other mountains, tortuous valleys and precipitous slopes covered by dense vegetation.

Gradually, I got to know the British Crown Colony. It consisted of the Island, and, to the north, across a narrow channel and Victoria Harbour, the Hong Kong Mainland which bordered China. The Japanese were in occupation beyond the border. North of Kowloon were the New Territories of about 360 square miles. They had been leased to Britain in 1898 for a period of 99 years. The only airport was at Kai Tak to the east of Kowloon; it was used for both commercial and military purposes. Since the dockyard in Victoria Harbour was vulnerable to attack from the Mainland, an alternative naval base had been prepared to the southwest of the Island at Aberdeen. This area also came under me for some engineer support.

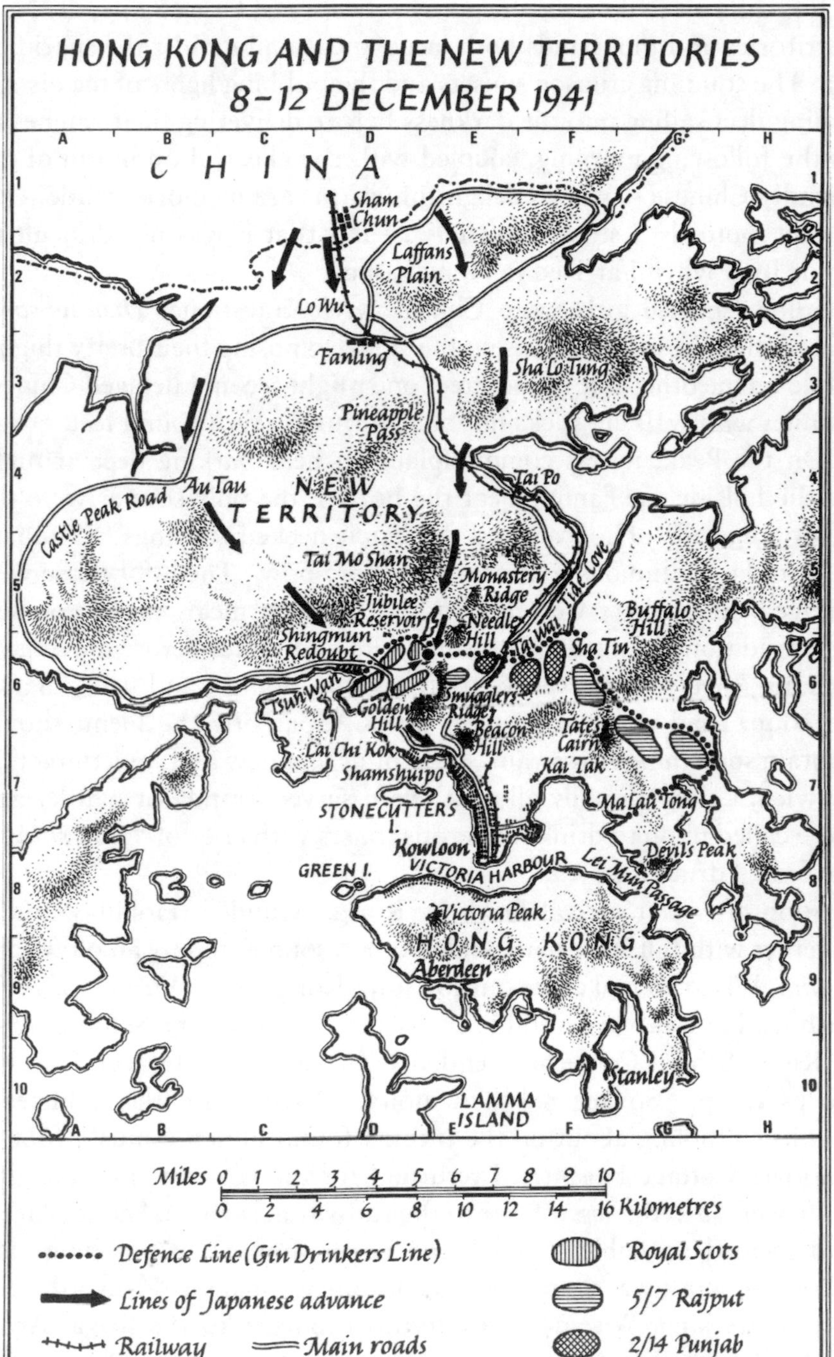

Hong Kong and the New Territories 8th–12th December 1941

It is difficult to describe the pre-war beauty of Hong Kong, the New Territories and the islands both large and small amidst the sparkling sea. The stunning crimson sunsets and the bobbing lights of the distant fishing fleet sailing into the darkness before delivering their catches to us the following morning, coupled with the cheerful optimism of the friendly Chinese – of such delightful visions are memories made. Our family motto is 'I strive cheerfully'. I felt that it was not difficult to abide by it when I arrived in Hong Kong.

Some Chinese girls wore Chinese style traditional *cheung sarm* tight fitting dresses with slits up the sides, exposing their pretty thighs, while on the other side of the street one might see middle-aged Chinese women with walking sticks hobbling along on tiny bound feet.

On the Peak, it was commonplace to hear barking deer at night on the hillside. At Fanling near the border, the only sounds were the whooping calls of coucals and the black-necked starlings. (Compare that to the continuous roar of traffic there now.) Then, for those who enjoyed them, there were the formal Chinese meals of 12 courses; they traditionally started with small bits and pieces before moving on to soup, then to meat (pork, beef, pigeon, poultry and fish), shark's fin soup, fried rice and a sweet dish. Apparently the menu should contain something that swam, something that flew and something that crawled. Guests, usually all men, were served brandy or whisky and were called upon to drink numerous toasts with cries of "*yum shing*", meaning "drink it all".[2]

Soon after our arrival in Hong Kong, Arundell, Holliday and I, together with Bill Wiseman, pooled our resources to buy an old yacht, *Diana*. Wiseman had come out to Hong Kong on the *Viceroy of India* with us. He was a remarkable character. "As usual the Summer term at King's School Canterbury ended with the annual Officer Training Corps camp." So began his memoirs. "I never got there. Instead, thanks to fooling about on the train, I found myself minus a foot in Andover Cottage Hospital. I returned for the Easter term managing quite well on a 'tin' leg... Prior to the railway accident, a Service career had seemed probable – and I had never thought of anything else. Choice of work was no problem as no one wanted me." Nevertheless, four years later, Wiseman was commissioned into the Royal Army Service Corps (TA) and posted to Hong Kong.[3]

Diana cost only 20 pounds plus the boat boy's wages. We used to sail regularly together, but, for some reason, Wiseman had to celebrate his 23rd birthday alone. "However, with the aid of Ah Su and a bottle of Gordon's Gin, I managed to circumnavigate the Island in record time, or so I always claimed," he wrote. "By October 1941 mounting debts forced us to sell *Diana*. Her massive lead keel brought in a small fortune, settling our debts just in time."

Meanwhile I, with my father's financial help, had bought a 25-foot Sparkman Stephens yacht with a cabin for two. At weekends I visited most of the bays on or around the Island. My friends and I slept on the boat.

I also had a small Morris car and so enjoyed travelling across the ferry to the New Territories or driving gently on the few roads on the Island. I often walked around the water catchments and reservoirs and so came to know the Island pretty well. I still kept up my painting which I had started at Harrow.

There was ample time to do what we liked because we seldom worked in the afternoon. As Bill Wiseman put it: "Off duty life was great. Although my pay and allowances totalled less than 300 pounds a year, I lived like a lord! I lodged in a comfortable and respectable Kowloon hotel, belonged to three or four clubs and went 'on the town' most weekends."

Anthony Hewitt, the Adjutant of the Middlesex Regiment, fondly remembered that Hong Kong was still "a festive place, a refuge for enjoyment. The top hotels and restaurants were the best anywhere, the night life exciting. 'The Grips' was a social centre where dinner jackets were mandatory. Overlooking an exquisite coastline, the Repulse Bay Hotel with its old fashioned style was the epitome of colonial living. In Kowloon, the Peninsula Hotel was our nearest haven, only two miles from our barracks at Shamshuipo."[4] The Peninsula was built at the end of the Trans-Siberian railway which would link Dover with Hong Kong.

For those who liked team sports, there was cricket, rugby and drag hunting. However, I was more than happy with my sailing and playing golf at Fanling in the New Territories. It was a golden time in Hong Kong; everything was very inexpensive. Commander Rex Young, a Royal Navy wireless expert, was amazed to discover on arriving in the Colony that "Hong Kong did not seem to know there was a war on... business seemed to be flourishing." The General Officer Commanding Hong Kong, A E Grasett, had a reputation for being easy-going. It would seem from the war diaries of Field Marshal Lord Alanbrooke that this attitude even prevailed in some quarters of England in June

1940, despite the collapse of France and the invasion of England appearing imminent. "Motored over to Salisbury where I spent rest of the day with Bertie Fisher, taking over Southern Command," he noted in his diary on 26th June. "The main impression I had was that the Command had a long way to be put on a war footing and that a peacetime atmosphere was still prevailing."[5]

In that same month, June 1940, Hong Kong did have a nasty warning of what might happen to us. The Japanese were then fighting the Chinese just beyond the border; several schools in Kowloon were converted to become hospitals for wounded Chinese brought over in Red Cross trucks. The smell of dead Chinese beyond the border was unmistakeable and unbearable: they had not been buried properly, if at all.

A Japanese attack was expected any day, so the Hong Kong Colonial Government demanded that all women and children leave the Colony immediately. Within days the giant Canadian *Empress of Asia*, her funnels spouting black smoke, sailed for Australia crammed with evacuees. Rickshaws overloaded with suitcases and anxious, tearful women had hastened towards the Kowloon docks to board her and the *President Coolidge*.

Later, the husbands held mass meetings to demand their wives' return. The daily press was filled with letters criticising the Government and complaining about so-called discrimination in allowing so many women to remain in Hong Kong – women who had enlisted almost overnight as auxiliary nurses, air raid wardens, stenographers and cipher clerks in order to stay there. "Too many wangled exemption and some deliberately flouted the orders," recalls one nurse who stayed. "They were the ones who loudly bemoaned their fate later in Japanese captivity. Children were kept in the Colony and suffered the horrors of war and the privations of subsequent internment, solely through their parents' selfishness."[6]

I am not convinced that the above criticism is fair; some of my married Service friends in Hong Kong kept their children there for good reasons.

Those who did not take soldiering too seriously in Hong Kong took comfort from the views expressed by Air Chief Marshal Sir Robert Brooke-Popham who was appointed to the new post of Commander-in-Chief, Far East, stationed at Singapore. He was a retired officer who had been Governor of Kenya.

After he had inspected defensive installations in Hong Kong, we were all assembled in the main theatre in the rather disreputable Wanchai District to hear the great man speak. He addressed us all, painting a picture that the Japanese fighting qualities were greatly inferior to ours. Having seen the "dirty uniforms" worn by the Japanese troops, he confidently announced that they were "sub-human specimens" and that he could not "believe they would form an intelligent fighting force".[7] According to one military authority on the war in the Far East, Brooke-Popham, though aged only 62, "had developed a habit of falling asleep at any time... often in the middle of a conference at which he presided, therefore often missing much of the subject under discussion. Although a man of great charm, he had clearly passed his prime."[8]

Brooke-Popham was certainly awake when one of our officers had the nerve to ask him how we could defend Hong Kong when the RAF had only five planes: two Walrus amphibians and three Vickers Vildebeeste torpedo bombers, all over ten years old with a maximum speed of 100 miles an hour. (The RAF had given orders that they were not to be flown operationally unless an opportunity occurred either at first light or at dusk.)

I heard the Air Chief Marshal reply briskly: "You must carry out the defence of Hong Kong with what you have got." We did not find this encouraging, but were reassured by his remarks that the "slit-eyed" Japanese could not fly at night and that their soldiers were of very poor calibre.

We were aware, of course, of the shocking atrocities committed by the Japanese. In July 1937, after their numerous clashes with Chinese Nationalist troops in north China, Japan had invaded the interior. On capturing the Nationalist capital, Nanking, they had massacred about 300,000 Chinese civilians and raped some 50,000 women. They had earlier slaughtered approximately 6,000 Chinese troops and civilians at Jinan.

But not everything was 'doom and gloom'. On 16th November, those of us at the bottom of the military ladder, not 'in the know', had a most marvellous surprise: two full-strength battalions of Canadian troops with a Canadian Brigade Headquarters suddenly arrived. I saw them parading after disembarking from the *Awatea* troopship. I felt that nothing but good could arise from these most unexpected reinforcements.

"It was a grand day," recalled Rifleman Ken Cambon of the Royal Rifles of Canada. "The sun shone but not oppressively, in a cloudless sky. The magnificent Peak and surrounding hills confirmed that it must be... a solid citadel indeed. Our two battalions marched down Nathan Road steel-helmeted and obviously invincible. The main street of Kowloon was lined by cheering crowds waving small Union Jacks. My platoon was halfway between two bands, which were unsynchronised to the same beat. The two-mile march to Shamshuipo Military Barracks was a continuous ballet of changing step."[9]

Another Canadian soldier takes up the story: "Sham Shui Po Barracks, white and shimmering in the heat. A Kiplingesque film set with its broad avenues stretching out towards the distant mountains," wrote William Allister. "Brigade HQ was privileged to be quartered in the Jubilee Building at the harbor's edge, with rooms and balconies overlooking large parade grounds. Where the good life began. Where we tasted the fruits of Empire. Where servants, at the lordly salary of 25 cents a week, did your laundry, shaved you as you slept and brought you tea in bed."[10]

A few Canadians, on arrival, concluded that they were in a form of paradise, with visions of delight everywhere. They were not the only ones. The *Times* correspondent felt that the islands and coastline to the west resembled "in appearance rather like a piece of the Western Isles of Scotland, but with a climate not unlike that of Florida".

"After the arrival of a few thousand Canadians, everybody felt that the Crown Colony could and would be defended successfully," wrote a Dutch-born construction engineer, Jan Henrik Marsman, who had the misfortune to arrive in Hong Kong six days before the Japanese onslaught. "It was a psychological miracle."[11]

I felt the same.

Notes

1. *History of the Corps of Royal Engineers*, Vol. 9, R.E. Institution, 1958, p. 124.
2. Wilson, Brian, *Hong Kong Then*, Durham: The Pentland Press, 2000, p. 54.
3. Wiseman, E P ('Bill'), *Hong Kong: Recollections of a British POW*, Ontario, Veterans Publications, 2001, p. 14.
4. Hewitt, Tony, *Corridors of Time: Distant Footsteps through the Empire 1914–1948*, Durham: The Pentland Press, 1993, p. 74.
5. Alanbrooke, FM, *War Diaries 1939–1945*, London: Weidenfeld & Nicolson, 2001, p. 89.
6. Diary of M Redwood, Imperial War Museum, London.

7. Kirby, S Woodburn, *Singapore: the Chain of Disaster*, London: Cassell, 1971, pp. 55–6.
8. Ibid.
9. Cambon, K, *Guest of Hirohito*, Vancouver, 1990, p. 5.
10. Allister, William, *When Life and Death Held Hands*, Toronto, 1989, pp. 6–8.
11. Marsman, J H, *I Escaped from Hong Kong*, New York, 1942, p. 9.

Part 3

REMEMBER THEM WITH PRIDE

by Oliver Lindsay

We drink the memory of the brave,
The faithful, and the few;
Some lie far off beyond the wave;
Some sleep in Ireland, too.
All, all are gone; but still lives on
The fame of those who died;
And true men, like you men,
Remember them with pride.

CHAPTER 6

The Vulnerable Outpost

In December 1939 the Japanese Army was told to prepare plans to invade Hong Kong should the decision be made to go to war. Seven months later Captain Sejima Ryuzo began spying in the Colony. He saw that work on the forward defensive Gin Drinkers' Line had ceased several years earlier. Construction of this line had started in 1937 when consideration was given to a division from Singapore reinforcing the garrison. About six miles north of Kowloon a chain of pill-boxes on the Mainland were to be built, zig-zagging 11 miles across the rocky and precipitous hillside. The line was so named because its left sector began at the scene of alcoholic picnics in happier days. Some trenches, particularly those on the west at the Shingmun Redoubt, were laboriously dug, cement overhead protection added and fields of fire studied. However, since the garrison could expect no reinforcements, the British concept of fighting well forward was stillborn, as the Japanese discovered.

Sejima recommended that the Army should capture the Mainland, consisting of the New Territories and Kowloon. But he was not confident that a Japanese assault from Kowloon on the Island's northern shore would be successful. A frontal assault in the face of British artillery and machine-gun fire would be a risky operation, he felt. However, Chinese Triad spies, well paid by the Japanese, had watched a British military exercise, in which a direct attack had been successfully staged on the north shore. Sejima's suggestions that the Army should invade on the south shore were therefore overruled.

Two months later, on 23rd September 1940, Japan invaded northern French Indo-China, marked on Map 1. (The US Army's Signal Intelligence service had broken the Japanese codes and accurately predicted an invasion. Unfortunately a cipher clerk had muddled the code names; Churchill was told by President Roosevelt that England was to be invaded by Germany at 3.00 p.m. on 23rd September.)

Four days later Japan signed the Tripartite pact with Germany and Italy, thereby recognising the 'new order' in Europe and gaining encouragement in turn for her aggressive policy in the Far East.

In July 1941 the Japanese Government sought agreement from the French Vichy regime to enable her forces to occupy all Indo-China including the bases at Camrahn and Saigon which were potential invasion springboards to attack Siam, Singapore, Malaya and the Dutch East Indies. France meekly agreed. Meanwhile Hitler had invaded Russia, thereby ensuring that the Japanese had nothing to fear from their northern flank.

Just when Japan felt that everything was falling neatly into place, on 26th July the United States froze all Japanese assets in its territories in order to persuade Tokyo to leave China and Indo-China. Britain and the Dutch did likewise, thereby cutting off all tin, rubber, oil and steel to Japan.

At an Imperial Conference in Tokyo on 6th September 1941, the decision was taken to complete preparation for war against Britain, America and the Netherlands. The alternative, of withdrawing Japanese troops from China and Indo-China, was quite unacceptable. Japan recognised that America would never surrender; their hope was that Japan's initial successes, coupled with Hitler's victories in Europe, would force the Americans to accept a compromise peace, leaving Japan supreme in East Asia.

Hong Kong was a valuable prize because the harbour would provide an important anchorage for Japanese shipping. Moreover war materials could no longer be delivered to China to support Chiang Kai-shek's Nationalist Government. After the fall of Canton, when the railway route was cut, innumerable junks in Hong Kong endeavoured to smuggle what they could to those fighting in China. Tokyo estimated that the junks were channelling 6,000 tons of munitions to the interior each month. If Hong Kong could be captured, the Japanese optimistically believed that China might despair of getting help from the West and come to terms.

Japan's spies in Hong Kong were fairly unsuccessful. Sakata Seisho, sent by Major Okada Yoshimasa to gather intelligence, was imprisoned by the Hong Kong police, but escaped to the Portuguese territory of Macao thanks to Triad connections. Maizuno, who ran a sports shop in Wanchai, turned out to be a Japanese Lieutenant. There were others like him. In 1949 Colonel Tosaka expressed dissatisfaction with the information provided by his agents. True, Colonel Suzuki, based in the Japanese Consulate, had picked up details of where the signal cables were laid and the location of some of the pill-boxes and guns, but his activities had been exposed. Tosaka had to fall back upon the Wanchai brothel girls, the Japanese jeweller in the Queen's Arcade, the Italian waiter at the Peninsula Hotel and the Japanese barber at the Hong Kong Hotel, who reappeared after the fighting in the uniform of a Lieutenant Commander as the Commandant of the Stanley internment camp.

So much for the Japanese preliminary plans and their intelligence, or rather the lack of it. Let us now turn to the British and Hong Kong Governments' priorities, relate them to later years, and consider the success or otherwise of their intelligence gathering.

* * * * *

The Chiefs of Staff in London had long recognised that Hong Kong could not be held without considerable reinforcements. They considered evacuating or reducing the garrison, but decided instead to make no change to its strength and simply ordered that the outpost should be defended for as long as possible.

In 1938 Major General A W Bartholomew, the General Officer Commanding (GOC) in Hong Kong, told the War Office: "I still regard the building of defences as unnecessary. I have also made it clear that troops must resist with arms any sudden attack on themselves or their charge, but this is not to apply to any properly-organized and authoritative request by a military command to enter the concessions... "[1]

To ensure that the virtual hopelessness of the position was understood in London, General Bartholomew signalled the War Office on 13th April 1938: "In event of wanton attack on Hong Kong, the garrison would have no option but to fight... the chances of effecting a prolonged resistance even in the best circumstances seem slight." The War Office needed no convincing. The vulnerability of the outpost was well understood. It was again confirmed that the Hong Kong garrison would have to do the best it could with what it had. By the Summer of 1940 it was even suggested in some quarters that the option be considered of reducing the garrison to cut down on the casualties they would suffer in a hopeless attempt to fight the Japanese off.

It could be argued that Britain was considering almost an 'open city' scenario. A precedent for such a policy was set later when Japanese forces were allowed to enter the British and French concessions at Tianjin (Tientsin). In mid-August 1940 the British Chiefs of Staff withdrew the two infantry battalions that were contributing to the security of Shanghai's International Settlement. That same month they recognised that: "We should resist the strong pressure to reinforce Hong Kong and we should certainly be unable to relieve it. Militarily our position in the Far East would be stronger without this unsatisfactory commitment."[2]

On 15th August the Chiefs of Staff in London summed it all up in a dispatch which stated that "Hong Kong is not a vital interest and the garrison could not long withstand a Japanese attack. Even if we had a strong fleet in the Far East, it is doubtful whether Hong Kong could be held now that the Japanese are firmly established on the Mainland of China; and it could not be used as an advance base. In the event of war, Hong Kong must be regarded as an outpost and held as long as possible."[3]

This dispatch was sent to the Commander in Chief Far East with other documents on *Automendon*, a British cargo liner en route from Liverpool to Singapore and Hong Kong. The crew of a German sea raider attacked and boarded the liner 300 miles from Sumatra and captured all the documents despite frantic British efforts to sink the dispatches. German officials handed the most secret documents to the Japanese in Tokyo.[4] The Japanese therefore had precise knowledge in late 1940 of Britain's inability to hold Hong Kong.

* * * * *

It is relevant to compare the position then to the 1970s and 80s when, again, there would be no opportunity of sending significant reinforcements to Hong Kong quickly. Let us examine the two periods in question.

In January 1975 I was Second in Command of 2nd Battalion Grenadier Guards. We were taking over from 1st Battalion The King's Regiment on arrival in Hong Kong. I asked what secret tactical plans existed in the safe to cover any aggression from China. I was told there was no plan held at Battalion level. This did not worry me unduly because there was no apparent threat whatsoever from the People's Liberation Army. Moreover there would presumably be time to issue the necessary orders, deploy the battalion, undertake reconnaissance of our areas and prepare for battle. All our more senior Officers and

Warrant Officers had some experience of all phases of war after innumerable peacetime training in the British Army of the Rhine. I recently asked the then Battalion Commander, Colonel David Fanshawe, if he felt the Grenadiers would have given a good account of themselves in a limited war scenario in Hong Kong. He gave an emphatic "Yes," and added one point which is particularly relevant to the fate which awaited the Canadians in December 1941.

David Fanshawe emphasised the vital necessity of building up Infantry soldiers' mental robustness and physical stamina. In extremis soldiers are likely to be required to march long distances, often in atrocious conditions, carrying heavy loads and then fighting for their lives. Armchair critics are all too ready to condemn when things go wrong – as inevitably they may do. Such people must appreciate that the soldiers involved 'at the coal face' are usually young, often exhausted, cold and hungry and probably exceedingly scared. They are held together by effective training, discipline and by their junior leaders.

The British Army's experience for 30 years in Northern Ireland – and more recently in Iraq – sometimes tested men to their limits and beyond. Political people and their lawyers in cosy offices suffer no lack of enthusiasm in finding fault. They and indeed historians in the longer term, having no experience whatever of the horrors of war, must appreciate the condition of those who put their life on the line for King, or Queen, and Country. The Canadians did their best in the most adverse circumstances. The same can be said for those today fighting in Iraq.

The British, Canadian, Indian and Chinese soldiers would be called upon in Hong Kong to face the pandemonium of battle – the explosions of shells and mortars, machine-gun fire, hearing the screams of the wounded and the loss of close friends to their left and right – such was the full horror of war in December 1941.

Luckily for us in the mid 1970s no Chinese threat developed and we concentrated on internal security scenarios, jungle warfare, counter-revolutionary war and civil assistance. Nevertheless some of us recognised that any limited war involving the withdrawal from the border through built up areas towards Victoria Harbour, regardless of civilian casualties, chased by the Chinese Communist Army, was a concept which was scarcely credible.

I recently asked Lieutenant General Sir Peter Duffell, the Commander of the British Forces in Hong Kong in 1990, what the concept of operations amounted to in his day. Had he favoured an 'open city scenario' as Major General Bartholomew had proposed in 1938, or to even reduce the garrison, as suggested by some in the War Office, in 1940? General Duffell replied as follows.

"In the mid 1980s when I became Brigade Commander in Hong Kong under Major General Derek Boorman who was Commander British Forces, the negotiations on the 1997 agreement were in hand. I had inherited a defence plan that saw the brigade fighting a classic withdrawal battle down to Kowloon (and through the Gin Drinkers' Line) and the Island in the face of an all out invasion by the People's Liberation Army. This seemed to me to be both an unlikely and impracticable scenario and one that was out of touch with military and political reality. We did not have the military strength to take on the PLA even if such a scenario was likely and anyway for the Chinese there were other ways to skin a cat or exert their will. It seemed to me that the British were not going to go to war to attempt to save Hong Kong. I saw in defence terms that the threat lay in the potential for the Chinese government to exert pressure on the British and Hong Kong governments in a variety of ways and that the border and its security and integrity was the key to any plans that we had. This ignored the possibility of air and maritime incursions which were also a possibility. On the former, unless we had a good deal of warning, we had no means to counter such an incursion. On the maritime front the best we could do was to shadow and confront any such maritime adventure with our patrol craft.

"On land my assessment was that the Chinese might exert some form of threatening pressure on the border to extract diplomatic advantage during negotiations with the British. I sketched an escalatory series of possible scenarios that started with verbal exchanges and stone throwing/banners, etc. from across the border and moved through mass illegal immigrant and civilian incursions, militia and PLA troop movements to the north of the border, closing up to the border; possible attempted incitement of military exchanges and eventually some form of military incursion. For each scenario I outlined a series of non-escalatory responses designed to hold the line – in a non-confrontational manner – that would allow us to maintain the sovereignty of the territory within the closed area while diplomatic measures to defuse the situation were put in hand. Our response was to be controlled and disciplined, limited, until military life was threatened, and in the style of our response to the border problems that occurred during the cultural revolution. I could not see any advantage in taking on the PLA full frontal and escalating matters to a situation where the whole territory could possibly be laid bare and diplomatic opportunity thrown away. We needed to buy time with our response. I put this plan to Derek Boorman who told me it was music to his ears.

"Later when I returned as CBF in 1990 I found that the brigade had reverted to the old defence plans. I reintroduced my original 1985 plans in the tense post-Tiananmen situation. We had one such confrontation where the Chinese after some difficulties with the Hong Kong Government in one aspect of our negotiations suddenly decided that they would not take back captured illegal immigrants. The result was a mass influx. We responded by upping our presence on the border, opening holding camps and holding the line while diplomatic exchanges continued. A few days afterwards the Chinese reverted to the old procedure and announced that they had 'taught us a lesson'. The realities were plain enough. As Kissinger used to say, 'There is a China card and China holds it.'"

* * * * *

To revert back to the situation 40 years earlier, why didn't the British declare an 'open city' in 1940 in the face of the overwhelming threat posed by the highly experienced Japanese forces just beyond the border, saving many thousands of British, Canadian, Indian and Chinese lives thereby? Why take on the Japanese Army "full frontal – and escalating matters to a situation where the whole territory could possibly be laid bare..." – an option General Duffell sought to avoid, in quite different circumstances, in the 1980s?

The Chiefs of Staff wanted the garrison to fight in 1940 because it was all a matter of Britain's prestige. For political and moral reasons Hong Kong had to be defended. Moreover many Chinese would have been seriously discouraged from continuing their weary and interminable struggle against Japan, if Britain had lacked the courage and determination to resist and had abandoned the Colony to the mercy of the Japanese before they had even declared war. Such a sordid act of appeasement would also have shaken the neutral Americans who were then strengthening their forces in the Pacific while critically assessing Britain's determination to fight on. The Chiefs of Staff had no wish to blatantly broadcast the extent of Britain's military weakness not only in the Far East, but throughout the world.

But other considerations were at play – those in Hong Kong and Singapore gradually came to believe that the Japanese Army was a second rate, contemptible force. Major General A E Grasett, Bartholomew's successor, urged that his garrison be strengthened by one more battalion. It would enable him to defend the Mainland, he said, against Japanese incursions from the north. Air Chief Marshal Sir Robert Brooke-Popham, as indicated earlier, also believed that greater robustness would defeat the Japanese.

Grasett was a Canadian who had graduated from the Royal Military College in 1909, having won the Sword of Honour before being granted a British commission in the Royal Engineers (John Harris's Corps). He had won the DSO and MC during the First World War after which he had attended the Staff College at Camberley and the tri-service Imperial Defence College when he and his colleagues studied the Hong Kong situation in 1934. It was remarkable how closely the exercise mirrored the actual development of events through to 1941. Their prophetic conclusion had been that the risks involved in holding Hong Kong were unjustifiable.

Yet, strangely, Grasett throughout 1940 became convinced that the Colony was defensible, believing that the Japanese troops were vastly inferior to Westerners in training, equipment and leadership. Japan's inability to defeat Chiang Kai-shek's Nationalists in battle was put down to incompetence.

In August 1941 Grasett was posted back to Britain, travelling via Ottawa where he held long discussions with his Royal Military College classmate, Major General H D G Crerar, Chief of the Canadian General Staff. Crerar subsequently told the Royal Commission convened in March 1942 that "Major General Grasett informed me... that the addition of two or more battalions to the forces then at Hong Kong would render the garrison strong enough to withstand for an extensive period of siege an attack by such forces as the Japanese could bring to bear against it."[5]

Grasett briefed the Chiefs of Staff on 5th September 1941 to persuade them to reverse their policy and recommend to the Prime Minister that significant reinforcements be provided.

The existing force in Hong Kong, he argued, was quite insufficient to deter an attack, or even delay the enemy sufficiently to destroy the port and installations, while the addition of two battalions would enable a full brigade of three battalions to deploy on the Mainland, with a second brigade defending the Island from a seaward assault. In addition, the Chinese would be encouraged by confirmation that Britain and her Empire were determined to fight for their possessions in the Far East.

"The Chiefs of Staff heard an interesting account on the present situation in Hong Kong from General Grasett," read the memorandum to Winston Churchill. "He pointed out the great advantages to be derived from the addition of one or two battalions, and suggested that these might be supplied by Canada. The Chiefs of Staff have previously advised against despatch of more reinforcements to Hong Kong because they considered that it would only have been to throw good money after bad, but the position in the Far East has now changed. Our defences in Malaya have been improved and Japan has latterly shown a certain weakness in her attitude towards Great Britain and the United States .... The Chiefs of Staff are in favour of the suggestion that Canada should be asked to send one or two battalions... "[6] Some five months earlier Churchill had advocated that the isolated Hong Kong garrison be reduced to a symbolic scale: "We must avoid frittering away our resources on untenable positions," he had argued.[7] But now he was not sure whether to agree or not to the new suggestion that Hong Kong, if reinforced, could be held after all. "It is a question of timing," he replied a week later. "There is no objection to the approach being made [to the Canadians for two battalions] as proposed; but further decisions should be taken before the battalions actually sail."

On 19th September the Dominion Office cabled Ottawa stating that "Approved policy has been that Hong Kong should be regarded as an outpost... a small re-enforcement of the garrison of Hong Kong, e.g. by one or two battalions, would be very fully justified. It would increase the strength of the garrison out of all proportion to the actual numbers involved and it would provide a very strong stimulus to the garrison and to the Colony, it would further have a very great moral effect in the whole of the Far East and would reassure Chiang Kai-shek as to the reality of our intent to hold the Island."

* * * * *

With the benefit of hindsight, we must ask ourselves how was it that Britain's, and in particular Hong Kong's and Singapore's, intelligence gathering was so bad in the months leading up to the Japanese onslaught throughout the Far East?

Major General C M Maltby, Grasett's successor as GOC Hong Kong, reassured by further reports from his staff of the inferior quality and material of the Japanese, and by the prospect of reinforcements from Canada, decided to deploy almost half his force forward on the Mainland. He referred in a signal to the War Office to holding the Gin Drinkers' Line "permanently" in order to protect Kai Tak airfield, simplify civil defence problems and make possible eventual offensive operations. Maltby posed the question a month before the catastrophic defeat by the Japanese: "Is not the value of Hong Kong as a bridgehead increasing every day? Looking at the future, a complete mobile brigade group could undertake offensive operations to assist Chinese forces operating in Japanese-occupied territories."[8]

Maltby saw Hong Kong as the potential springboard for Britain, Canada and her allies to liberate South China from the Japanese. A month later in Shamshuipo prisoner of war camp, the terrible anguish and despair he felt at his defeat was so much greater because, through no fault of his own perhaps, the Japanese threat had been so misrepresented to him.

A heavy responsibility for the misreading of the intelligence, it appears, must fall on Maltby's senior officer, Major Charles R Boxer, arguably the most experienced Intelligence Officer in the Far East.

Educated at Wellington College, Boxer had been commissioned in 1923 into The Lincolnshire Regiment after 18 months at the Royal Military College, Sandhurst. Over the next seven years he successfully developed two careers – his military one, and secondly as an historian and author, learning Dutch, Portuguese and Japanese.

Boxer learnt Japanese at the School of Oriental Studies at the University of London. In 1930 he undertook an additional year of intense instruction in Tokyo before being assigned to a Japanese regiment as a Military Language Officer where, it was confidently believed by the British Ambassador in Japan, Sir Robert Craigie, that the British Language Officers were in a much better position to understand the minds and ambitions of their Japanese hosts than were the ordinary British Military Attachés on his staff. In the months to come,

Boxer formed lasting friendships with fellow Japanese army officers, and scholars who shared his academic interests.

By 1931 he was serving with the 38th Nara infantry regiment at Kyoto, living with his Japanese hosts in their barracks. They 'leased' him a cook-concubine who saw to his needs and improved his colloquial Japanese. In mid 1933 he returned to his regiment in Yorkshire before a posting to the Intelligence division of the War Office in London.

This then was the man who became a key member of the intelligence-gathering Far East Combined Bureau (FECB), and the GOC's principal Intelligence Officer and Interpreter. He travelled extensively in China and became highly thought of, despite his remarkable private life. After his wife had been despatched to Australia with others, he took an American journalist and one time opium addict, Emily Hahn, as his lover, having an illegitimate child with her. As we will see, he was probably responsible for one of the most erroneous signals ever sent on the eve of battle to the War Office.

The other important Intelligence Officer in Hong Kong was Flight Lieutenant H T 'Alf' Bennett, also a Japanese linguist.

In September 1990 I was running a major two-day battlefield tour for British Servicemen in Hong Kong. While waiting to be taken by helicopter for a reconnaissance of the Shingmun Redoubt with veterans of the campaign, Bennett approached me unexpectedly. "You should be aware why the intelligence was so bad before the war," he told me. "It was the fault of the British Ambassador's staff in Tokyo. They had been there much too long, and had become complacent, some marrying Japanese. Confined to restricted areas of Japan, they were fed false intelligence by Japanese agents. And so it was that we were misled."

Sir Sydney Giffard, who served four tours with the Foreign Office in Japan between 1952 and 1980 ending up as the Ambassador, disagrees with Bennett's assessment "because it had been clear to experienced observers for many years (since the Manchurian Incident and the murder of Prime Minister Inukai) that the Japanese Government was coming under increasing pressure from extreme nationalist elements, especially in the army, bent on expansion in China and against Western interests in Asia".

There is no evidence that the British staff had been in Tokyo too long before the war.

Major General Maltby found it easy to blame the Embassy in Tokyo. He stated in his post war report that the civil defence plan was not fully implemented before Japan's invasion because of "the belief that Japan was bluffing… the true gravity of the state of affairs was not reflected in the Embassy despatches from Tokyo."[9] Yet the British and American Ambassadors were giving London and Washington grim warnings of impending Japanese operations, and at least one British Military Attaché in Tokyo from 1938, Colonel G T Wards, had accurate views. He was another Japanese linguist who, like Boxer, had been attached to a Japanese regiment. Lecturing to the officers in Singapore in April 1941, he had emphasised the excellent morale and thorough training of the Japanese, condemning the common belief that they would be no match for British soldiers. However, the senior officer present vehemently disagreed, announcing that Wards' views were "far from the truth" and "in no way a correct appreciation of the situation".[10]

Whether Alf Bennett was right to blame the Military Attachés in Tokyo is therefore highly questionable. Both he and Boxer were frequently across the border in China with their Japanese friends. Surely they were in a good position to discover what was going on?

Just as Prime Minister Blair and President Bush were seemingly misled, it would appear, by their Intelligence and Secret Service Officers before the 2003 Iraqi war on the question of Weapons of Mass Destruction, so General Maltby must, it appears, have been ill informed by his senior staff responsible for advising him on Japanese intentions and capabilities. Nobody in Hong Kong knew what the Japanese were up to. They were soon to find out.

Notes

1. File 106/2375, Public Record Office (now the National Archives), London.
2. PRO CAB 80/15, COS (40) 592 (revise), dated 15th August 1940.
3. Ibid.
4. Elphick, Peter, *Far Eastern File: The Intelligence War in the Far East*, London: Hodder & Stoughton, 1997, p. 256.
5. Duff, Sir Lyman P, *Report on the Canadian Expeditionary Force to the Crown Colony of Hong Kong*, Ottawa, 1942, p. 14.
6. Memo Mr Hollis to the PM, dated 10.9.41 (PRO).
7. Churchill, W S, *The Grand Alliance*, London: Cassell, 1950, p. 157.
8. File 106/2400 signal 1488, dated 27.11.41 (PRO).
9. *Operations in Hong Kong from 8th to 25th December 1941*, supplement to the *London Gazette*, 27.1.48.
10. Kirby, S Woodburn, *Singapore: the Chain of Disaster*, London: Cassell, 1971, pp. 74–5.

CHAPTER 7

Battle Stations

Major General C M Maltby arrived in Hong Kong in July 1941. The GOC had gained useful experience fighting the Pathans on India's northwest frontier. "He was fit, wiry and lightly-built, rather bowlegged with a slightly rolling gait. His blue eyes could be very kindly or very frosty, always betraying the mood he was in," remembers his ADC, Captain Iain MacGregor Royal Scots. "His hair, cut very short, was sandy tinged with grey. He had a trim moustache and a complexion like the mellowed red brick of an Elizabethan English country house. He was not amused by caustic or esoteric wit; never by smut. He was almost a British caricature in some ways."[1]

General Maltby's idea of a peaceful Sunday afternoon in the hot weather was "a stroll round the Island". Taking up to half a dozen staff officers, most of whom would rather be playing golf or sleeping, he would clamber along the most inaccessible hillsides and the roughest paths, nullahs and catch-waters for three hours, studying the possible battlefields. General Maltby hated all forms of protocol and detested snobbery, pretentiousness, boasters and pomposity. He had instructed at the Indian Staff College at Quetta (but, contrary to some accounts, he had not been the Commandant there). His subsequent appointment was as a District Commander in India. He had been led to expect further promotion after his tour in Hong Kong.

Before the arrival of the Canadians in November 1941, Maltby had only four Regular Army battalions – 2nd Battalion Royal Scots, 1st Battalion the Middlesex Regiment, 5/7th Rajputs and 2/14th Punjabis.

His new plan, when the Canadians arrived, was that three battalions would fight on the Gin Drinkers' Line on the Mainland, leaving the Middlesex Regiment, a machine-gun battalion, to man the pill-boxes round the Island, and the two Canadian battalions on the Island to oppose any landings from the sea. The Island Brigade would be under command of the Canadian Brigadier J K Lawson. When necessary, after holding the Japanese for as long as possible, certainly not less than a week, the Mainland battalions would withdraw to the Island, leaving only an Indian battalion to hold the Devil's Peak in the south-east. See Map on page 37.

The Mainland Brigade was commanded by the newly promoted Brigadier Cedric Wallis. He became the most controversial soldier in the battle for Hong Kong. Wallis had enlisted in the Royal Horse Guards in the First World War, been commissioned into the Sherwood Foresters and served in the Lancashire Regiment before joining the Indian Army in 1917. He had fought in Iraq; at the end of the First World War he was appointed the Chief Political Officer in Mosul before a posting to southwest Persia. He next served in south India and Burma. At the beginning of the Second World War, he commanded an internal security force in Bombay before moving to Hong Kong in 1940. He was promoted to Brigadier from Lieutenant Colonel in command of 5/7 Rajputs, shortly before the Canadians arrived. (Some books state erroneously that he had the Military Cross.)

Wallis was a slim, tough, very determined and ambitious soldier who wore a black patch or a dark monocle over his left eye, which he had lost in the First World War. He felt there were too many cocktail parties in Hong Kong and too little time was spent in hard training. Like John Harris, he had listened to Brooke-Popham's optimistic views. "I felt the Air Marshal must be very badly informed and making a great mistake in belittling the Japs," he wrote afterwards. "This sort of nonsense fitted in very nicely with what many liked to hear and believe in, as they could not bear to think that their carefree, elegant life-styles could be interfered with."[2]

Early in November 1941, Wallis committed his three battalions to occupy and work on the Gin Drinkers' Line, instead of going to camps on the frontier. He felt that defence preparations should take priority over all else. "With many young and inexperienced officers and newly arrived recruits in Indian units, all units were badly in need of training also," he wrote. "Camps were consequently postponed until after Christmas 1941, so that units could live and work in their battle positions, in itself one of the best forms of training."

The 2nd Battalion the Royal Scots, the oldest and senior British Infantry Regiment of the Line, was responsible for the west, including the Shingmun Redoubt, and for covering the southern slopes of Tai Mo Shan mountain. The 2/14 Punjabis covered the centre of the Mainland and the 5/7 Rajputs were on the right (east). See Map on page 37.

The Royal Scots "worked hard wiring, digging and on camouflage and were in good form except that their strength was sadly reduced by sickness," wrote Wallis. "Malarial cases were the heaviest and their defensive area was badly infested with mosquitoes. At one time 110 cases were being treated.

"Both Indian battalions had been weakened by repeated 'milkings' for new units and had just received 150–180 partially trained recruits as reinforcements. The Rajputs received new 3 inch mortars only after deployment."

All units registered possible artillery targets by bringing down live fire and then adjusting it for range. The targets included for example likely enemy approaches or forming up points before an attack. The artillery batteries were either mobile ones or in static gun emplacements.

With a frontage of ten miles along the Gin Drinkers' Line, no reserve unit could be found to stop the enemy should they break through.

Previously the Royal Scots' war role had been on the Island and so the officers and soldiers were unfamiliar with the ground in their new position. They were responsible for a frontage of over 5,000 yards although the textbook norm was 1,000 yards. The abandoned 1937 plan envisaged that at least two divisions would be required to hold the line properly. Wallis had less than one sixth of this strength. The Royal Scots Battalion was issued with only 90 anti-personnel mines – far too few. It had been 'milked' like the Indian Battalions, losing ten experienced officers and receiving territorial or emergency commissioned replacements, many of whom had only just taken up their new appointments before the war started; the Battalion was left with just four officers possessing regular commissions.

On 25th October, two days before the Canadians sailed from Vancouver, a brief reached Ottawa from the War Office which read: "The task of the Hong Kong garrison is to defend the Colony against internal attack and to deny the use of the harbour and dry dock to the enemy.

"The threat: the Japanese are established on the Mainland, are carrying out operations in the vicinity of the frontier, and are in possession of a number of air bases within easy reach of the Colony. They also hold command of the sea and are therefore in a position to occupy the surrounding islands at will… "

This frank, rather pessimistic report ensured that the Canadians were aware of the true situation. Crerar, the Canadian CGS, had earlier announced that there was "no military risk" in sending two battalions to Hong Kong. Nevertheless he "had many high-level British contacts, who, at the strategic level, had a thorough understanding of the risks involved," wrote Brereton Greenhous, who worked for 25 years in Ottawa's Department of National Defence's Directorate of History. "They could have told him at any time during the past two or three years that the garrison was no more than a hostage to fortune." [4]

On 16th November 1941 the Canadians reached Hong Kong, ten days before Cordell Hull, the American Secretary of State, rejected the Japanese attempt to prolong diplomatic negotiations. Hull was still insisting that all Japanese troops be withdrawn from China and Indo-China before Washington would release any assets or permit the importation of oil.

Four days after the Canadians arrived, they occupied their battle positions during a night exercise. Starting in early December, one of the three platoons in each company spent a few days in turn manning these positions after a further reconnaissance. The British had no knowledge of the level of training of the Canadians on their arrival. The account which follows may seem harsh and critical of them.

It is often forgotten that there was a Canadian Army to fight in northwest Europe from the D-Day beaches onwards. Moreover 623 high grade young Canadian officers commanded British platoons in 140 battalions in Italy, France, Belgium, Holland and Germany.[5] Canadian officers had also served earlier in North Africa to gain experience. Well trained, well led and uncommitted Canadian battalions, impatient for action, were not chosen for Hong Kong because the imminence of hostilities there was not understood; the fact that the international situation had become so precarious was not recognised. Canada deserves infinite gratitude for sending reinforcements – all volunteers – to Hong Kong.

Many Canadian soldiers, if properly trained, were outstanding. Field Marshal Lord Alanbrooke, who had a critical eye and no respect for the second rate, wrote in his diary on 5th September 1941: "Motored down to Tilshead to visit the Canadian Army Tank Brigade. They have not been in the country long and are consequently in the early stages, but promise very well ..." [6]

On 3rd December Maltby and Lawson toured the frontier and, watching the Japanese through binoculars, thought them to be scruffy, lazy and uninterested. Nevertheless two independent reports from China stated that between 10,000 and 20,000 Japanese were expected to arrive at Sham Chun, five miles north of Fanling close to the border, on 4th December for an attack on the Colony.[7] Maltby did not believe these reports, preferring, presumably, the reassuring views from Major Charles Boxer and "people of all kinds and nationalities from all over China, MI6, consular agents, Secret Intelligence Service, cloak-and-dagger types from Shanghai, Canton and elsewhere" whom Maltby's ADC was admitting at night direct into the General's study. [8]

Maltby was responsible for the defence of Hong Kong but was answerable to the Governor, who was also the King's Representative and Commander in Chief. It was the previous Governor, Sir Geoffrey Northcote, who had proposed to the British War Cabinet that Hong Kong should be declared an open city and the Japanese forces allowed to march in. The closing months of his tour had been clouded by two scandals involving mishandled immigration and air raid shelters which failed to match up to specifications. Some expatriates believed that the entire Government apparatus was riddled with graft. In September 1941 Northcote left Hong Kong with "a nasty taste in my mouth".

His successor was Sir Mark Young. After initial training in Ceylon, he had served in the West Indies and the Middle East for 13 years, ending up as Governor of Tanganyika before coming to Hong Kong. He was a very able, tough, courageous, unflappable, austere and awe-inspiring figure who did not suffer fools gladly. Sir Mark was of medium height, slim and always immaculately dressed, befitting perhaps his background of Eton and the Rifle Brigade.

During the months before the Japanese invasion, the Hong Kong Government, in keeping with the War Office's policy, did not take rigorous action in the face of blatant Japanese hostile provocation. For example the Governor, then Northcote, reported that Formosans were entering the Colony as fifth columnists. He wanted to deport them, but the Foreign Office cautioned against such action, fearing reprisals. He also complained about low-level bomber flights over Hong Kong's fortifications, but the Foreign Office again advised against taking decisive action. The Japanese proceeded to sink junks carrying food for the Colony, to occupy two islands immediately south of Hong Kong, to send a naval party to seize temporarily a British lighthouse and to insert a virtual naval encirclement around the Colony. Northcote told London that these unfriendly actions warranted a vigorous response, though he did not request permission to undertake retaliatory action for he had no modern aircraft and, should hostilities break out, the outcome would be a bloody one.

Could the British and Hong Kong Governments be accused of a degree of appeasement in not taking vigorous action against extreme Japanese provocation? Field Marshal Alanbrooke took over from Field Marshal Dill as CIGS on 1st December 1941 and noted in his diary that he had discussed the possibility of Japan entering the war with Dill. "He had told me frankly that he had done practically nothing to meet this threat," wrote Alanbrooke. "He said we were already so weak on all fronts that it was impossible to denude them any further to meet a possible threat." Alanbrooke thought Dill was right in his dispositions and that he could not have done more to meet the probable Japanese entry into the war.

Stalin, on the other hand, could have mobilised his vast forces before the German onslaught – Operation Barbarossa. He could have moved his aircraft from vulnerable airfields where they remained wing-tip to wing-tip; he could have committed his divisions to battle stations instead of leaving them to face giant German encirclements; he could have listened to Stafford Cripps, the British Ambassador in Moscow, who had earlier delivered a letter from Churchill warning of the invasion. But Stalin believed that Britain was trying to entrap Russia and concluded that "they're playing us off against each other".[9]

Sir Mark Young appreciated that vigorous protests in Hong Kong could not be backed up by force. Had definitive information been available weeks before Japan went to war, there was little he or Maltby could have done about it, unlike Stalin.

As mentioned in Chapter 1, on Saturday 6th December a cablegram from Singapore reached Alanbrooke and Maltby with news that two convoys of Japanese transports, escorted by cruisers and destroyers, were southwest of Saigon in Indo-China (now Vietnam). That evening a British officer on Hong Kong's frontier received a police message that three Japanese divisions of 38,000 men had arrived at To Kat, only eight miles from the frontier. That same evening at 7.20 p.m. Singapore ordered the RAF in Hong Kong to assume "No. 1 degree of readiness". That night all the Anti Aircraft guns in the Colony were manned.

The Church Parade at St John's Cathedral in Victoria on Sunday 7th December started no differently from any other. General Maltby was there with many of his officers. Hurried twitterings of conversation among the ladies confirmed that the Chinese Charity Ball at the Peninsula Hotel the night before had been a great success. The latest rumours about the Japanese caused anxious, worried frowns. An officer suddenly entered the Cathedral and whispered to Maltby in the front pew. He got up and strode from the Church followed by others. The Service had not even reached the prayers for peace.

The Defence Council was hurriedly summoned to a lengthy meeting at Government House. Sir Mark Young and Major General Maltby agreed that war was imminent, and the entire garrison was ordered to war stations. Deployment began.

On that same morning, John Harris drove in his small Morris car to Fanling, close to the Chinese border, because he had heard rumours of a large Japanese fleet nearby. Accompanied by Jimmy Wakefield, Willie Clarkson and Dickie Arundell, he indeed saw the ships unloading in an adjacent bay. They felt certain that war was imminent. After a picnic they returned that evening, passing barbed wire concentration points, concrete pill-boxes and ammunition dumps nestling under camouflage nets among the hills.

Well to the south, the Royal Rifles of Canada and Winnipeg Grenadiers moved to their trenches along the mountainous range of the Island, to oppose any landing from the sea. On the Mainland, the Royal Scots, Punjabis and Rajputs similarly manned their battle stations, watching the rapidly changing shadows as the clouds raced across the moon. Victoria Peak was usually a sparkling Christmas tree of lights; that night it was in darkness, sullen and unfriendly. Covered by the massive guns of Stanley Fort, Motor Torpedo Boats patrolled far out into the South China Sea to give early warning of the enemy's approach. In the misty, heavily camouflaged pill-boxes of Hong Kong Island, the machine-gun battalion of the Middlesex Regiment stood-to. The Hong Kong garrison was ready for war.

After darkness that night Major Charles Boxer, together with Geoffrey S Wilson who was Head of the New Territories Constabulary, went to the top of a hill overlooking the Japanese frontier positions a few thousand yards away. They could not see any movement, not even a lighted cigarette. Boxer remarked that it did not look as if anything was going to happen that night. He returned to Victoria to the Battlebox Headquarters for night duty.

Even at this eleventh hour, the possible concentration of at least a Japanese division close to the border was contemptuously dismissed by at least one senior staff officer that day: an astonishingly erroneous intelligence summary was sent to the War Office from Hong Kong stating that "the reports are certainly exaggerated and have the appearance of being deliberately fostered by the Japanese who, judging by their defensive preparations around Canton, appear distinctly nervous of being attacked."[10] There is no proof that Boxer drafted that cable, but it seems highly unlikely that, being the garrison's senior Intelligence Officer in Hong Kong, he would not have approved its contents. This suggests that some officers were totally out of touch with reality.

Notes

1. Letter MacGregor to author, 1977.
2. Letter Wallis to author, 1977.
3. File 593 (D14) MO10, National Defence Headquarters (NDHQ), Ottawa.
4. Greenhous, Brereton, "C" *Force to Hong Kong: A Canadian Catastrophe 1941–1945*, Canadian War Museum Historical Publication, No. 30, 1997, p. 19.
5. Burd, Frederick, 'CANLOAN', *The Guards Magazine*, Winter 1996, p. 244.
6. Alanbrooke, F M, *War Diaries 1939–1945*, London: Weidenfeld & Nicolson, 2001, p. 181.
7. File 106/2400 (PRO).
8. Letter MacGregor to author.
9. Sebag Montefiore, Simon, *Stalin: the Court of the Red Tsar*, London: Weidenfeld & Nicolson, 2003, p. 309.
10. File 106/2400 op. cit. (PRO).

CHAPTER 8

Shingmun Redoubt: The Vital Ground

8th–10th December 1941

The story which follows reflects great courage, which Churchill recognised, and considerable controversy. Was if fair that only one of the British Regiments should be awarded the Battle Honour 'Hong Kong' to be emblazoned on their Colours for ever more, when the other Regiment was denied this coveted honour? Was it appropriate for the Canadian battalions to be so severely criticised that Montgomery had to intervene on their behalf to have the Official History altered? Is it possible to produce convincing new evidence, 64 years after the fall of Hong Kong, that some soldiers' reputations were needlessly maligned? At the conclusion of Part 3 of this book, the reader can make his own mind up on these issues.

* * * * *

The Japanese attacked three nations almost concurrently. Masanobu Tsuji, Chief of Operations 25th Japanese Army, Malaya, stated that the first landings at Kota Bharu on the east coast of Siam and Malaya took place 80 minutes before the initial raid on Pearl Harbor (7.53 a.m. local time).

At 4.45 a.m. local time on Monday 8th December in Hong Kong, Major Charles Boxer heard on a Tokyo broadcast instructions in code to their nationals that war was imminent with Great Britain and America. Sir Mark Young was immediately informed and the garrison alerted.

Major G E Grey, commanding the border force of C Company 2/14 Punjabis and the Engineer demolition parties to the east and north of Fanling, immediately and successfully blew up all forward demolitions, having received orders to do so at 5 a.m.

At 6.45 a.m. the garrison was told that the British Empire and Japan were at war. Some 75 minutes later the loud crescendo of an air raid warning ominously disturbed the bright sunny morning. Practice alerts had never taken place at that hour before.

John Harris went out onto the veranda of his flat in May Road, halfway up the Peak, in time to see planes circling over Kai Tak airport. The loud rattle of anti-aircraft and machine-gun fire mingled with the explosions of falling bombs. So sudden was the attack that people elsewhere at first thought that "the bloody Royal Air Force was practising for a display". He also saw bombs landing very close to a Royal Navy ship in Victoria Harbour. She was moored fore and aft and was trying frantically to sail to safety. He had never seen the Navy unloose a ship so quickly.

John drove in his Morris car to his battle position at the Dairy Farm, close to the Royal Artillery gun positions on Mount Davis in the northwest of the Island and near Queen Mary Hospital. He met there about a dozen other Sappers. The Dairy Farm was a well-built, single-storey agricultural building on a beautiful site overlooking the Canton Delta. His role was to repair any structural damage and to maintain the pumps which carried water to the Gunners. He did not anticipate that he would have to undertake infantry patrols when more and more men were lost in the desperate days ahead. We will return to his adventures in due course.

The Japanese attack on Kai Tak had been most successful. All but one of the five ancient Vildebeeste and Walrus aircraft were left blazing on the airfield close to wooden buildings which had crumbled into sheets of flame. Eight civilian aircraft had also been destroyed. The implications of losing so much so soon were serious: Maltby no longer had the ability to mount air reconnaissance to discover the location of the Japanese. Attempts to camouflage the dispersed aircraft were futile; no dispersal bays had been built due to the expense involved.

The Japanese then switched to their secondary targets. Ignoring the port, gun positions and troop emplacements on the Gin Drinkers' Line, they chose to attack the 2,000 Canadians still in Shamshuipo camp. Heavy bombs descended upon the barracks while fighter aircraft machine-gunned the huts from 60 feet. But the Japanese intelligence was faulty: both Canadian battalions had moved on the previous day. There were only two Canadian casualties – Sergeant Routledge and Signalman Fairley. They were the first Canadian soldiers to be wounded in the Second World War.

The Japanese had over-estimated the strength of the RAF in Hong Kong. They gleefully reported on Radio Tokyo the destruction of 14 large and 12 medium planes.

The Hong Kong scene had changed dramatically. Trucks, cars, buses, wagons, carts and rickshaws still ran through the narrow streets, but air raid wardens, auxiliary nurses and uniformed Volunteers of the Hong Kong Volunteer Defence Corps were already at their posts.

Conscription for British residents had been introduced in Hong Kong in 1941. Most had joined the Hong Kong Volunteer Defence Corps, referred to hereafter as 'the Volunteers'. They had become something very special, for they alone were training to fight for their families and homes. They came from many professions: there were humble clerks and dockyard artisans as well as prosperous bankers and the *taipans* of the big trading firms. All parts of the British Isles were represented in their ranks, which also included Chinese, Free French, Russians and Portuguese. There were also Scandinavians and Americans who can even more truly have been considered Volunteers since their nations were then neutral.

As Hong Kong prepared for its first morning of war, Sawyers, Churchill's butler at Chequers, carried in a cheap portable radio to the Prime Minister's dining room. A programme of music was suddenly interrupted by a warning to listeners to stand by for an important announcement. Averell Harriman from Washington and Churchill heard the calm, grave voice of the BBC announcer tell Britain that Pearl Harbor had been attacked. The Stars and Stripes and Union Flag were now irrevocably entwined.

In Hong Kong furious work continued on the demolition of the railway bridges over the Sham Chin river. (See Map on page 37) The British could see the Japanese quite clearly, scarcely 300 yards away to their front – well within shot. But the Japanese made no attempt to rush the bridges or open fire, since they too were equally busy preparing their own bridge which they would push across when the British had blown theirs and departed.

As the dust settled after two enormous explosions, the British and Japanese alike saw that both bridges had been destroyed. The Japanese eagerly rushed forward with their replacement as the demolition party pulled back behind Major Grey's covering force.

Forward observation posts reported hundreds of Japanese sweeping south in two separate thrusts at best possible speed, travelling across country rather than by roads when necessary. At 6.30 p.m. the railway tunnel south of Tai Po was destroyed, while defensive positions were taken up for the night on the higher ground to the south.

Despite the inevitable loss of the obsolete RAF aircraft, the first day of the battle for Hong Kong had gone to plan, thanks to Major General Maltby and his garrison. The 12,000 British, Canadian, Indian and Chinese troops were in their defensive positions and the ships at battle stations in good time. Maltby had ordered the blowing up of the demolitions four hours before the Japanese 38th Division had attacked.

* * * * *

This should be compared to developments elsewhere. We have seen how the British Expeditionary Force in France had no warning of the German onslaught; at Singapore the first Japanese air raid on the installations was an instant success; everything was beautifully lit up because the man responsible for blacking everything out had gone off duty taking the key to the electricity power station with him.

An American radar unit at Pearl Harbor had detected the approach of aircraft. Close to the island an American warship had sunk a Japanese submarine. Nevertheless the alarm was not raised. When the Japanese started positioning themselves to attack the US Pacific Fleet at Hawaii several Americans started making out low infringement flying reports, still believing the aircraft must be their own. There subsequently occurred one of the strangest episodes in American military history: the destruction of General Douglas MacArthur's air force, on the ground, nine hours after word had reached him of the disaster at Pearl Harbor. The need for momentous decisions in Manila that morning proved to be too much for him. The United States lost most of their aircraft in the Philippines, practically all the B-17s and most of their fighters, surprised on the ground, with negligible cost to the Japanese.[1]

* * * * *

By dawn on 9th December, Major Grey's forward troops were between the northeast of Needle Hill, on Monastery Ridge and Sha Tin – the last of their delaying positions. They had fulfilled their role admirably. Communications had been well maintained, over 100 casualties inflicted on the enemy and 16 major demolitions carried out on the bridges, roads and railway. By dusk they withdrew behind the Royal Scots, Rajputs and Punjabi Battalions on the Gin Drinkers' Line. But the Japanese were clearly fit, skilful and well led. The ability of the Japanese to move rapidly and stealthily, particularly at night, disturbed and probably surprised Maltby.

On the Island, theatres, cinemas and some restaurants still functioned normally. At the Palace Floating Restaurant, which resembled a Mississippi steamboat, diners leisurely chose their lobsters, shrimps, crabs, scallops, oysters, squids, prawns and garoupa, all of which wallowed alive in large cages beneath the restaurant, a few paces from the toilets which spilt their contents into the static, stagnating water.

The *South China Morning Post* on Tuesday 9th December was as reassuring as always. Life went on as normal on the Island "as if we were taking part in yet another exercise", recalled Captain A G Hewitt, the Adjutant of the Middlesex. "We were not very concerned that the Japanese had advanced rapidly. I drove round the Island with the RSM and visited our companies and the Winnipeg Grenadiers, drinking Scotch with our people and Canadian rye with the others. Morale was high."[2]

To what extent they were influenced by Air Chief Marshal Sir Robert Brooke-Popham's stirring Order of the Day is doubtful. It read: "We are ready. We have had plenty of warning and our preparations are made and tested... We are confident. Our defences are strong and our weapons efficient. Whatever our race, we have one aim and one aim only. It is to defend these shores, to destroy such of our enemies as may set foot on our soil..."

General Maltby's Order of the Day was "... I expect each and every man of my force to stick it out unflinchingly, and that my force will become a great example of high-hearted courage to all the rest of the Empire who are fighting to preserve truth, justice and liberty for the world."

By 9th December the Japanese closed up to the Gin Drinkers' Line. The blow was to fall on the Royal Scots' Shingmun Redoubt – the 'vital ground' to the British and Japanese alike, the key to the defensive position on the Mainland. The redoubt was the dominating ground which, if captured by the enemy, would enable them to choose the most advantageous approach into Kowloon City itself, bypassing the Rajputs and Punjabis to the east.

Brigadier Wallis commanding the Mainland Brigade was well aware of the extreme vulnerability of the redoubt. He had participated in exercises earlier in the year when his Rajput Battalion broke through the position. Little did he realise that the tracks he was using would be used by the Japanese some months later. A Royal Scots officer made a 'dummy' attack on the Redoubt in early December to practise the defences. He had no difficulty in getting a section through the perimeter wire onto the position undetected. There are two reasons why this vital ground was so vulnerable. The principal one is that only No. 8 Platoon Royal Scots, an artillery observation post and A Company Headquarters, 42 men in all, could be spared to hold the position because all Maltby's forces, in particular those on the Gin Drinkers' Line, were spread too thinly. Secondly, the ground favoured the attacker because the front consisted of a confusing complex of defiles, re-entrants, bowls, sloughs and streams, varying in height between sea level on the west to over 1,000 feet on the east. There was, therefore, no prospect of many of the platoons being able to support each other.

In keeping with Brigadier Wallis's orders, the Commanding Officer of the Royal Scots, Lieutenant Colonel S E H E White, impressed on all ranks that the concrete defensive works were only to be used for Vickers machine-gun teams in the special weapon bays, for storage and, as a last resort, as protection against artillery or mortar fire. The need for sustained patrol activity was stressed. No mines could be spared for the redoubt's front.

The Royal Scots clearly had their problems, but so did Colonel Doi Teihichi and his 228th Regiment, whose leading battalion was advancing towards Tai Wai at the foot of Tide Cove.

* * * * *

To digress very briefly by introducing a personal note, having served in Hong Kong in the mid 1970s, I was posted at my request to Ottawa to serve 'on exchange' for two years in the Canadian National Defence Headquarters. Knowing that I was about to meet veterans of the

Winnipeg Grenadiers, which had much in common with my own Regiment including the same cap badge and Regimental March, I visited the Canadian Historical Branch. I enquired there if they had any files in their archives on the Winnipeg Grenadiers who had fought in Hong Kong. To my amazement, Brereton Greenhous showed me shelves of dusty files which contained all I needed, including numerous files with personal accounts by the senior surviving Japanese officers. These accounts are in no other archive. It transpired that the Japanese officers in question were brought back to Hong Kong after the war to face trials on the atrocities they had allegedly committed. Canadian prosecuting teams met them there and they all frequently walked the ground together with interpreters, and so the accounts ended up in Ottawa. The Japanese first-hand stories which follow in this book can therefore be relied upon.

* * * * *

By 3.00 p.m. on the 9th, Colonel Doi, ahead of his two other battalions, was on Needle Hill watching the Gin Drinkers' Line. "For about two hours we carried out a reconnaissance of the main line of defence," he recalled. "Although the enemy was not to be seen, a good view of the trenches and defensive positions was obtained, and a sighting of something like white clothes being dried gave a clue to the likely presence of enemy troops. My impression was that the enemy was still inactive perhaps because of their estimate that it would take at least several more days for the Japanese troops to approach their position. Heavy fog suddenly limited the visibility to about 20 metres, and as the rain began to fall and the wind was increasing it became utterly impossible to continue the recce."[3]

Colonel Doi's communications had failed and he had lost touch with his three battalions. Moreover, although he was being drawn irresistibly to attack the Shingmun Redoubt, it lay firmly in another Japanese regiment's sector. In the Japanese army, orders, once issued, had to be rigidly obeyed forthwith; there was no flexibility, or opportunity for commanders to use their discretion.

At last Doi located his battalions, which had already had an exhausting approach march; his supporting artillery had been delayed well back due to the British demolitions on the Tai Po Road and would not be available.

Near Jubilee Reservoir he ordered his 2nd Battalion on the left to recce the enemy. The 3rd Battalion was to attack at 11.00 p.m., with two Companies, containing at least 150 soldiers, leading. Obstacle-clearing teams moved forward to clear the pathways through the wire entanglements; this would take them an hour. As the Japanese prepared to attack the vital ground, Colonel Doi wondered what the British were up to.

At 8.00 p.m. 2nd Lieutenant J S R Thomson left the Redoubt with a patrol of nine soldiers. The remaining 17 men of his platoon were largely manning the Vickers machine guns or on sentry duty in the pill-boxes, of which there were five – all constructed of concrete and steel and connected to each other by underground tunnels.

The Company Commander, Captain C R Jones, had received orders from Colonel White that his Company should patrol to the north, to check on any enemy being on the southern slopes of Needle Hill and in the Shing Mun Valley, and that his patrols should then return via Captain H R Newton's D Company of the 5/7 Rajputs. It had been moved earlier that day to Smuggler's Ridge, which lay to the southeast of the Redoubt.

Thomson returned at 10.20 p.m. having spent some time with Captain Newton. "It seems beyond doubt, in view of the short time that had elapsed, that Thomson did not patrol towards the Shingmun river or Needle Hill. If he had, he would have run head-on into the advancing Japanese," recorded the history of the Royal Scots.[4] Had Thomson discovered that Doi's battalions were massing for an attack, he could have sent runners to the Forward Observation Officer, Lieutenant L C Wilcox, on the Redoubt. The FOO could then have brought artillery fire down on the Japanese, while all the mortars within range could have lobbed explosive projectiles at a high angle into the Japanese forming up points. Instead, Thomson reported to Jones in the artillery observation post, which was located underground alongside the Company Headquarters, stating that there was no indication that the enemy was near.

Ten minutes later Jones received a message that F W Kendall, who was nearby with another platoon, wanted to speak to him. Kendall was in charge of 'Z' Force, which had received some training to sabotage the enemy behind their lines. Because of the poor visibility, Jones ordered his runner, Private Wyllie, to guide Kendall to the observation post. Wyllie, contrary to orders, borrowed the key to the grille at the entrance of the post from the sentry there and, *on departing locked the gate on the outside and went off with the key.* The only other entrance was by the 'trap', or upper grille. "Although those inside the observation post were not aware of the situation the reality was they were trapped below ground. Thomson was the first to discover this predicament when he tried to return to his platoon," continues the Royal Scots' history.

At 11.00 p.m. Corporal Laird, on sentry nearest to the Shingmun river, saw lights and a group of shadowy figures approaching the wire. He challenged them. Receiving no reply, he opened fire with a sub-machine gun. Grenades were flung at him and his fire was returned. Laird alerted his section commander and shouted to the signaller to inform Sergeant Robb and Captain Jones of the situation.

"The Companies leading the attack," wrote Colonel Doi, "assaulted the eastern position. First, a small number of troops threw hand grenades into the air ventilation chimneys of the connecting tunnels, and the infiltrating teams went into the tunnels and engaged in fierce close-quarter fighting."

Jones told Brigadier Wallis on the field telephone that he had heard muffled explosions and shouts. Wallis ordered that this serious situation must be quickly dealt with and told Jones "to get out with all his men to evict the enemy quickly". Never, to his dying day, did Wallis ever discover that Jones was trapped inside the post with the Platoon Commander and Forward Observation Officer. The Japanese started to drop grenades down through the grille. The field telephone line became silent at 1.30 a.m. Over an hour later there was a large explosion which blew the roof off the observation post. By that time the three officers within the position, Jones, Thomson and Wilcox, were all wounded as were six soldiers, while two Indian Gunners had been killed. In these circumstances Captain Jones decided to surrender. They were virtually on their own because 18 men of the Royal Scots had decided to 'live and fight another day' by moving southeast up to a mile away to join Captain Newton's Rajputs, whom they reached at 3.30 a.m. on 10th December.

The last Royal Scots section post on the Redoubt held out for a further 11 hours before a British shell caused the concrete pill-boxes to cave in. Four soldiers were dug out alive by the Japanese.

"The capture by surprise of this key position which dominated a large portion of the left flank and the importance of which had been so frequently stressed beforehand, directly and gravely affected subsequent events and prejudiced Naval, Military and Civil defence arrangements," wrote General Maltby. "The possibility of mounting an immediate counter attack that night was considered but was ruled out as the nearest troops were a mile away, the ground precipitous and broken, and the redoubt very obscure."

The collapse of the Redoubt, which Maltby had hoped would be held for seven days, was one of the major disasters of the campaign, and "really caused chaos in Fortress HQ. I have never seen General Maltby more shocked or angry," recalled one of his staff officers.

So, where does the blame lie – with Captain Jones, inadvertently locked in the artillery post? With the Royal Scots platoon of 27 men facing three battalions of highly experienced Japanese soldiers? Or with Brigadier Wallis who had first-hand knowledge of the extreme vulnerability of the position and no reserves, yet expected a handful of men to achieve the impossible?

Notes

1. Manchester, William, *American Caesar*, New York: Dell, 1978, p. 238.
2. Interview Hewitt with author.
3. Colonel Doi's progress report in National Defence Headquarters (NDHQ) Directorate of History, Ottawa.
4. Paterson, R H,*Pontius Pilate's Bodyguard*, Vol. 2, The Royal Scots History Committee, 2000, p. 107.

CHAPTER 9

Nothing but Darkness Ahead

10th–13th December 1941

Following the collapse of the Shingmun Redoubt, the Royal Scots were ordered to withdraw to a new line farther to the rear between Golden Hill and Lai Chi Kok. (See Map on page 37.)

Paradoxically, having punched a gaping hole in the Gin Drinkers' Line, Colonel Doi, to his astonishment and dismay, was ordered that same morning of 10th December to withdraw from it immediately. His Divisional Commander told him that he had flouted the orders given to him by entering 230 Regiment's sector. Doi refused to obey two specific orders to abandon the position. His initiative was later censured. The Divisional staff officer, Oyadomani, was "sharply rebuked" for not curbing Doi's enthusiasm. By midday, however, Doi's achievement was recognised and he was permitted to remain on the Redoubt.

The Japanese were suffering casualties: their advance south of the Gin Drinkers' Line was stopped by artillery fire and the vigorous action taken by Captain Newton's Rajputs. One enemy company attacked and was driven back into the redoubt, which was then shelled by 6-inch Howitzers. The gunboat, HMS *Cicala*, built in 1916 and of 616 tons, had been covering the left flank of the Royal Scots during the last three days, and discovered a Japanese working party clearing demolitions. Fire was opened with 6-inch guns and direct hits obtained.

That afternoon the last of the Eastern Telegraph Company cables between Hong Kong and the outside world were cut by enemy action.

During 10th December Japanese torpedo boats, minesweepers, one cruiser and four destroyers were observed. This increased Maltby's uncertainty as to whether he should concentrate his forces to face further attacks from the Mainland in the north, or leave the two Canadian battalions, and the Middlesex in their pill-boxes, all spread around the Island. Meanwhile the battle for the Mainland continued, with the Japanese attacks falling again only on the Royal Scots. 2nd Lieutenant J A Ford in D Company was ordered to establish his platoon on the highest point of Golden Hill. The appalling strain of that climb in the dark was never forgotten. The soldiers, burdened by equipment and ammunition, and weak as some of them were with malaria, were in a state of exhaustion as they crawled on hands and knees over rocks and scrub to the bare hilltop. There they found a few shallow weapon pits dug over three years previously. There were no mines and the broken, rusted wire was valueless.[1] Yet this position was to be referred to as "the strong Golden Hill Line" in Maltby's despatches. Sentries were posted, while others tried to rest despite the bitter cold. No food could be carried up to them. Each man received a tot of rum for breakfast, while they stood to awaiting the next Japanese attack.

Captain D Pinkerton commanded D Company. Ford had nothing but praise for him: "It was his courage, his cool insistence on standing fast under merciless Japanese mortaring that gave D Company the reputation they won on Golden Hill. Pinkerton was a tall, unbending man, sparing of words and unsparing of our energies as well as his own... We were proud of him, perhaps partly because he made us proud of ourselves."

The remainder of the Battalion was to the west of Ford's platoon, on lower ground. At 7.30 a.m. on 11th December, the Japanese 230 Regiment attacked in great strength the whole Battalion front. "I saw Captain Pinkerton lead a bayonet charge to clear the top of Golden Hill ridge. From then on throughout the day we were heavily mortared," Ford continues. "There could be no fighting back. And the mortaring was carried out with deadly accuracy."

The Companies had been unable to establish field cable communications. The Official Report, published over seven years later as a supplement to *The London Gazette*, deals inadequately with what happened: "11th December – On the mainland at dawn the enemy opened up mortar fire and then attacked the left flank of the 2 Royal Scots, driving them back in disorder and exposing the junction of the Castle Peak and Taipo Road, thus seriously endangering the withdrawal of all the troops based on the Taipo Road... The situation was critical but the company of the 1 Winnipeg Grenadiers and the Bren carriers from Kai Tak aerodrome defences were moved into position covering the gap." As an afterthought, probably prompted by someone else, a note was added that both Royal Scots Company Commanders were killed. They were Captains W R T Rose and F S Richardson.

During this action, the Battalion Signals Officer, Captain Douglas Ford, went forward to a southern spur on Golden Hill because he knew that the supporting artillery had misjudged the range: British shells were falling amidst the Royal Scots. He found a field telephone and through Colonel White had the range increased. At 7.30 a.m. C Company had been 35 strong. Within three hours it had received 25 more casualties.

At 10.00 a.m. Brigadier Wallis told Colonel White that "the good name of the Battalion was at stake. It was emphatically stressed that further withdrawals must stop or all troops based on the Tai Po road to the east would be cut off."[2]

At this critical moment, one can but wonder why Wallis, less than three miles away from Colonel White's Battalion Headquarters, with the good Castle Peak Road between them, could not have visited him to discuss the rapidly deteriorating situation. This also applies to General Maltby in his 'battlebox' in Victoria. Should Maltby have gone forward, as some other generals in different circumstances certainly would have done? He could have discovered what was going on, with a view to planning accordingly. A Motor Torpedo Boat would have carried him across the harbour to the Mainland very quickly. Wallis's headquarters was three miles beyond, so the entire journey would have taken less than half an hour.

Throughout the day 2nd Lieutenant Ford had commanded the troops defending the summit of Golden Hill. "In the end he was literally blown off the hill by Japanese mortar fire. When he withdrew, under orders, he found that both his Company Commander and Second in Command had been wounded and that his two fellow platoon commanders had been killed," continues the Royal Scots' history. "When he reached Battalion Headquarters with the remnants of the Company he was given a large whisky by the Commanding Officer and, not surprisingly in his famished and semi-exhausted condition, he immediately fell asleep."

The Commanding Officer, Lieutenant Colonel S E H E White MC, was a bluff Irishman, known to his officers as 'Scram', his favourite order of dismissal. He was a tallish man, dark-skinned from years of exposure to the sun. During the 18 days of war in Hong Kong he was to see his Battalion almost literally blown to bits.

When the news reached him of the virtual disintegration of B and C Companies, he went forward to meet the survivors of D Company, upon which the full Japanese attacks had now fallen; the Company was ordered to fall back to less exposed ground closer to Kowloon.

The Royal Scots had already received casualties amounting to about one sixth of their effective strength. The ratio of officer casualties was significantly greater.

At 11.00 a.m. the Royal Scots, with the supporting Company of the Winnipeg Grenadiers, were ordered to withdraw to a line extending obliquely back almost to Shamshuipo in Kowloon. On their far right, the two Indian battalions were still relatively unscathed on the Gin Drinkers' Line.

Alarming reports reached Fortress HQ of a possible invasion by sea. The enemy had landed on Lantau Island, to the southwest of Hong Kong. They were fired on by the heavy guns at Aberdeen. An enemy party in sampans attempted a surprise landing at Aberdeen Island within 300 yards of the Naval Base. They were driven off by machine-gun fire from a platoon of the Winnipeg Grenadiers and by 3 Battery of the Volunteers. Orders were given to the Royal Engineers to lay anti-personnel mines on the beaches on the southern shores. After the surrender some of these mines were to be defused by Jimmy Wakefield, by order of the Japanese.

At midday on 11th December, General Maltby made the momentous decision to withdraw all his troops from the Mainland that night, except for 5/7 Rajputs which would remain on the isolated but commanding position on the Devil's Peak Peninsula indefinitely, in accordance with previous orders.

The Kowloon denial plan was being implemented as quickly as possible. The cement works, power station and dockyards were all destroyed. Merchant ships, including a Swedish vessel, were sunk.

In Kowloon an unpleasant stench filled the air since the bodies of the dead, following the Japanese bombing and shelling, were rotting in the bright sun. Sewage seeped into the streets from broken mains. The refrigeration system had broken down in the godowns: the goods stored there began to rot. Exhausted soldiers buried their faces in their arms to keep out the stench of death, excreta and putrefaction.

Doctor Isaac Newton in Kowloon noted in his diary: "11/12 December. Unfortunately much valuable time that was spent collecting stores, food and drugs was frittered away by an order from Hong Kong to prepare a camp for 10,000 evacuees from the Island. 60 to 70 casualties admitted and two operating theatres in continuous use for 12 hours. All lights have gone except for emergency installations in the hospital.

"Terrible riots have broken out in Kowloon and it is most dangerous to go out. As I stood in the compound this evening, I could hear the roar of the looting in the Nathan Road. It was a very nasty sound. No sooner was the camp for the evacuees stacked with food, when rioters broke in."

A few looters were shot, their crumpled bodies being left on the ground as an example to others. But law and order was disintegrating and, as the fighting drew nearer, less attempt was made to control the chaos.

The withdrawal of the Mainland Brigade went ahead as planned with little interference from the enemy, who failed to follow up. The Royal Scots began to embark at Kowloon City pier at 7.30 p.m. and, by 10.00 p.m., it was back on the Island. "A strange journey," wrote 2nd Lieutenant Ford. "After all the Battalion had been through, we left the battlefield in buses, as if we were going back to barracks after an exercise in the hills. The ferry boats were waiting for us at the pier. We looked across the water, usually ablaze with the lights of the Island. That night there was nothing but darkness ahead."

D Company Winnipeg Grenadiers crossed over to the Island after midnight. All armoured cars, some trucks and nearly all the Bren carriers were successfully evacuated.

The difficult withdrawal of the Rajputs and Punjabis the same night, with all their equipment, towards the Devil's Peak in the southeast was also successful despite a strong Japanese blocking position on Tate's Cairn. One group of Punjabis became lost and found themselves on the outskirts of Kowloon fighting Japanese patrols and fifth columnists. Fortunately RAF launches picked them up from the wharf just as the Japanese were closing in.

By dawn on 12th December, the Rajput Battalion was holding the Ma Lau Tong defensive line, last fortified in 1941; it was an extension of the Gin Drinkers' Line. Behind them Brigadier Wallis had his small headquarters. Fresh rations and ammunition were ferried forward to them all. The Punjabis meanwhile were gradually evacuated to the Island.

At 5.45 p.m. the Japanese launched a battalion attack on the Rajputs but failed to break through and received heavy casualties due to machine-gun and artillery fire supported by the 6-inch battery of howitzers.

At 4.30 a.m. on 13th December, General Maltby decided that the Devil's Peak Peninsula would not be held after all. He asked the Rajput Commanding Officer, Lieutenant Colonel R C Rawlinson, if he could withdraw his entire Battalion during the next two hours of darkness. Rawlinson replied that it would be difficult, but fortunately the enemy had taken a nasty knock.

The evacuation presented additional problems because the reliability of the Chinese boats' crews was such that they had to be under guard to prevent them from deserting. Chinese engineers had already run away; staff officers from Fortress HQ went forward to operate the boats in their absence. The withdrawal fell behind schedule, despite the efforts of four Motor Torpedo Boats.

At 8.30 a.m. the last covering troops were withdrawn in broad daylight in MTBs. The 120 mules which had carried heavy equipment had to be left on the Mainland because of the desertion of the crews of the ship to carry them. There had been no Japanese air activity or any attempt to follow up the withdrawal; the evacuation had been completed without casualties.

Brigadier Wallis was the last to leave the Mainland. He deserves credit for planning the successful withdrawal following the defeat at the Shingmun Redoubt.

When Brigadier Wallis took over from his predecessor, Brigadier Reeve, a little over a month earlier, he had asked him his views of the Royal Scots. Reeve had replied that Lieutenant Colonel White "would be a good average Commanding Officer and one the men knew and trusted". Wallis replied that he was "none too happy with the discipline of the Battalion as exemplified by the number of courts martial, some of them officers; the high rate of venereal disease and the high percentage of malaria." Brigadier Reeve replied that "he thought in the event the Battalion would fight well – after all they are Jocks".

Wallis wrote in the War Diary of the Mainland Brigade that he attributed the weaknesses in the Royal Scots to be due first to too many inexperienced officers – "perhaps 'milking' had been too great?" he wondered. "Secondly the Battalion had been left too long overseas without relief – 12 years in all." Third that the previous Commanding Officer, "Lieutenant Colonel D J McDougall, was a bad CO. He drank heavily himself and did not control his Battalion. It caused great astonishment in Hong Kong when it was learned that on vacation of command this officer was to command an officers' school in Burma."[3]

In short, Brigadier Wallis blamed the Royal Scots for the failure to hold the Gin Drinkers' Line and positions to the south. Even if the Japanese had been a third rate force and unable to fight at night, as Air Chief Marshal Brooke-Popham and others had earlier claimed, there would still have been no justification for Brigadier Wallis to expect that one platoon could defend the Shingmun Redoubt. This is because the advantage and initiative invariably lies with the attacker. The defenders, too few in numbers and too thinly spread, have no knowledge where the weight of the attack is to be anticipated. So it can only be expected that an assault, with the advantage of surprise, pressed forward in great strength at a few points, will succeed in breaking through. The Japanese 38th Division consisted of highly trained troops with a wealth of battle experience from years of fighting in China. Their artillery was greatly reinforced beyond the normal establishment.

Brooke-Popham stated in his despatch that at least two divisions – some nine brigades – would have been required to hold the Gin Drinkers' Line. In fact only one brigade was available. The Shingmun Redoubt was insufficiently supported by fire and was located with an open flank.

The Royal Scots had been asked to achieve the impossible. The Battalion received over 100 casualties on the Mainland. To anticipate events, the Royal Scots had well over 200 more casualties in the battle for the Island. Thereafter, three officers and 59 soldiers died in captivity and, as will be related, a horrifying total of three officers and 178 soldiers died at sea when the ship taking the POWs to Japan was sunk by an American submarine.

Many officers and soldiers of the Royal Scots gave of their best. For that, and for their conduct during nearly four years of dreadful captivity, the 2nd Battalion Royal Scots occupies a special place in the long history of the Regiment.

Notes

1. Interview Ford with author.
2. War Diary and Narrative, Mainland Infantry Brigade and attached troops, p. 37.
3. Mainland War Diary, p. 88.

CHAPTER 10

"Clay Pigeons in a Shooting Range"

13th–17th December 1941

The speed of the Japanese thrusts in Hong Kong and Malaya, and the success of their operations against Pearl Harbor, were being studied by Hitler at Berchtesgaden. He followed with jubilation every development in the war in Asia and congratulated himself on declaring war on America following the Pearl Harbor fiasco. Hitler eagerly awaited his share of the plunder of tin, rubber and oil to be captured in Malaya, Burma and the Dutch East Indies. Possibly the key positions of Ceylon and Port Darwin would eventually fall too. The glittering prizes were endless. As Churchill put it in a different context: "All sorts of greedy appetites have been excited, and many itching fingers are stretching and scratching at the vast pillage of a derelict Empire."

"We are watching day by day and hour by hour your stubborn defence of the port and fortress of Hong Kong," signalled Churchill to Sir Mark Young. "You guard a vital link long famous in world civilization between the Far East and Europe. All our hearts are with you in your ordeal. Every day your resistance brings nearer our certain victory."

As the exhausted Rajputs and the last of the guns were being evacuated from the Devil's Peak Peninsula, Lieutenant General Sakai despatched at 9.00 a.m. on 13th December a launch flying a white truce flag. Aboard were two Japanese officials, a civilian administrator, and two British hostages – Mrs Macdonald who was very pregnant, and Mrs C R Lee, the wife of the Secretary to the Governor, who brought her two dachshunds, Otto and Mitzi, with her. A young American reporter of the *Detroit News*, Gwen Dew, obtained a notable scoop by running to the scene at Queen's Pier to report the conversation. The Japanese leader politely introduced himself as Colonel Tala of Military Information. The bespectacled, younger, stocky figure clutching the flag was Lieutenant Mizuno while the third Japanese carrying a portfolio was Mr Othsu Dak.

Major Charles Boxer met the delegation and immediately recognised the dark, thickset Mr Othsu, whom he had come to know during his frequent liaison trips to the Japanese at the border. To the dismay of some observers including Gwen Dew, Boxer and the Japanese spent some time bowing and saluting each other. Gwen Dew asked Mr Othsu what the conditions were for the surrender offer. "Equitable terms for both sides and safe conduct for all," was his reply. Boxer quickly intervened with "Let's leave the terms to the Governor." Travelling by staff car, he took the surrender terms to Sir Mark Young in Government House. The terms consisted of General Sakai demanding the Island's immediate surrender, with threats of unrestricted bombardment if he refused.

An hour later Boxer returned with the Governor's categorical rejection of the terms. The Japanese, expecting such a reply, said that their forces would refrain from resuming the bombardment until 4.00 p.m. to give Sir Mark Young time to reconsider. After further salutes and bows, they re-boarded their launch and returned to Kowloon with Mrs Lee and the two dogs.

General Sakai, who commanded the forces attacking Hong Kong, read the Governor's reply with growing irritation and impatience. "Not only is this Colony strong enough to resist all attempts at invasion, but it has the backing of the people of the British Empire, of the United States of America and of the Republic of China. British subjects and all who have sought the protection of the British Empire can rest assured that there will never be any surrender to the Japanese."

Sakai reluctantly contemplated the many problems of invading the Island, but he never doubted the success of his mission, knowing that Hong Kong was cut off and could not be reinforced, for the Japanese had complete control of the air and seas.

After all, three days before, torpedo and bombing attacks on *Repulse* and the *Prince of Wales* had sunk both ships off Malaya. Admiral Phillips had been keeping wireless silence and so no fighter aircraft had been sent from Singapore because the RAF did not know his position until it was too late. "The efficiency of the Japanese in air warfare was at this time greatly under-estimated both by ourselves and by the Americans," recorded Churchill. "In all the war I never received a more direct shock. As I turned over and twisted in bed the full horror of the news sank in upon me. There were no British or American capital ships in the Indian Ocean or the Pacific except for the American survivors of Pearl Harbor, who were hastening back to California. Over all this vast expanse of waters Japan was supreme, and we everywhere were weak and naked."

When most people in Hong Kong heard of the loss of these two great ships, their morale was badly shaken. However, a new hope arose: the local Hong Kong radio announced that the Nationalist Chinese Seventh army was only a little more than 100 miles away and rushing to relieve the Colony. Many prayed that this was true. Certainly, the constant hope that Chinese armies were marching south encouraged the garrison and civilians to sustain their efforts. General Maltby was not confident that Chiang Kai-Shek's divisions would arrive in time, if at all. Nevertheless, according to Japanese records examined in 1946, the Chinese did step up their guerrilla campaign and attempt to divert attention from the Hong Kong operation. They also sent reinforcements to the Canton area and moved a force, about one and a half divisions strong, towards Hong Kong.[1]

General Sakai took the Chinese threat to his rear very seriously and ensured that a Japanese regimental group, the Akari Detachment, was positioned some 40 miles northeast of Hong Kong to prevent Chinese interference. They reported later that the Chinese effort to reach Hong Kong was minimal.

General Maltby appeared confident that the Colony could be held; the battle for the Mainland had not amounted to a major defeat, in as much as the enemy had received more casualties than they had inflicted. Numerically, he had a force equal in number to the Japanese. It is only with the benefit of hindsight that we know the truth: the complete lack of air support and inadequate sea power, referred to earlier, made the defeat of the Colony a foregone conclusion.

Maltby's dilemma on how best to defend the Island was acute. Lieutenant General Percival in Singapore favoured putting his troops well forward to overlook the beaches. Similarly, Field Marshal Rommel in the Spring of 1944 wanted to hold his Panzer Corps close to the coastal defences in Normandy, knowing that the Allied air forces would bomb any subsequent forward movement.

The factors facing Maltby were, first, lack of transport. Secondly, the narrow roads over mountain passes were quite inadequate to move any battalion quickly in any direction. He anticipated the enemy attacking from the northwest, across the harbour, landing in Victoria. This was because the distance was short; Victoria was within easy reach of the Japanese mortars, and mobile artillery was already starting to destroy one pill-box after another with remarkable accuracy.

Maltby therefore deployed his troops, after many confusing changes. (See Map overleaf.) The Punjabis and Rajputs would man the forward defences on the left and right respectively. The Royal Scots would be held centrally, well forward. His greatest strength therefore covered the threat to Victoria. The Winnipeg Grenadiers and Royal Rifles would be spread out behind them, guarding against an invasion from the sea. Maltby believed his best plan involved the Middlesex machine-gunners, supported by scattered companies including the Volunteers, who would hold and destroy the enemy while 'flying columns', consisting of Winnipeg Grenadier reserve companies, hurried forward. The General felt that a Japanese landing on the northeast coast was improbable because ships sunk under the demolition plan would hinder any approach.

The RAF had earlier destroyed their last remaining aircraft on the ground to prevent the Japanese capturing it and so reconnaissance from the air was impossible. When Japan first attacked the Colony, the cruiser squadron and submarine flotilla had immediately been despatched to Singapore. One destroyer, *Thracian,* four gun boats, eight Motor Torpedo Boats, seven auxiliary patrol vessels and an auxiliary craft used for minefield duty were the only ships left in Hong Kong. Naval personnel numbered 1,300 British and 300 Chinese. The naval base at Aberdeen was sheltered from enemy artillery firing from the Mainland, being protected by the massive mountain, Victoria Peak. As many sea approaches as possible had been mined.

Hong Kong was divided by a narrow, winding road which led from Happy Valley, close to the Wanchai, and ran between Mount Nicholson and Jardine's Lookout. (See Map overleaf.) From there the road met with three others at Wong Nei Chong Gap before dropping 300 feet towards the beautiful Repulse Bay and its famous hotel. Three miles farther to the south, beyond Stanley Mound, lay the Chung Hom Kok peninsula and Stanley Village. Stanley Fort was on the most southern tip of Hong Kong.

By 14th December, West Brigade consisted of the Royal Scots, Punjabis and Winnipeg Grenadiers. East Brigade comprised the Rajputs and the Royal Rifles of Canada. Both Brigades contained units of the Hong Kong Volunteer Defence Corps, which consisted of five batteries and seven rifle companies in defensive positions spread throughout the Island.

The inter-brigade boundary lay largely to the east of Happy Valley, Jardine's Lookout, Wong Nei Chong Reservoir to Chung Hom Kok.

Eastern Brigade was commanded by Brigadier J K Lawson MC. He had been born in England, but his family had emigrated to Canada when he was still a child. He had served in the Canadian Expeditionary Force and the Motor Machine Gun Brigade in the First World War. In 1941 he was the Canadian Army's Director of Military Training before being promoted to Brigadier to command the 2,000 men destined for Hong Kong. He lacked experience of handling anything more than a Company – 100 men. He was largely responsible for selecting the two Canadian Battalions for Hong Kong.

Western Brigade was commanded by Brigadier Wallis, who had no knowledge of the ground in Hong Kong Island because he had always been stationed with his Rajputs on the Mainland. He also had not met any of the officers or men of the Royal Rifles of Canada and through no fault of his own never discovered, before the Japanese attacked the Island, what the Battalion might achieve.

Neither Canadian Battalion had radios, 3-inch mortars or transport. Although the Force had been allotted 212 vehicles in Canada, the *Awatea* was a troopship not a freighter: there was room for only 20 vehicles in her holds. Owing to incompetence, none of the 20 reached Vancouver before the *Awatea* sailed. The 212 vehicles were loaded on another ship, which was diverted to Manila and never reached Hong Kong.

The Commanding Officer of the Royal Rifles was a veteran of the First World War – Lieutenant Colonel W J Home MC. He had been removed from command of a company of the Royal Canadian Regiment in 1939 as "unfit to command in war".[2]

The Royal Rifles had spent ten months in Newfoundland, mostly guarding a railway line and airport. There was neither time nor opportunity for worthwhile training. Three months before arriving in Hong Kong they were on coast defence in New Brunswick where "anything more complicated than section or platoon tactics was abandoned".

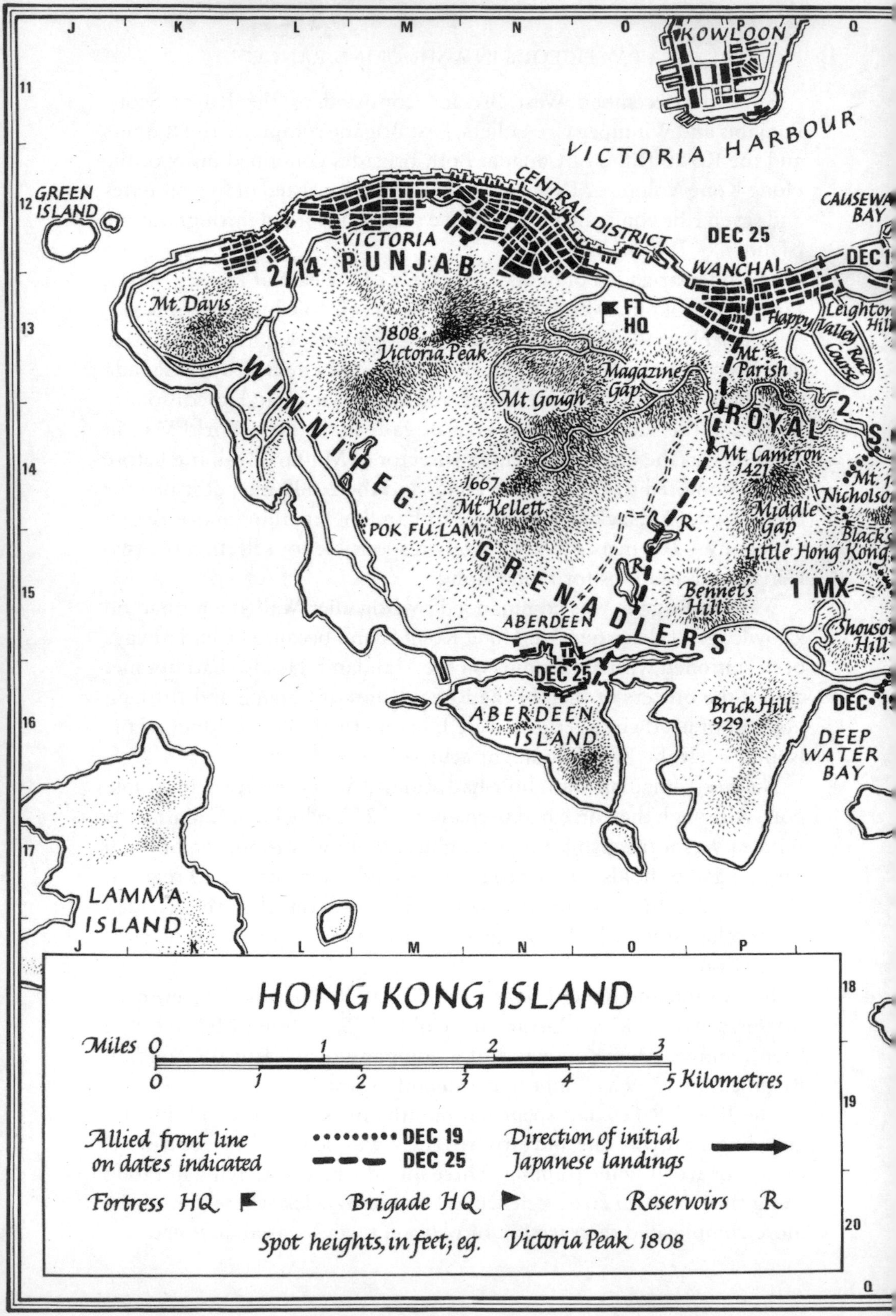

KOWLOON
VICTORIA HARBOUR
GREEN ISLAND
CENTRAL DISTRICT
VICTORIA
2/14 PUNJAB
DEC 25
WANCHAI
Mt. Davis
FT HQ
1808
Victoria Peak
Happy Valley Race Course
Mt. Parish
Magazine Gap
Mt. Gough
WINNIPEG GRENADIERS
ROYAL
Mt Cameron 1421
1667
Mt. Kellett
POK FU LAM
Middle Gap
Little Hong Kong
Bennet's Hill
1 MX
ABERDEEN
DEC 25
ABERDEEN ISLAND
Brick Hill 929
DEEP WATER BAY
LAMMA ISLAND
HONG KONG ISLAND
Miles 0 1 2 3
0 1 2 3 4 5 Kilometres
Allied front line on dates indicated
DEC 19
DEC 25
Direction of initial Japanese landings
Fortress HQ
Brigade HQ
Reservoirs R
Spot heights, in feet; eg. Victoria Peak 1808

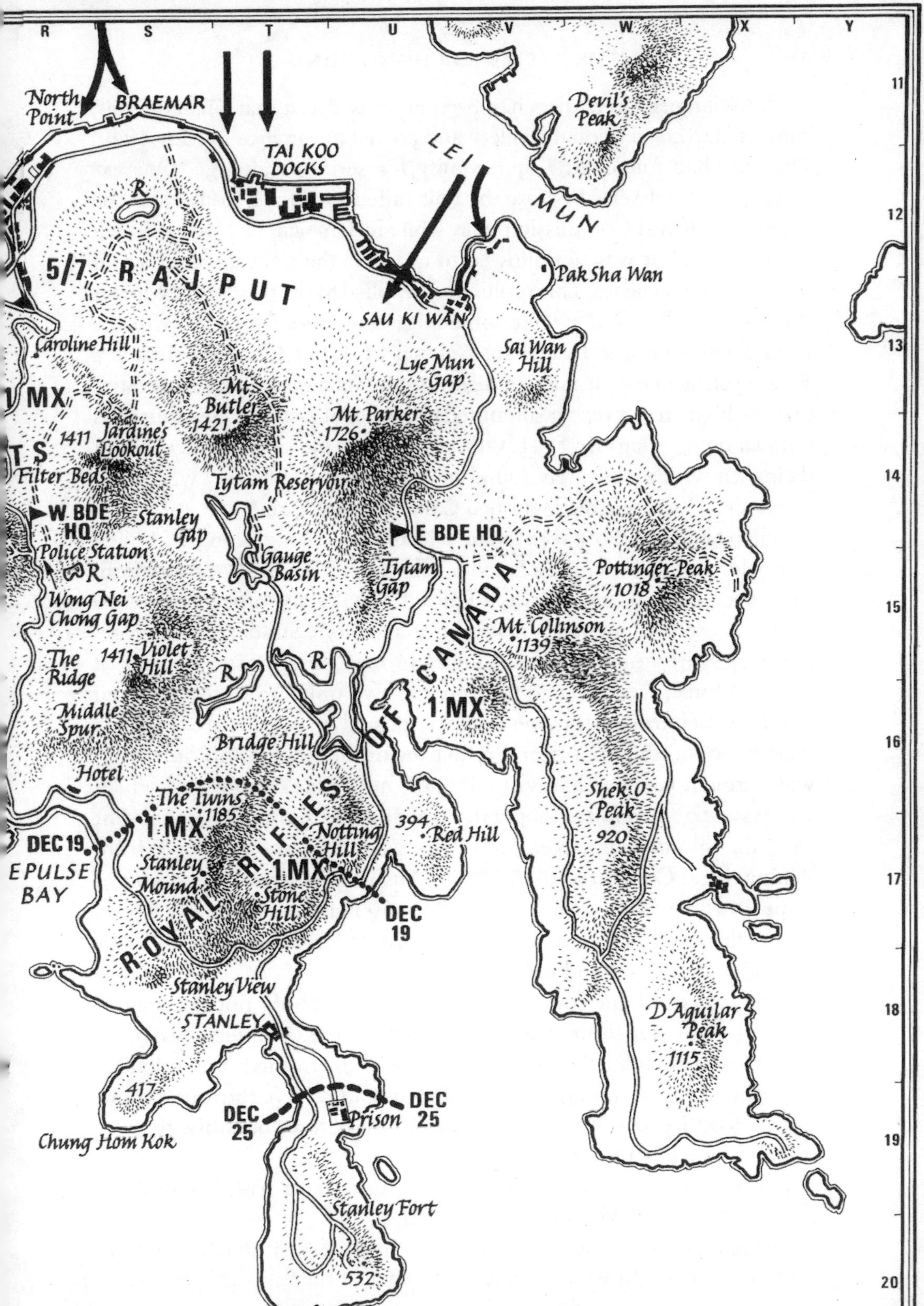

R
S
T
U
V
W
X
Y
North Point
BRAEMAR
TAI KOO DOCKS
Devil's Peak
LEI MUN
Pak Sha Wan
SAU KI WAN
Sai Wan Hill
Lye Mun Gap
5/7 RAJPUT
Caroline Hill
Mt. Butler 1421
Mt. Parker 1726
1 MX
1411 Jardine's Lookout
T S
Filter Beds
Tytam Reservoir
W. BDE HQ
Stanley Gap
E BDE HQ
Police Station
Gauge Basin
Tytam Gap
Pottinger Peak 1018
Wong Nei Chong Gap
Mt. Collinson 1139
The Ridge
1411 Violet Hill
WINNIPEG GRENADIERS
Middle Spur
1 MX
Bridge Hill
Hotel
The Twins 1185
1 MX
ROYAL RIFLES OF CANADA
Shek O Peak 920
Notting Hill
394 Red Hill
DEC 19
EPULSE BAY
Stanley Mound
1 MX
Stone Hill
DEC 19
Stanley View
STANLEY
D'Aguilar Peak 1115
417
DEC 25
Prison
DEC 25
Chung Hom Kok
Stanley Fort
532
11
12
13
14
15
16
17
18
19
20

The Winnipeg Grenadiers had been mobilised as a machine-gun unit, converted to conventional artillery and posted to Jamaica in May 1940. They too had found little opportunity for serious training. "One ex-corporal (who deserted before the unit sailed for Hong Kong) told the subsequent Royal Commission that, while in Jamaica, he 'saw' a 3-inch mortar once, but was not allowed to examine the sight as he was told that it was too delicate. This prohibition applied to the men of the Mortar Platoon as well."[3] There were some misgivings about the ability of the Commanding Officer, Lieutenant Colonel J L R Sutcliffe, who "made a series of elementary mistakes in regard to the state of training and equipment of his men in a report submitted to National Defence Headquarters Ottawa on 6th October 1941. Officers who get the simplest facts about their men wrong are rarely found in command of efficient, well motivated units," wrote a distinguished Canadian historian.[4]

When the two Battalions were selected for Hong Kong 151 men were eliminated when they failed a subsequent medical examination. Moreover, each Battalion was required to take six officers and 150 men over establishment as "first reinforcements". Suddenly, therefore, at the eleventh hour 16 officers and 436 men, or almost a quarter of the total force, were needed to bring the two units up to the required numbers. Reinforcements were quickly posted in; most had completed their basic training, but nearly a quarter of them were still only part-way through it. They had virtually no knowledge of mortars, which were essential for Hong Kong. Fifty Canadians attempted to go absent from the ship in Vancouver and others were restrained by force from joining them. Compared to the 1,000 Australians who went absent at Cape Town en route to Britain in 1941, 50 may seem a paltry figure. These, then, were the Canadians whom Brigadiers Lawson and Wallis were about to command in battle.[5]

Who was to blame for such a shambles? Certainly not the men of the Royal Rifles or Winnipeg Grenadiers who had volunteered to fight. Nor, to some extent, those who had chosen or 'trained' the individuals, because it was anticipated that they would receive thorough training in Hong Kong for perhaps a year or two before, possibly, the war spread to the Far East.

Can similarities be drawn with other theatres of war, both during the Second World War and more recently?

Lieutenant General Charles Foulkes, the CGS in Canada, stated in a report to the Minister of National Defence on 9th February 1948 that a unit which contains men who have not completed their recruit training is not fit for battle. "We found, in training formations for war, that even after recruit training, section, platoon, company and battalion exercises had to be carried out," he said. "Then battle inoculation using live ammunition and exercises in every phase of operations were necessary. I can say without fear of contradiction that even after four years of arduous training I found the 2nd Canadian Division just ready for battle when we landed in North West Europe, and even after the first battle it was necessary for me to make several very serious changes in order to win further battles. The training of men for war is like training a racehorse for a race. It is necessary to re-train after each battle, eliminate the weak, tired or battle-weary, and correcting the mistakes in the last battle to ensure victory in the next."

The above was, and is, equally applicable, of course, to any other army. From the end of the Dunkirk evacuation in 1940 to the start of the fighting in France in 1944, the Guards battalions in the British Army, for example, undertook exhaustive exercises to prepare for battle. Tactics evolved, they felt, to best defeat the Germans. Yet at their very first major operation, in the breakout southeast of Caen during Operation Goodwood, it became immediately apparent from the British defeat then, that the Guards Armoured Division's organisation was faulty. Lorried infantry following the advancing armour should instead fight alongside, if not in front of, the tanks in the close bocage country of hedgerows and ditches, behind which lurked the deadly German anti-tank weapons.

The Territorial Army units sent earlier to fight in the British Expeditionary Force in France and Belgium in 1939 and 1940 were found to be woefully ill-trained, just as the men fighting in Malaya, Burma and Singapore in 1941 and 1942, against a smaller Japanese force, proved to be unable to move fast across country or fight against an enemy which was trained to bypass and then set up road blocks behind the road-bound British formations.

The 1982 Falklands War can certainly be contrasted to the despatch of the Canadians to Hong Kong. The 2nd Battalion Scots Guards and 1st Battalion Welsh Guards were Public Duty battalions on London ceremonial duties when the possibility of their being sent 8,000 miles to the South Atlantic arose. "Few really believed that they would actually leave Britain (a view apparently shared at a high level within the Ministry of Defence) and, if they did, the battalions' role was expected to be that of garrison troops, the Argentinians being assumed to have surrendered [to the Royal Marines and Parachute battalions] long before 5th Infantry Brigade could arrive to influence events," wrote Major General Murray Naylor in the Scots Guards Regimental History.[6] As so often happens in war, plans went awry. At the vital battle of Tumbledown Mountain, on the approaches to Port Stanley, the Scots Guards on 13th June 1982 had to undertake a night attack against a strong, motivated enemy, sited on dominating and often insurmountable crags, well-entrenched with machine guns covering their minefields. Due to the outstanding courage and leadership of the officers and NCOs, such as Lieutenant Colonel Mike Scott DSO and Major John Kiszely MC, the Guardsmen overwhelmed the enemy. The following day all the Argentinians in the Falklands surrendered. (By 2005 Lieutenant General Sir John Kiszely was commanding all the British forces in Iraq.)

Just as the Canadians en route to Hong Kong were told in 1941, "Don't worry, lads, you will be training in Hong Kong, there's ample time," and the Guardsmen 41 years later were assured, "the Argies will have surrendered; it's garrison troops for you," so recriminations in the 21st century, as to where the blame lies, will not get us far.

* * * * *

On 17th December, four days after the withdrawal from the Mainland to Hong Kong Island, Lieutenant Zempei Masushima led a patrol of four Japanese to choose landing sites on the Island's north shore. Dressed in Chinese clothes, they approached the Tai Koo Docks in the northeast. A British searchlight spotted them; a Rajput pill-box quickly opened fire, so the patrol jumped into the water and swam on, pulling the boat behind them. After landing at the docks, which had a 600-yard frontage with a Rajput pill-box at each end, Zempei carried out a full reconnaissance. He noted the location of pill-boxes, obstacles and wire and found several pill-boxes to be empty. The patrol then returned to Kowloon, being fired upon once more. Zempei was decorated for his gallantry. "Owing to the success of this officer's patrol it was decided to make the landings at this point," concluded the citation.[7]

Ironically, Captain C M M Man of the Middlesex Regiment was also in the area of the Tai Koo Docks that night because it was regarded as a possible enemy landing point. "I shall never forget the eerie sensation of walking through this large complex of sheds and workshops, all apparently empty with no sight of life," he wrote. "All the time I was conscious of the feeling that I was being observed. Try as I could I could not see anyone."[8]

Brigadier Wallis had established his East Brigade HQ alongside the Royal Rifles HQ at Tytam Gap well to the east of the Island, nearly two miles from the Tai Koo Docks. Sir Mark Young, the Governor, visited him there and asked him for his frank opinion on what the chances were. "I told him that once again we were spread too thin with little depth," recalled Wallis. "That lacking air cover and with widely dispersed machine-gun posts, and as the Japanese had ample artillery and mortars, while our own men had had little rest from incessant bombardment, it would only be a matter of time before we were forced back. I think Sir Mark was shocked by my reply."[9]

Brigadier Lawson had moved his West Brigade HQ from the Wanchai to the Wong Nei Chong Gap where several steel-doored anti-aircraft shelters cut into the rock. He had, unwittingly, placed himself on the vital ground which was a key Japanese objective because whoever controlled the Gap and the high ground which overlooked it, controlled the key crossroads, the very heart of Hong Kong Island. The harbour to the north and Repulse Bay to the south were both within 15 minutes' drive.

The Royal Scots on the waterfront in the Wanchai became difficult to supply due to the intense shell fire. Some loaves and stew occasionally reached them. Chinese prostitutes, some of whom knew them in happier days, came out of their densely built-up Chinese quarters, oblivious to the danger, and offered flasks of green tea. They had no food to give, but they offered little gifts of aspirin tablets and safety-razor blades.

Some of the Wanchai streets were piled up with dead bodies; attempts were made to cart them off for burial in communal graves. "Refuse was gathering in heaps everywhere," wrote 2nd Lieutenant Ford, who had rejoined D Company from hospital. "On one rubbish heap I saw a dead monkey and alongside it a dead baby, side by side."

Each day was a terrible nightmare, particularly for the Chinese. Mrs Mabel Redwood, an Auxiliary nurse, was working day and night in a makeshift hospital at the racecourse and wrote in her diary, which is now at the Imperial War Museum in London: "After prolonged shelling, the planes came. They seemed to be directed at the communal kitchens where Chinese were being supplied daily with cooked rice. Later I ventured home. I saw more horror in that journey than I ever want to see again. They had got the Chinese queuing for the rice well and truly. I had to step over mutilated bodies. Poor things had no chance and there were no military objectives nearby."

Fortress HQ suddenly received a message late at night that a large force of 'Japanese cavalry' was advancing across Happy Valley racecourse. Captains Iain MacGregor and Peter MacMillan, both on duty at the HQ, were sent with a small scratch force in a lorry with machine guns to engage them. Captain MacGregor saw "shapes of dozens of wraith-like animals which might have been cavalry. A number of bursts of machine-gun fire killed many of them; it transpired that the horses, terrified and bewildered, had escaped from the Jockey Club's stables. One of my own Australian ponies was among those killed. It seems silly and illogical now, with all the smell and sight of human death constantly around us then, to have felt so much pity, disgust and compassion for those slaughtered animals."[10]

MacGregor's force was next ordered to fight off an enemy landing in the Wanchai. They discovered that the three large boats they saw contained friendly Chinese who had escaped from the Mainland. Another landing had apparently taken place on 17th December when retreating Gunner personnel at Pak Sha Wan, opposite Devil's Peak in the northeast, had reported that "the enemy are as thick as leaves in the battery position". Concentrated fire was brought down on over 100 people in small rubber boats and rafts. All were killed in the water and the position was reoccupied without opposition four hours later. It is likely that it was more fleeing Chinese rather than Japanese who were annihilated that night.

As the Japanese indiscriminately shelled and bombed Hong Kong, their armed fifth columnists became increasingly active. They attacked an AA searchlight position and incited the Chinese to riot. Transport drivers, among others, were encouraged to desert, sabotaging their vehicles before running away. Several traitors with primitive lamps "operated from a dry battery, with a small but adequate mirror, were reported signalling from the Island to the Mainland," recorded General Maltby. "When these operators were intercepted they were shot... The morale of the civilian population remained shaky, chiefly due to rice distribution difficulties. The Chungking Government representatives had been most helpful in assisting in the maintenance of order... In the A.R.P. tunnels in certain cases armed gangs of robbers were operating. Pamphlets were dropped by the Japanese."

On 17th December, on the same day that Zempei Masushima had chosen the landing sites on Hong Kong Island after swimming across the harbour, two Japanese launches carried their 'peace party' to Victoria. Sir Mark Young replied that he declined "absolutely to enter into negotiations for the surrender of Hong Kong, and takes this opportunity of notifying Lieutenant General Sakai and Vice Admiral Masaichi Mimi that he is not prepared to receive any further communications from them on the subject."

"Jap envoys came over and said all military installations have been destroyed, no use going on fighting," wrote Brigadier Lawson in his diary, which was lodged after the war in Wolsey Barracks, London, Ontario. "Governor told them to go back and destroy some more."

Japanese bombers intensified their attacks; one bomb alone in a built-up area caused 150 serious civilian casualties. The long nightmare continued. "We were," observed Gwen Dew, the young American journalist who had witnessed the first Japanese 'peace mission', "clay pigeons in a tiny shooting range".

General Sakai lost patience with the Colony and reluctantly decided that he would have to invade the Island. He gave out orders accordingly: the sands of time were rapidly running out for the attackers and defenders alike.

Notes

1. File 982.013 (D3), NDHQ.
2. Report by Lt Gen. C Foulkes (CGS to the Minister of National Defence), 9.2.48, reproduced as Annex C in Vincent, C, *No Reason Why*, Ontario: Canada's Wings, 1981.
3. Vincent, op. cit., p. 60.
4. Greenhous, B, *"C" Force to Hong Kong: A Canadian Catastrophe 1941–1945*, Canadian War Museum Historical Publication No. 30, 1997, p. 23.
5. Details of the Australian absentees are in Clarke, Michael, *My War*, self published, 1990, p. 152.
6. Naylor, Murray, *Among Friends: the Scots Guards 1956–1993*, London: Leo Cooper, 1995, p. 135.
7. *Japan Times Weekly*, 17.9.42.
8. Letter Man to author.
9. Letter Wallis to author.
10. Letter MacGregor to author.

CHAPTER 11

Triumph or Disaster: The Japanese Landings

18th–19th December 1941

Sakai discussed his plans in Kowloon with Major General Sano, the Divisional Commander, who gave out the orders to regimental and battalion commanders. The landings would start at 10.00 p.m. on 18th December; they would all be launched against the northeast of the Island, whereas General Maltby expected the attack in the northwest.

The Japanese Division consisted of three Regiments, each equivalent to a Brigade, and each of which was to commit two of its three battalions to the attack.

Each battalion was organised on a four-company basis and was up to 1,000 men strong. It also contained a company of 12 heavy machine guns and a platoon of 70-mm support guns. Each battalion was supported by 12 75-mm field guns from the divisional artillery regiment.

The Shoji Regiment (230) was to attack 500 yards east of North Point, after embarking from west of the Kai Tak area. (See Map on pages 90–1.)

The Doi Regiment (228), following its success at the Shingmun Redoubt, was to embark from east of Kai Tak and land in the centre at Braemar.

Finally, the Tanaka Regiment (229) was to embark from the Devil's Peak peninsula and land at Sau Ki Wan.[1]

Each regiment was to cross the harbour in two waves: the first in collapsible rowing boats, each of which carried 14 men. The second wave and follow-up troops were to cross by powered landing boats which would tow more assault craft. One hour was allowed for the first wave to cross. "The sunken shipping offered some concealment, but apprehension was felt that small bands of the British enemy might hide amidst the wrecks in a desperate effort to obstruct the crossing."

The Japanese were acutely conscious that up to now their plans had not proved as successful as they wished on the Mainland. Compared to fighting against the Chinese, they had suffered considerable casualties. "Two or three British gunboats were active along the flank of our attacking unit during the offensive (on the Mainland), menacing by bombardment and obstructing our action considerably," Colonel Tosaka recalled. "Their long range fortress artillery bombardments were extremely effective. The Japanese Army was greatly hampered, especially in moving its heavy guns. Little thought had been given to an attack on Hong Kong Island if indeed the British should entrench themselves there. In actuality the British Army did not show great resistance on the expected Gin Drinkers' Line. However the Japanese Army at that time was thrown into considerable confusion in making adjustments to the situation and new attack preparations."[2]

* * * * *

The 18th December was a cool, overcast and rather miserable day. Father F J Deloughery, the Roman Catholic Chaplain to the Canadians, who had been among the first to be bombed during his Communion service at Shamshuipo Barracks, heard confessions, administered Holy Communion and comforted the soldiers as best he could. He had spent the last week visiting the companies by day and wounded in hospital by night.

That evening he had a long chat at Wong Nei Chong Gap with Brigadier Lawson. Both were worried about the Canadian companies, several of which had not received a hot meal for at least 24 hours. Why had the administration of the battalions tended to break down already? What were the Quartermasters, Company Second in Commands, Company Quartermaster Sergeants and others doing to ensure that in the five days before the Japanese attacked the Island, they could provide, at least, hot meals and drinks to their men? It was their responsibility. The Punjabis, Royal Scots and Rajputs were largely in the very front line overlooking the harbour. Couldn't those well behind them meet the challenge of delivering hot meals to their soldiers?

The desertion of Chinese drivers, referred to earlier, was a factor. Under the defence scheme it had been decided that the NAAFI (Navy, Army, Air Force Institutes) would open canteen services in accessible areas. (This did not remove the responsibility of battalions to feed their own.) Alternative plans for NAAFI to send mobile canteens to visit troops in their positions fell through due to the lack of transport.

The food re-supply organisation included Wenzell Brown, a Hong Kong University professor, and Mrs Gwen Priestwood. The former recorded in his memoirs that, despite his best efforts, he was unable to find any of the Canadian "food distribution centres". Mrs Priestwood was given a brilliant yellow milk wagon with pictures of cows plastered on it, and was asked to move tobacco, arms and food between stores. With an armed escort she raced through air raids, past barbed wire, wrecked buildings, shell holes and road blocks. Eventually the van was painted a dull, inconspicuous grey; she missed the cows' calm, imperturbable faces.

* * * * *

Between 5.00 and 6.00 p.m. about 200 Japanese were seen to be approaching the Devil's Peak pier in the far northeast. They were fired at by the Gunners. The Japanese retaliated just before dusk with an extremely heavy bombardment of Lei Mun. The soldiers there felt sure that the Japanese attack would come in a matter of hours straight at them. They were right.

That night Brigadier Lawson realised that his position at the Wong Nei Chong Gap was much too vulnerable. He decided to move it the following morning to a less exposed area half a mile to the west on Black's Link. A new site had already been chosen and a telegraph link had been laid to it.

In the gathering darkness, the Japanese soldiers silently entered their assault craft while Rifleman Sydney Skelton scribbled in his diary; it eventually ended up in National Defence Headquarters, Ottawa. High in the mountains above Tytam Reservoir, the Rifleman had entered in his diary ten days earlier: "Our heavy guns can be heard now. They are firing at Japanese ships. With us are the Middlesex Regiment. They are a good bunch of chaps. Two of our boys have lost their minds. Gone crazy in the head. The bombing has snapped their minds. Some have been machine-gunned from the diving Japanese planes. Sixty-five per cent of us have had to be awake at night and no one is allowed to undress."

As Colonel Doi stood at the water's edge as his first boats pushed off from Kai Tak into the darkness, Sydney Skelton made the penultimate entry in his diary: "Huge fires are raging in Victoria. The bombardment is still on. This one day I shall never forget. Tomorrow will tell another story." It did.

* * * * *

Fifty-four years later in the military cemetery at Stanley, John Harris and I were attending a moving ceremony arranged by the Royal British Legion. Wreaths were laid, prayers were said. A band softly played, *Oh God, our help in ages past...* We stood on the grass amidst the graves and flowers. Glancing to my side, I saw the grave closest to me. I read the name upon it – Rifleman S Skelton. My reaction? It was no sense of horror. Having become so familiar with the short entries in his diary over the years, I looked around me – to gather my thoughts, perhaps. I then looked at my friends on my left and right; their heads were bowed for we were praying for all those buried there. I looked at the blue sky, and then again at Sydney's grave. He had come a long way from Canada, "the land of the free... ". Even now, ten years on, I feel that he had found an eternal peace there – in a 'foreign field', it is true, but a more beautiful well-kept spot it would be hard to find. He is remembered now, in these pages. Indeed, to use the words familiar to all of us "... At the going down of the sun and in the morning, we will remember them." So remember Rifleman Sydney Skelton. Remember also the other 500 Canadians who were killed, died of wounds or sickness or were reported missing.[3]

* * * * *

At 7.00 p.m. on the 18th, the 2nd Battalion 228 Regiment in groups of 14 silently embarked in the small collapsible assault craft. Colonel Doi climbed on a large barge which carried 80 officers and men of his tactical HQ.

The night was exceptionally dark. The sky was overcast with frequent showers of rain. Thick black smoke was being blown across the harbour from the burning oil tanks at North Point.

Colonel Doi gave the following account: "Halfway across the harbour, our attempt had gone undetected because the grounded ships concealed our move. But time and again the water was lit as brightly as broad daylight by the flare of burning heavy oil in the storage tanks on the opposite shore. Searchlight beams from Lyemun Point also played on the harbour. Streams of enemy machine-gun fire from the opposite shore and Lyemun Point slowed the boats, and since they failed to take a straight course, units were either mixed up or separated while they were still in the water. The resultant confusion made it almost impossible to maintain complete command of the battalion. Some boats had their oars broken and men rowed with their entrenching shovels. When exposed to enemy fire on the water, which offers no shelter, it is absolutely useless to turn the boats away from the direction of enemy fire, but perhaps it is only normal human psychology to react that way.

"It was a spectacular and grim crossing, but for the most part men went ashore on schedule. The assault boat carrying my leading battalion commander reached the spot (to the east of Braemar Point near the Taikoo Docks) where an enemy pill-box was located. He was wounded. The situation ashore was such that the squad leaders didn't know the whereabouts of platoon leaders and the latter in turn did not know the position of company commanders. It was very difficult to maintain the battalion under complete command. The only chance under the circumstances was for the men, on reaching the shore in their assault boats, to form up as a group and charge into the enemy immediately."

As the first wave approached the Island, they signalled to the second, still at Kai Tak, to start their crossing: "The harbour was still being illuminated by the searchlights and the flare of the burning oil. The enemy machine-gun fire was all the more intense. I, the Regimental Commander, led the 1st Battalion in the crossing. When we landed I found a wire net fence, something like the one ordinarily found around a tennis court. It blocked our advance inland. Unlike ordinary wire entanglements, the net could not be cut by wire cutters, and we spent some time climbing over it with a ladder which we had brought with us.

"Enemy machine-gun fire was as intense as ever. Our second wave was forced to lie prone at the water's edge for a time after the landing. The anti-tank Company lost so many men that only one gun could be manned. It took three hours for the commander of the 1st Battalion to regain complete control of his battalion. The main reason for the delay in restoring command was that our shouting at the time of landing invited the enemy fire. Also runners who were dispatched failed to establish contact because of rampaging enemy Bren carriers. The only alternative was to join up and regroup by a slow process of communicating from one adjoining unit to another." Their objectives were Jardine's Lookout and beyond to Wong Nei Chong Gap.

On each side of Colonel Doi the first waves of the flanking regiments pushed inland. Colonel Shoji's 230 Regiment was soon in considerable confusion among several concrete pill-boxes half a mile to the west at North Point. Shoji remained on the shore as his companies moved towards their objective – Mount Nicholson to the west of the Gap. The leading platoons quickly became pinned down by artillery fire.

On the extreme east, Colonel Tanaka's 229 Regiment had a shorter crossing and landed between Sau Ki Wan and Lyemun Fort. They too headed rapidly inland with Mount Parker as one of their objectives.

The battalions, once ashore, were ordered to bypass opposition, secure the high ground well inland, and take the commanding features of Mount Parker, Mount Butler, Jardine's Lookout and Wong Nei Chong Gap. On the following night – the 19th/20th of December, they were to attack west and southwest to capture Mount Nicholson and Repulse Bay. The three battalions not committed to the invasion were to remain in Kowloon to garrison the City and provide subsequent reinforcements.

No specific orders were issued regarding the disposal of prisoners.

* * * * *

"The landing of the enemy at North Point and Lyemun at approximately 20.30 hours appears to have been simultaneous and was closely followed by landings at Aldrich Bay, Taikoo Docks and the Sugar Refinery Wharf," was the entry in the Fortress HQ War Diary Preliminary Summary.[4]

The next few hours were vital if Hong Kong Island was to be held. Or had General Maltby already left it too late? As already stated, 200 Japanese had been seen several hours earlier approaching the water's edge from the Devil's Peak peninsula – men of Colonel Tanaka's No. 229 Regiment. Yet Maltby still clung to the belief that it was Victoria which was to be attacked from Kowloon. So he did not react to the visible threat. The British post-war Official History would criticise him for this error.

When it was obvious that the enemy was landing, one Rajput reserve company was moved forward and three Hong Kong Volunteer Defence Corps (HKVDC) armoured cars were sent to Brigadier Wallis's HQ as a mobile reserve. At midnight two Canadian platoons of the Royal Rifles with artillery support tried to recapture the Sai Wan position but were unsuccessful. By now the Rajputs manning the pill-boxes on the shore line had all been overwhelmed or bypassed. Could Brigadier Lawson have committed the Royal Scots to counter-attack? Where were his 'flying columns' of the Winnipeg Grenadiers? Had these units been speedily despatched, the roads were still reasonably clear of debris but the vehicles carrying such a force would have been extremely vulnerable. In any event, the Japanese were deploying inland across country, led by fifth column guides, en route for the mountainous, inaccessible areas of Mount Parker, Mount Butler and Jardine's Lookout, which lay between the two Brigade HQs and overlooked the Wong Nei Chong Gap.

At about 4.00 a.m. on 19th December Colonel Shoji gave out fresh orders to his two leading battalion commanders: his 2nd Battalion was to attack east through the Lookout towards the five-road junction at the Gap. The 3rd Battalion was to attack to the right and capture the north slope of Mount Nicholson beyond the Gap. The Japanese had clearly advanced with astonishing speed.

Jardine's Lookout had initially been held by only two HKVDC platoons. Realising their vulnerability, Brigadier Lawson had committed at 2.00 a.m. three platoons of the Winnipeg Grenadiers, one of the 'flying columns', to reinforce the Volunteers. Lieutenant S A Birkett found the ascent up to the Lookout impossible in rain and darkness; he decided to wait until daybreak. The leading Japanese patrols and main body close behind, under a barrage of grenades, swept the Volunteers from their positions.

Brigadier Lawson sent for his only other reserve – A Company of the Winnipeg Grenadiers at Little Hong Kong. He briefed the Company Commander, Major A B Gresham, at the Wong Nei Chong Gap, ordering him to move across Jardine's Lookout to secure the massive Mount Butler. Neither Maltby nor Lawson appreciated that the Japanese had several thousand troops on the high ground moving fast towards the Gap. Nevertheless A Company reached Mount Butler where they forced at the point of the bayonet scattered Japanese sections to withdraw.

Company Sergeant Major J R Osborn personally led the assault on the mountain and held it for three hours until the position became untenable due to three companies of the Japanese being in the area. When Major Gresham ordered a partial withdrawal, Osborn alone engaged the enemy, enabling the other Canadians to rejoin the Company. He then had to run the gauntlet of heavy rifle and machine-gun fire to get back himself. He had been in tight corners before. He was a lean, granite-jawed ex-able seaman, aged 41. Born in Norfolk, he had joined the RNVR and fought in the Battle of Jutland. After farming in Saskatchewan and working on the railroad in Manitoba, he had enlisted in the Winnipeg Grenadiers in 1933. The Battalion, although militia, had a small nucleus of regular NCOs.

During the afternoon the Company continued to be cut off from the rest of the Battalion. The enemy surrounded them, throwing grenades. Sergeant W J Pugsley wrote afterwards: "CSM Osborn and I were discussing what was to be done now, when a grenade dropped beside him. He yelled at me and gave me a shove and I rolled down the hill. He rolled over onto the grenade and was killed. I firmly believe he did this on purpose and by his action saved the lives of myself and at least six other men who were in our group." Corporal W A Hall also saw the grenade fall in their midst. "CSM Osborn on my right threw himself on it. Speaking for myself and the rest of the men who are still alive today, it is hard to say in words the admiration which we have for his gallant sacrifice."

CSM Osborn was certainly an inspiring example of courage. In his death he displayed the highest quality of heroism and self-sacrifice. Shortly afterwards, the Japanese rushed the position and took the survivors prisoner.

A different kind of unique courage was shown earlier that morning by 80 elderly men of the Volunteers, called Hughesiliers after their founder. They had been given the sedentary role of preventing sabotage of the electrical plant at the North Point power station. When Colonel Shoji's most western battalion stormed ashore, the Hughesiliers found themselves in the very front line. A Middlesex platoon of 24 men reinforced them, despite the three vehicles carrying them forward being hit. Forty-four other Volunteers linked up with them, too. Even so, the Japanese surrounded the exhausted defenders, who decided to fight their way out after being under concentrated attack for 18 hours.

A derelict bus in the King's Road outside offered some cover. Private 'Tam' Pearce, aged 67, the Chairman of the prestigious J D Hutchison & Co. and Secretary of the Jockey Club, told Major the Hon. J J Paterson, the Chairman of Jardine, Matheson & Co. and the senior member of the Legislative Council, that he would as soon be killed under a bus as roasted alive inside the burning power station, and "at the time there seemed to be quite a bit in what he said – not much choice either way". Five men reached the bus, but all became casualties, one being killed, and were captured with the others.

The Hughesiliers' battle was remarkable, not only because the elderly veterans had sought action rather than safety, but also because they had won time for fresh defences to be established in their rear. Maltby was full of praise for them. Their courage was typical of most who fought on in isolated positions long after there was no hope of relief or reinforcements. Bullet-scarred, impersonal pill-boxes hidden by overgrown vegetation in long forgotten gullies are today a mute reminder in Hong Kong of other less celebrated actions. The long list of 'missing in action' is indicative of their courage. All too often there was no survivor, and so there is no possibility of recording their no less gallant deeds.

* * * * *

By about 6.00 a.m. on the 19th, the Japanese were closing fast on Wong Nei Chong Gap. Photograph No. 6 shows Brigadier Lawson's Brigade HQ on the road which lay between Happy Valley and the road junction above which was the police station, marked on the photograph. Beyond, the road led to Repulse Bay. Also in the photograph are shelters held by D Company Winnipeg Grenadiers (or D Company HQ and two platoons to be precise).

At 6.30 a.m. a party of 70 British and 70 Chinese soldiers of the Royal Engineers under Lieutenant Colonel R G Lamb arrived as reinforcements at the Gap and reported that the area was under heavy mortar and machine-gun fire. An hour later, states the Fortress War Diary, A Company Royal Scots left Wanchai Gap in trucks and then on foot to counter-attack the Japanese but was pinned down by heavy fire from Jardine's Lookout. A few of the Royal Scots succeeded in fighting their way forward and joined the Brigadier.

Lawson had, as said earlier, placed his Brigade Headquarters on the vital ground. He was clearly now in the very front line while the Winnipeg Grenadiers, commanded by Lieutenant Colonel J L R Sutcliffe, were well over a mile behind it, to the west, a reversal of the normal arrangement.

"Why did Lawson move so far forward?... We shall never know why he virtually abdicated his responsibility as Brigade Commander and chose to act instead as a Company Commander. Did he recognise the desperate need to hold the Gap, and believe that the sight of their Brigadier in the front line would hearten his men?" ponders Brereton Greenhous of Canada's Directorate of History.[5] "Whatever his reasoning, his action was a mistake."

Lawson telephoned Brigadier Wallis at Tytam Gap and "told me his HQ was being threatened and could I try and put in a counter attack to relieve the pressure. I managed to collect a small force of Volunteers and artillery personnel under a Gunner officer, but Lawson was some two miles away over mountainous country," recalled Wallis. "This counter attack never got further than the lower slopes of Mount Parker. A little later he called me again and said his HQ was almost surrounded and that he and his staff were going outside to fight it out, rather than be killed inside like rats. I told him of the failure of the counter attack."[6]

Brigadier Lawson also appealed for help from Sutcliffe of the Winnipeg Grenadiers, and then, at 10.00 a.m. he told Maltby that the enemy was firing on his shelter at point blank range. Lawson's Brigade Major, C A Lyndon, told Fortress HQ that the Headquarters was being evacuated to Black's Link. It was arranged that D Company Winnipeg Grenadiers would give covering fire. The Brigade telephone exchange was destroyed and the HQ totally abandoned.

Some of the Winnipeg Grenadiers watched Lawson and others run for cover. Japanese machine gunners also caught sight of him in his distinctive Brigadier's uniform. Sergeant R Manchester, 100 yards away, saw him stagger and fall. The Japanese continued to fire into the small, broken group.

Four days later Colonel Shoji received reports of the discovery of Lawson's body. The Japanese medical officer, Captain Kimura, wrapped the dead Brigadier, the former commander of the Canadian Forces, in the blanket of Lieutenant Okada, the nearest Japanese Company Commander. "He had died of a wound to the right leg and loss of blood," wrote Shoji. "I ordered the temporary burial of the officer on the battle ground on which he had died so heroically."

Notes

1. The Japanese plans and reports quoted in this and subsequent chapters are taken from personal accounts and interrogation reports of Lt Gen. Ito Takeo in July 1947; Maj. Gen. Shoji Toshishige in November 1946 to Capt. E C Watson; Maj. Gen. Tanaka in January/February 1947. All these accounts are in NDHQ as are Col. Doi Teihichi's notes and statements.
2. Statement taken by GHQ Far East Comd M 1 SECGS, NDHQ.
3. The figures quoted are taken from the War Office report on operations in Hong Kong, 8th–25th December, in the Supplement to *The London Gazette* dated 27.1.48. The figures, the Supplement states, are approximate.
4. The diary is undated, typed on Army Form C 2118, marked Copy No. 3, headed 'Preliminary Summary', and has numerous additional references and some notes added in manuscript.
5. Greenhous, B, *"C" Force to Hong Kong: A Canadian Catastrophe 1941–1945*, Canadian War Museum Historical Publication No. 30, 1997, p. 86.
6. Letter Wallis to author, 21.8.77.

CHAPTER 12

Hell's Destruction

19th–20th December 1941

By 10.00 a.m. on 19th December, the Japanese were in possession of much of the high ground in the east of the Island, including most of Jardine's Lookout, the lower slopes of Mount Butler and the northern slopes of Mount Parker. They were fanning out towards Leighton Hill, and the Wanchai which contained the most filthy overcrowded slums in Hong Kong.

Major General Maltby learnt from Brigadier Wallis that the Royal Rifles were having immense difficulty in holding their positions in the northeast. C Company's war diary recorded on 19th December: "No one had had a hot meal for five days owing to the destruction of the cooking arrangements. They had been doing continuous manning for over a week with no chance to sleep but in weapon pits. Some would fall down in the roadway and go to sleep. It took several shakes to get them going again."[1] The breakdown of the feeding arrangements, already commented upon, was extraordinary considering that for four of those five days the Japanese were on the other side of the harbour still on the Mainland. The "continuous manning" was also unfortunate. The inference that men in weapon pits could get no sleep is implausible because those fighting in northwest Europe or Italy, when close to the enemy, invariably slept in the bottom of their slit trenches. (Those who slept in the open would be vulnerable to enemy artillery, mortars and fighting patrols.)

After Colonel Tanaka's 229 Regiment had landed at Sau Ki Wan and infiltrated through the Rajputs, it had come up against C Company of the Royal Rifles commanded by Major W A Bishop. The enemy greatly outnumbered the Canadians. Bishop withdrew his force to prevent Tanaka's men breaking through to Tytam Gap. Even so, the Company had gone into action at 10.00 p.m. on 18th December with five officers and 172 men, whereas when the roll was called 18 hours later, only four officers and 64 men were present, their history tells us.

Brigadier Wallis had not expected the withdrawal. He began to realise that the Battalion was simply not trained for war. This is not surprising because, as already noted, it had come from coast defence duties where "attempts at anything more complicated than section or platoon tactics were abandoned".

At 10.00 a.m. on the 19th, Maltby "conferred with Brigadier Wallis about the stabilisation of the position," as Maltby put it. There was the grave danger that if the enemy staged a serious attack on the combined Headquarters of Wallis's East Brigade HQ and the adjacent Royal Artillery HQ, they would probably suffer the same fate as Lawson's HQ and his co-located artillery personnel. Not only would these HQs be lost, but also the Battalion Headquarters of the Royal Rifles.

The Japanese could then sweep on south, thereby "cutting off all the troops in the area Collinson Battery–d'Aguilar Peninsula included in which were the wireless personnel of the Civil Government at d'Aguilar wireless station," continues Maltby. "Accordingly I authorised Brigadier Wallis to withdraw his HQ to the Stonehill Company HQ."

Almost everyone who has ever written a book about Hong Kong over the last 60 years has severely criticised Maltby and Wallis for moving south, thereby enabling the enemy to penetrate between the two Brigades, splitting the defences. The critics, or "armchair warriors" as Colonel David Fanshawe put it earlier, have boldly announced that Wallis should instead have moved due west to Wong Nei Chong Gap to link up with West Brigade. These critics have failed to appreciate that up to six strong, battle-hardened battalions of Japanese were already between the two Brigades; we have seen how Lawson's Brigade HQ had already been wiped out there; the Royal Scots' determined counter attack towards the Gap had failed, as had Wallis's earlier attempt to move west to relieve Lawson.

Virtually all the critics have another thing in common: they have not visited Hong Kong, let alone 'walked the ground' to appreciate the difficulties which exhausted, ill-trained troops, unfit after a long sea voyage from Vancouver, with no communications, would have in moving west across rugged, mountainous terrain split by precipitous valleys, nullahs and gullies. May I express the hope, with genuine humility, that those who plan to write about the battle for Hong Kong in the future first visit all the battlefields, as I have done on over a dozen occasions? (The military cemeteries should be visited, too.)

* * * * *

Maltby planned that Wallis's East Brigade should carry out "offensive operations from the area of Red Hill and the Tytam Reservoirs and connecting up with Wong Nei Chong Gap when cleared... or to operate via Repulse Bay area in order to link up with West Brigade."

Since the two Brigades were now split, we will follow the fortunes of West Brigade first, before returning to Wallis's Brigade in the south.

* * * * *

At 1.30 p.m. on 19th December General Maltby issued orders to Western Brigade for a general advance to commence 90 minutes later. 2/14 Punjabis were to attack east towards North Point to relieve the Hughesiliers at the power station. Lieutenant Colonel G R Kidd, commanding the Punjabis, was already heavily engaged to the east of Leighton Hill with two companies; the orders never reached him. This left the Royal Scots, who were ordered to fight south to recapture Jardine's Lookout and the Wong Nei Chong Gap. Eight field guns were promised for the attack but none materialised. There was too little time for proper reconnaissance, the coordination of all arms, or adequate briefings of the men.

A composite force of HQ and B Companies commanded by Captain Douglas Ford advanced via the south of Mount Nicholson, while C Company was ordered to attack the southwest side of Jardine's Lookout with Captain Pinkerton's D Company on its left. However, Pinkerton was suddenly told, much to his surprise, to attack the Gap immediately as it was apparently lightly held. As a result some trucks with Vickers machine guns mounted on them and the remaining three carriers led the advance. The carriers were open-topped, armour-plated caterpillar tracked vehicles armed with a light machine gun.

They reached the point about 200 yards north of the Gap where Captain K J Campbell's A Company had been ambushed earlier that morning, resulting in all the officers being killed or wounded and casualties reducing it from 76 to 15.

Pinkerton's D Company found the way blocked by a tangled mess of burnt-out vehicles and corpses. "Suddenly without any warning whatsoever," wrote one of his men, "the Japs brought down on top of us everything they had." A heavy mortar bomb hit the first carrier killing Captain A M S Slater-Brown and the Battalion Intelligence Officer. D Company, on foot behind the vehicles, crouched in the ditches and scrub alongside the road. "If one of us moved a hand, it brought down a tornado of lead on top of us from Jardine's Lookout." The Japanese were firing from pill-boxes captured earlier from the Volunteers.

Lieutenant Colonel White ordered his Royal Scots Companies to halt and wait until darkness. When night fell, the three Companies, Ford's composite one, C and D, advanced. Pinkerton stormed through the Gap and reached the steps of the police station shown on the left of photograph No. 6. 2nd Lieutenant J A Ford found him seriously wounded on the steps and carried him back to safety. A second battalion attack was no more successful; the leading platoon commander, A K MacKenzie, was blinded while V R Gordon was so severely wounded he died later. Captain Ford decided "to withdraw all Royal Scots from a hopeless position in which complete annihilation would be certain with the coming of daylight. Yet another 'gamble' had failed, though not for any lack of tenacity in those engaged."[2] During the fighting on the 19th, four Royal Scots officers and 20 soldiers were killed and four officers and 48 soldiers were wounded.

Thereafter the Battalion was withdrawn to positions on Mount Nicholson, from where it could overlook the Gap and prevent any movement to the west.

The Japanese were finding the fighting more difficult than they had anticipated. The six battalions ashore by dawn on the 19th had become uncoordinated due to the initial Rajput resistance and the unfamiliarity of the ground. Colonel Shoji's 3rd Battalion, short of ammunition, had suffered the heaviest casualties and was still unable to capture the Gap, where D Company of the Winnipeg Grenadiers was holding out. Shoji sent his apologies to the Divisional Commander at Tai Koo Docks. Colonel Doi's left battalion had been delayed by heavy artillery fire; many of the Japanese wounded had not been evacuated because the medical units had not arrived. The dying and wounded of all combatants were lying abandoned in the rain and darkness.

* * * * *

The map of Hong Kong Island shows the Allied front line on 19th December. It ran south of Causeway Bay to Mount Nicholson and on towards Deep Water Bay and was held by the Middlesex, Volunteers, Royal Scots and Punjabis.

In the south, Brigadier Wallis, with the Royal Rifles, Middlesex, Volunteers and Gunners, was holding the line from Repulse Bay to the east.

* * * * *

The Gloucester arcade in the centre of Victoria was packed day and night by Chinese sheltering on the cold concrete. Trash and ruin littered the streets, crumbled stone blocked the pavements. Fifth columnists, gangsters and thieves were busily at work, looting, murdering and sniping, adding to the chaos as best they could.

Government stocks of rice were being sold in Victoria at ten centsworth per person. Chinese University students tried to keep the crowds in orderly lines.

Air raid sirens screamed while the heavy rumble of guns gradually became louder. Numb despair crept over Europeans and Chinese alike. Most British families thought it too dangerous to stay in their houses; those who could fled to the leading hotels, although their servants were loath to see them go. All were now committed to war work. Americans and other foreigners had joined one or other of the various Volunteer Defence Auxiliary services. Nurses, air raid wardens, food and transport workers grimly stood to their posts.

* * * * *

Ten days earlier it had all been very different. The Americans had entered the war; the Chinese were said to be advancing south to relieve the Colony; encouraging reports were coming from the Mainland; a string of stirring, optimistic messages from Churchill, Brooke-Popham, Sir Mark Young, Maltby and others were eagerly relayed around the Crown Colony.

"The city carried on as usual," recalls John Harris of the Royal Engineers. "The shops and offices were all open. It was as if Hong Kong for centuries had seen these flaps before. The story still prevailed that the Japanese could neither move nor see at night! The very first morning that the enemy bombed Kai Tak, my watch broke so I went in uniform into Victoria, to Lane Crawford, the Asprey's of Hong Kong, to replace it. The staff there were in morning coats. The head of the department, an Englishman, asked me why I had chosen a cheap replacement. 'Oh!' he said. 'You can have any watch in the shop you like. And there's no need to pay.' Then he added the prophetic words, 'None of our watches will be here in a few weeks' time.' At least one man knew what was going on; they were all looted.

"Then I drove back in my Morris car to my position at the Dairy Farm near Mount Davis in the northwest of the Island.

"My job, as already related," (continues John Harris), "was to carry out engineering tasks of any description, with about a dozen others, in the northwest – keeping the water pumps going, repairing bomb damaged equipment, keeping the roads partly destroyed by shells open and so on.

"I particularly remember the night of 18th December. It was exceptionally dark; the sky was overcast, with frequent showers of rain. Thick black smoke was blown across the harbour from the burning oil tanks at North Point which the Japanese artillery had set alight to obscure their crossing. Occasionally there was a brilliant red flash across the sky as the enemy hit another strategic point, which burnt fiercely. It was like daylight for a minute; I could almost read from the glow.

"I was very close to Mount Davis, the Royal Artillery West Fire Command Headquarters, with its massive 9.2-inch guns, its Fire Command Post, Fortress and Battery Observation Posts, Plotting Rooms, encoder and much else. Learning later of the heavy casualties inflicted on the enemy by our artillery, I took great pride in their success, not that I really knew what was going on," remembers John Harris.

The Mount Davis gun position was clearly a key enemy objective to destroy at the first opportunity. At 4.00 p.m. on 13th December, the position was heavily shelled. The battery's top gun, which had been particularly useful for landwards firing, was hit by a dud shell which damaged the inside of the bore; if the gauge – a standard measure to which things must conform – would not pass, then a shell could not be fired.[3]

"Fortunately about one in three of the Japanese shells, throughout the battle for Hong Kong, failed to explode. A 9-inch shell had entered the Fortress HQ plotting room – the holy of holies – and did not go off. Eventually the shell was dislodged. Very plainly on the case were stamped the words 'Woolwich Arsenal, 1908'.

"On 14th December I could see that Mount Davis was being heavily shelled: the anti-aircraft gun site was severely damaged and nine men killed. One gun was demolished and the other could only fire over open sights with no assistance from height or range finding instruments," continues John Harris.

"Two days later the Mount Davis Battery Plotting Room was hit by another dud: it worked its way through a ventilation shaft and finished up covering the 20 men there with dust and debris, all lucky to be alive. Forty-eight hours later all communications with Royal Artillery Central at the Wong Nei Chong Gap were cut when Brigadier Lawson's HQ was overrun. Major G E S Proes was amongst the many Gunners killed there. (Some 40 years later Oliver Lindsay took Proes's son to the precise spot: the tragedy and sorrow can be imagined.) Attempts were made at Wong Nei Chong Gap to bring artillery fire onto the Japanese whom the Royal Scots were attacking but it proved impossible to support them with effective fire owing to the mountainous terrain.

"In due course the Mount Davis gun position was so heavily bombed all the guns were put out of action and the Gunners were swept up in the fighting elsewhere. This is typical of what happened to other artillery locations.

"During this period, I and the few other Sappers with me all slept as best we could on the concrete Dairy Farm floors by day in order to spend each night patrolling between Mount Davis and the Naval Base at Aberdeen. Our mission was to prevent the Japanese landing on the northwest shoreline and infiltrating through our lines. They had already tried an unsuccessful landing on Aberdeen Island," recalls John Harris.

"The Winnipeg Grenadiers, who had been there, and many Royal Navy personnel from their base, had all been committed to the battles to the east, and so our rather forlorn Royal Engineer patrol seemed to be the only one patrolling the area. The road running through the Wong Nei Chong Gap and centre of the Island was held by the Japanese, making the busy road we patrolled in the west important, for it was now the only one connecting the south of the Island – Stanley and Repulse Bay – with the north – Victoria and the Wanchai.

"On 19th December, after receiving a lot of contradictory orders, about ten of us under command of Major Parsons were ordered to climb the hills above Aberdeen, leaving our transport there. An officer told us to lie in a broad line amongst the scrub and rocks there. Our position gave no protection from the continuous shelling. We could see several fires and parts of the road which led from Repulse Bay to the Wong Nei Chong Gap. Clouds descended upon us from Victoria Peak; it was a miserable cold day. I felt helpless. I reflected on my life for I could see no way that I could survive the next few hours.

"At 6.00 p.m. my group was ordered to move to the Ridge which lies just south of the Gap. (It is marked on the map of Hong Kong Island and a photograph of the Ridge is at No. 7.) There were about five big houses there, all in a state of defence. It was under occasional heavy mortar bombardment because it was in a fairly important place, blocking any Japanese approach from the Gap.

"After a two-hour hard march we reached the Ridge and found up to 200 people running and firing in all directions. Some Japanese fired back from a catchwater 100 feet above us, inflicting some casualties. The position was being strengthened by barricades connecting one house to another and by stragglers, isolated from their units, drifting in.

"I saw quite clearly the attack on the Wong Nei Chong Gap police station, part of which was on fire. In the darkness amidst the chaos we didn't know what to do. I was carrying a large, heavy revolver which was awkward to manage and did not fill me with confidence. You must remember that we Sappers were not really intended to act as infantry; we were cold, wet and had had no food since early morning. To our relief the officer in charge, Lieutenant Colonel E C Frederick of the Royal Army Service Corps, told us that the Ridge was full and ordered us to 'get out' and return to the Dairy Farm and man the shoreline below it. We retraced our footsteps back down the narrow road cut through the rock, under cover of the rocks on the north side of the road, and eventually picked up our transport at Aberdeen; all the buildings were without light and there was no movement in the streets. We reached the Dairy Farm at about 2 a.m., lay down on the concrete floor and fell asleep instantly.

"I will describe what happened at the Ridge after we had gone because it was typical of the muddle which was going on at the Repulse Bay Hotel and elsewhere.

"Lieutenant Colonel R A P Macpherson had no confidence in the Ridge's defences and ordered a mixed group of Royal Navy and RASC to leave. On moving south they came across two crashed trucks which had been ambushed. The Japanese were beneath the vehicles firing at the group, some of whom returned to the Ridge. 'We were reduced to drinking water from the fire-buckets and what rain water we could catch,' reported Captain A H Potts.[4] 'The Japs had cut off the water supply. The stench was awful because the lavatories could not be flushed, and some of our foolish troops continued to use them instead of going outside.' Night came with pouring rain. The following morning, Sunday 21st December, was brighter. The Japanese had grown so confident that they had erected a tent within sight of the Ridge; their reconnaissance aircraft circled overhead. On Mount Nicholson they had spread out their flags to mark their positions.

"That afternoon Major C A Young of the Royal Rifles arrived, amidst cheers, at the Ridge with A Company after an unsuccessful attempt to break through to the Gap from Repulse Bay. Towards dusk two ambulances made the perilous run to evacuate wounded but the Japanese fired on them. Even so, after dark they were removed, apart from Macpherson who refused to leave despite himself being wounded.

"The telephones were still largely working; Macpherson was told by Maltby that he could abandon the position. Messages were relayed to Repulse Bay in French in case the Japanese were listening.

"The enemy decided to assault and surrounded the buildings, losing men in the process. Macpherson decided to surrender and went out with a white flag but was shot at so returned indoors. Captain Strellett of the Volunteers waved a white sheet fixed to a handle. He could feel the bullets hitting it so left the flag by a window. Macpherson went outside to hail the Japanese but fell wounded a second time. Fortunately some did succeed in escaping through a nullah later that night."

A Company of the Royal Rifles remained at another house called Altamira on the other side of the road. Major Young remembers that "The enemy closed in on us but we held them off for three hours until darkness came. I had the men remove their noisy boots, and we cut our way through 28 barbed wire entanglements trying to reach the Repulse Bay Hotel. I told the Company that from then on it was each man for himself and to filter through in small parties; it was almost daylight so we had to hide among rocks until the following night. Eventually four parties started out, each under an officer. Two of these officers were later found with their hands tied behind their backs – killed by bayonet wounds."

The Japanese hunted down those who had left the Ridge and other areas. One British officer was about to be executed when a Japanese noticed that he was wearing the First World War Victory Medal, which they had also received. "Ah! Japanese decoration! Let him go," they cried.

The prisoners were taken to Eucliffe, a Chinese millionaire's castle on the north shore of Repulse Bay. Having been beaten up by rifle butts, their hands were tightly bound behind their backs and they were prodded forward with bayonets to the edge of the cliff. They were then forced to sit facing the sea with their feet dangling over the edge. "We knew that we were going to be shot because on top of the bank were pools of blood and at the bottom of the cliff there were dozens of bodies," stated Company Sergeant Major Hamlon of the Royal Rifles at the post-war War Crimes Trial. "It was evident that they had been shot on top of the cliff and fallen down. Then a firing squad came forward and we were all shot. Owing to the fact that I turned my head to the left as I was being fired at, the bullet passed through my neck and came out of my right cheek. I did not lose consciousness and the force of the bullet hitting me knocked me free from the others and I rolled down the cliff." He lay at the cliff's foot bleeding all day until dark when he moved "a mess of blood" into a dank cave where he remained shivering as Japanese sentries patrolled above.

Later 54 bodies were found in the area. Many had been shot, others bayoneted to death and the rest beheaded.

The Japanese were to commit other horrifying atrocities elsewhere.

Notes

1. Garneau, Grant, *1st Battalion The Royal Rifles of Canada*, Bishop's University, 1971, p. 90.
2. Muir, A, *The First of Foot*, Edinburgh: The Royal Scots History Committee, 1961, p. 71.
3. Rollo, Denis, *The Guns and Gunners of Hong Kong*, The Gunners' Roll of Hong Kong, 1991, p. 132.
4. Luff, John, 'The Hidden Years', *South China Morning Post*, 1967, pp. 99–105.

CHAPTER 13

Slaughter and Manoeuvre: The Japanese Advance West and South

20th-24th December 1941

By dawn on 20th December Western Brigade was holding an ill-defined and confused line. In the north was Z Company of the Middlesex at Leighton Hill with Rajput survivors. The Royal Scots held the centre including part of Mount Nicholson. D Company of the Winnipeg Grenadiers, isolated and unsupported, were still hanging on at the Wong Nei Chong Gap. The line then swung south through Little Hong Kong and Shouson Hill. Most of the Winnipeg Grenadiers, less D Company, had withdrawn to reorganise on the slopes of Mount Cameron.

That morning the Japanese began to force their way west, first in the direction of the Naval Base at Aberdeen. Meanwhile, they continued to ferry troops across the harbour from Kowloon. The British shelled the likely crossing places, but direct observation of the landing points was now impossible.

Brigadier A Peffers, Maltby's senior staff officer, tried to encourage Lieutenant Colonel Sutcliffe commanding the Winnipeg Grenadiers, who had been ordered that night to clear all Mount Nicholson. The Battalion "had earlier withdrawn from its position somewhat precipitately. I spoke to Sutcliffe. He seemed tired, discouraged and distressed, saying his men were exhausted, as indeed they and everyone else were," Peffers stated. "I told him he could have six hours rest and that his Battalion must be ready after that to take its place again in the line. It did so and put up a grand show in the final days." [1]

Maltby's staff officers in the Fortress HQ battlebox were getting equally exhausted. The General Staff Officer Grade 1 (GSO1) there was Colonel L A Newnham MC, the former Commanding Officer of the Middlesex Battalion. He had a long record of outstanding service; in the First World War he had been twice wounded and later served in Egypt, the Rhineland and Bermuda. "Colonel Newnham was constantly everywhere seeing for himself what was happening," recalls a Warrant Officer of the Middlesex who was aware that Newnham had visited Wallis up on the Mainland during the fighting there. "He was very reserved and conscientious, a strict teetotaller, non-smoker and a man who kept himself fit with golf and tennis under normal conditions. A first-class soldier, in fact," wrote Captain Freddie Guest in his book, *Escape from the Bloodied Sun.*[2] Guest came across him in the battlebox; Newnham "had been at it for five days and nights without a minute's rest and was practically out on his feet. He simply refused to let up and the General was distinctly worried about him," recalled Guest, who offered Newnham a light ale. He drank it reluctantly, being a teetotaller, looked surprised and immediately flopped into a chair and was asleep. Guest had laced the drink with a stiff measure of neat whisky!

The temptation for Maltby's staff officers in Fortress HQ to survive the bitter fighting by remaining in total safety at their posts 20 feet underground was resisted by one and all.

On the 20th Major Charles Boxer took a staff car and drove, presumably by the western road patrolled by John Harris, to the Repulse Bay Hotel. He found that the celebrated cocktail bar had become an emergency hospital filled by many wounded, including sailors from the abandoned destroyer *Thracian*, which had been heavily damaged and deliberately grounded.

Boxer saw a company of Punjabis falling back in disorder after trying to attack Japanese Gunners on Brick Hill, to the southwest of the Ridge. The Company's officers had all become casualties. Impulsively, Boxer tried to lead them out of a gully but was shot in the back by a sniper. Boxer's biographer states he was wounded near Brick Hill, but this action could have taken place farther northeast. He lay seriously wounded for hours before he was rushed to a hospital's morgue.

Others on Maltby's staff who became casualties included Captain T M Pardoe, a brilliant Chinese and Japanese linguist; he was killed by a shell when visiting units. Major G E Neve with two other staff officers had been ambushed when on a reconnaissance. As they got out of the car grenades were thrown at them; Neve died a few days later.

These losses were irreplaceable and further increased both the strain in Fortress HQ and the difficulties of others trying to deal with them. Brigadier Wallis felt, justifiably or not, that they didn't trust his reports and that the HQ underestimated the problems, which led to piecemeal attacks and failure.

Fortress HQ was completely out of touch on one vital matter: what had happened to Brigadier Lawson? No new Brigade Commander had been appointed after he had closed down his HQ at the Gap. As a result, there were no proper orders given for coordinated counter-attacks, and they were indeed largely piecemeal. This was particularly unfortunate because many sailors and airmen, for example, were being sent to the front line although, like John Harris, they had received no training in infantry tactics. At last on the 20th Colonel H B Rose MC commanding the Volunteers was appointed to succeed Lawson.

One group which was holding out with great tenacity was D Company of the Winnipeg Grenadiers, still at the Gap close to where Lawson had been killed. Padre U Laite did his best to sustain the courage of the exhausted Canadians. Throughout each day and night this United Church Chaplain cared for the wounded in the kitchen shelter between the trenches. "The position was being fired upon from all sides. The main road running through the position was cluttered for hundreds of feet each way with abandoned trucks and cars," recalls Captain H Bush. "The Japanese were using mortars and hand grenades quite heavily. Casualties were steadily mounting, but at the same time reinforcements were trickling in, so that at the end of the day, while the killed and wounded were 25, the effective fighting strength was about the same."

Protecting the eastern approaches to Victoria was Z Company and Battalion HQ of the Middlesex on Leighton Hill. The other Middlesex machine-gun companies had barely yet been in action because they were continuing to man the coastal defences. It was appreciated that the main threat were the Japanese Regiments now on the Island and so the Middlesex were gradually withdrawn from their pill-boxes to be pitch-forked into the fighting.

Serious fires were now out of control in the Central District of Victoria. The Civil Fire Brigade asked Maltby for troops to tackle them; the General had to reply that none were available.

Early on 21st December the Winnipeg Grenadiers were ordered to try once more to recapture the Gap. They advanced under darkness, but were unsuccessful after meeting the enemy unexpectedly before deploying.

The Punjabis near Victoria were ordered to face southeast to prevent an enemy breakthrough from the Wanchai area. Those Indian soldiers in pill-boxes on the north shore were withdrawn to join the Battalion.

At about midnight a cable was received from the War Office emphasising the need to destroy all oil installations. This was largely carried out on the following day by artillery fire.

By 22nd December "morale had been seriously affected by the feeling that it was futile to continue resistance with insufficient equipment, with insufficient mobile artillery support and without both air support and air observation," wrote Maltby. The number of wounded increased; fighting continued for much of the day. "Battles are won by slaughter and manoeuvre," wrote Churchill in *The World Crisis*. "The greater the General, the more he contributes in manoeuvre, the less he demands in slaughter."

Shortly after midnight on the 23rd Colonel Rose, commanding West Brigade, was told that Mount Cameron had been lost and the troops were coming back in disorder but efforts were being made to rally them.

There was another serious blow: the Director of Public Works confirmed that "no water was coming from Tytam Reservoir; the Aberdeen supply was out of action for at least two days and only a trickle was coming from Pokfulam. The town of Victoria was now helpless." The troops were also feeling the shortage of water.

On the 23rd D Company Winnipeg Grenadiers was finally overrun. Ammunition was completely exhausted and the remaining men, 12 at the most, were worn out. Thirty-seven wounded were in the position. Padre Laite, being the only unwounded officer, surrendered the position.

Fortunately the Royal Engineers and two companies of the Volunteers with 40 Royal Marines were holding Magazine Gap; the Royal Scots were fighting off the enemy at Wanchai Gap and two small ammunition convoys had got through to Little Hong Kong during darkness and returned successfully with much needed supplies. Brigadier Wallis at Stanley was being sent ammunition by motor torpedo boats.

Captain C M M Man's Z Company of the Middlesex was holding on magnificently near Leighton Hill, although the Japanese were infiltrating into the houses and streets around them. He had only 40 men, drawn from the Band and others discarded by companies – the "odds and sods of the Battalion" as he put it. Six machine guns were helping to keep the enemy at bay. It proved impossible to evacuate the wounded, who had to remain in the Company position.

Captain Man's thoughts strayed to Topsy, his wife of 13 months. She was in the Nursing Auxiliary Service in a makeshift hospital in the University Buildings of Victoria. "In the early days I used to telephone her, using the civilian telephone to let her know that I was still in one piece. She ran even bigger risks, because the Japanese had no inhibitions about bombing hospitals and butchering nurses. On one occasion as a shell passed overhead, I said to her, 'Hang on a second, that was a near miss.' Her reply was, 'That wasn't over you, it was over me.'"

Man's next position, after being ordered to withdraw, was in the Wanchai in a Chinese VD clinic, "not the most salubrious of locations, especially as it had been hastily vacated." There the resolute Middlesex soldiers, still accompanied by several Canadians and Indians, bitterly contested every inch of the ground and resisted to the end, adding fresh laurels to the Regiment's proud history.[3]

* * * * *

By the morning of Christmas Eve, West Brigade's line stretched from the slums of the Wanchai, through the west slopes of Mount Cameron and the Wanchai Gap held by the Royal Scots, down to Aberdeen reservoir and Bennets Hill held by C Company, Winnipeg Grenadiers. A second line was held by two companies of the Volunteers.

* * * * *

We should now return to Brigadier Wallis's East Brigade which had moved from Tytam Gap to Stone Hill, north of Stanley, on the afternoon of the 19th. (Map on page 126 shows Repulse Bay and the Stanley Peninsula, while photograph No. 9 shows Colonel Tanaka above Repulse Bay.)

Wallis was determined to attack out of the Stanley area towards Repulse Bay and Wong Nei Chong Gap. At 10.00 p.m. on the19th, the

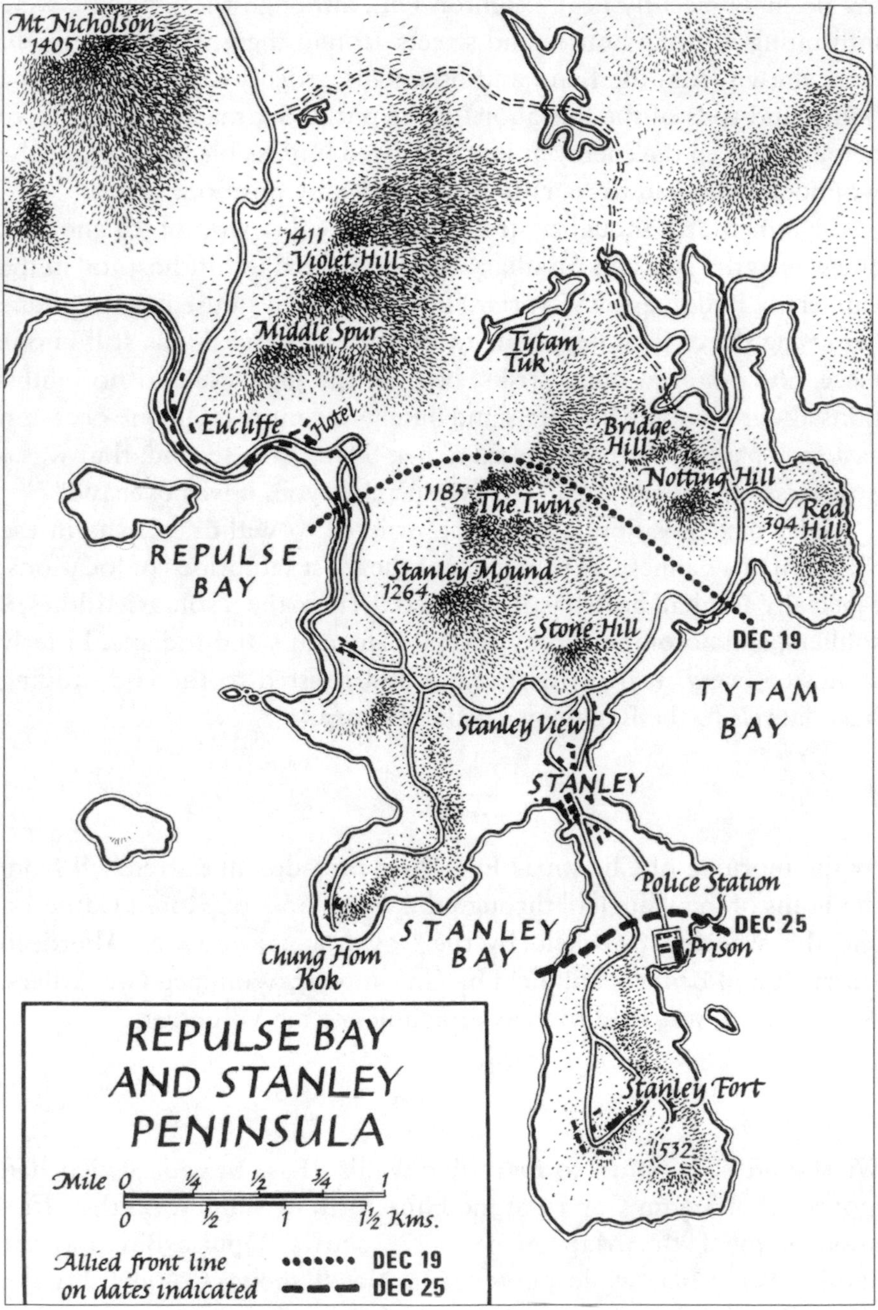

Repulse Bay and Stanley Peninsula

Royal Rifles, to be supported by two platoons of the Middlesex and three Bren carriers of the Volunteers, received orders to capture the Gap and join up with West Brigade, taking Violet Hill en route. Wallis pressed Lieutenant Colonel W J Home, commanding the Royal Rifles, to start his attack at 5.00 a.m. on the 20th. Home insisted he could not start before 8.00 a.m. as Companies were scattered and communications incomplete. Home had a good point: the Battalion had no proper wireless sets although the Brigade reserve of signals equipment had already been issued to the Battalion to replace what they had lost earlier. Various static pill-boxes and defences had buried cables leading to them providing telephones which still worked, but, once moving across country away from them, relaying messages became a major problem.

* * * * *

The Japanese usually took no steps to cut the telephone cable system, even when they had captured the cable huts where terminations were made; they presumably preferred listening to the conversations. The same applied to the civilian telephone system. Nevertheless the heavy bombing and shelling cut the cables, necessitating Royal Signals personnel carrying out immediate repairs, largely during darkness so that they were not picked off by the snipers, as Boxer had been. The telephones were therefore in continuous use in Hong Kong until almost the very end.[4]

It is of interest that this was also the case when the Russians were encircling Berlin and Hitler's Headquarters from mid-April 1945 onwards. The Führer's bunker, despite all the efforts and expense that had gone into its construction, lacked proper signalling equipment. As a result his staff officers had to ring civilian apartments around the periphery of Berlin whose telephone numbers were listed in the Berlin directory. If the inhabitants answered, they asked if they had seen any sign of the advancing Russians. And if a Russian voice replied, usually with a string of exuberant swearwords, then the conclusion was self-evident.[5] By this means Freytag von Loringhoven and others could establish the extent of the Red Army's advance before Hitler's situation conferences. Russian soldiers also used the telephones, but for fun rather than to gain information. While searching houses, they would ring numbers in Berlin at random. Whenever a German voice answered, they would announce their presence in unmistakable Russian tones or shout abuse as the mood took them.

* * * * *

Brigadier Wallis watched the Royal Rifles advance towards Violet Hill, seeing that it "was slow and overcautious. Men were taking cover every time a distant shot or burst of machine-gun was heard," recorded the Brigade Diary.[6] By 10.00 a.m. it was obvious that a strong party of Japanese had reached Violet Hill first. Attempts to push on to Middle Spur failed although the Japanese were cleared from Repulse Bay.

The hotel there was in an atmosphere of siege. A mixed force of Canadians, Volunteers, Middlesex Regiment, naval ratings and men of the Hong Kong Royal Navy Volunteer Reserve tried to defend the area. At one point a Gunner officer, Major C R Templer, was ordered to replace the local commander, who was drunk, but Templer's tactless remarks necessitated his temporary removal. The women and children who had gathered in the hotel were experiencing the worst days of their lives.

D Company Royal Rifles attempted to reach the Gap by going across country. After an exceedingly stiff climb, the Canadians advanced almost 3,000 yards through two water catchments before coming under heavy artillery fire. The Company gave up the attempt and returned badly disorganised and without their 3-inch mortars to Stanley View at 9.00 p.m.

By nightfall on the 20th, Colonel Tanaka's 3rd Battalion held Middle Spur and Violet Hill; more Japanese were moving to Stanley Mound. At 11.00 p.m. Colonel Newnham in Fortress HQ ordered Wallis to launch a major attack on a more easterly approach via Tytam Tuk and Gauge Basin. "Hold what you have, including Repulse Bay Hotel, and do what you can to get through. Boldness will pay especially if you get in the enemy's rear. Use your carriers boldly in recce," Wallis was told.

The following morning, two 3.7-inch howitzers were positioned near Stanley Prison and one 18-pounder from the beach defence role was manhandled forward to fire over open sights at the enemy. These three pieces were the only ones left. Major T G Macauley Royal Rifles commanded the advance guard with great energy. It consisted of one company each from the Volunteers and Royal Rifles; Macauley so impressed Wallis that he subsequently recommended him for an award. The remainder of the Brigade which followed consisted of two companies of the Royal Rifles and one of the Volunteers. In effect, therefore, it was a battalion battlegroup, rather than 'a brigade'. The Volunteers' carriers were slow in moving off, having failed to refuel overnight. In the meantime the enemy forestalled the column by occupying Red Hill and the Tytam Tuk crossroads. Brigadier Wallis wrote in the Brigade Diary that he went forward to the leading troops to find out what was happening, as Lieutenant Colonel Home was too far back. Wallis ordered Home to bring forward a second company to outflank the enemy. Home replied that he would send a runner back to call forward the company commander to give him orders. Wallis felt this would take too long and so "went himself, met the company commander and gave him orders direct".

It is not unknown in war for a battalion commander to go forward to take command of the leading company in exceptional and vital circumstances, but here we have the Brigade Commander, Wallis, running the Battalion.

"The morning was hot and steamy after the rain and the going very hard over rocky ground with few and bad tracks. The Royal Rifles, heavily clad in thick battledress, moved terribly slowly and held up the machine guns of No. 2 Company of the Volunteers. In spite of their heavier loads, these Volunteers were first on top of Notting Hill," continues the Brigade Diary. "The Brigade Commander went forward again to find Lieutenant Colonel Home sitting in a house and put him in the picture and then he went on to find Major Macauley, who had Major Templer with him, working hard. He was operating two 3-inch mortars."

At 1.00 p.m. Wallis spoke to Maltby in Fortress HQ on the field telephone, saying that he could at last see men of Macauley's D Company nearing the crest of Bridge Hill, where a hand-to-hand grenade fight was in progress. Wallis told Maltby that he was "very worried over the terrible slowness and lack of training of the Royal Rifles but that they were really doing their best that day at any rate and fighting gamely". Maltby ordered that all available men were to be sent to Repulse Bay with all carriers in a further attempt to break through and connect with West Brigade.

By dusk that night, the 21st, Wallis's only battalion was dispersed in three different directions. Fifty survivors of Major Young's A Company were pinned down at Altamira House, as related earlier, close to the Ridge and just south of the Gap. Sixty more Royal Rifles were in the

Repulse Bay Hotel, around which Japanese sniping was continuing. The rest were scattered about one mile northeast of Stone Hill. It is not surprising that they were making no progress because two Japanese battalions, on the commanding high ground facing them, were well supported by mobile howitzers and three light tanks. Major Macauley had been wounded and all the officers of No. 1 Volunteer Company lost. A further advance was impossible. There was a grave danger of Stanley Mound and Stone Hill being captured, in which case the enemy could cut off all troops to the east. Wallis therefore withdrew his forces to Stanley. This was his last serious attempt to recapture the Gap or break through to relieve Repulse Bay Hotel where Major Templer had taken command.

Japanese aircraft occasionally flew over the bay. John Harris at the Dairy Farm saw the anti aircraft Gunners nearby shoot down a Japanese aircraft. An abandoned Motor Torpedo Boat, disabled earlier, had been grounded on a small island; the Japanese bombed it regularly several times each day.

Templer received orders to remove his force from the hotel so that the women and children, if abandoned there, would not remain mixed up with the military and be killed in the ensuing battle. On the first floor, around a single screened candle, a few families sat in silence. Lights were suddenly seen flashing in one of the rooms in the north wing; an enemy patrol was going from room to room.

Templer took Bombardier Guy and a few others to investigate. He heard Japanese conversing at the other end of a corridor. "So I bowled several hand grenades down it, withdrawing into a doorway as they exploded," he wrote later. "It was a grand scene in the pitch dark. The Japs left and I resumed my post at the front door waiting for the moon to set."[7] The military escaped via a drain tunnel which led to the beach, and then south along the road or across country to Stanley.

The small group of residents awaited the enemy's arrival. Only the formidable snoring of Mr Hogdon broke the silence. He had been banished to sleep in a large clothes closet because he prevented anyone else sleeping. The tension grew. Jan Marsman, a Dutch engineer who had been due to fly to Manila the very moment the Japanese bombed Kai Tak, repeatedly called out into the eerie emptiness: "Come in… Come in… No soldiers here… No soldiers here!" At last a door opened. Two Japanese entered menacingly; hands were raised. A section with fixed bayonets approached a few badly wounded in their beds.

Four days earlier at the Silesian Mission at Sau Ki Wan the same men had overrun a non-combatants' Advanced Dressing Station medical post; on a hillside they had bayoneted the "unsuspecting men from the rear amidst cheers from enemy onlookers. Some had been bayoneted three times before they would fall. All the while, the Japanese were talking and laughing," recalled Captain Osler Thomas of the Volunteers who feigned death in a ditch, drenched in blood.

As the Japanese approached the helpless wounded in the Repulse Bay Hotel, the thin, elderly, white-haired figure of Miss Mosey in her white nurse's uniform barred their path. She stared straight through the Japanese as though they did not exist. "You will have to kill me first before you kill them," she said. They hesitated and then abruptly turned away.

The decision to abandon the families proved fully justified. The Japanese respected both her courage and the fortitude of the dejected and bedraggled families.

The successful defence of Repulse Bay for over 72 hours had interfered with the Japanese timetable and delayed their drive to the south against Stanley.

* * * * *

At 10.00 p.m. on 21st December Lieutenant Colonel Home told Brigadier Wallis he wished to speak to the Governor, Sir Mark Young. He said the Royal Rifles were "dead beat and he felt further resistance would only result in the wasting of valuable lives. He explained that, as the senior Canadian officer, now that Brigadier Lawson was reported killed in action, he felt a grave responsibility." Wallis tried to dissuade him from such a course and said that he should first inform General Maltby. Home had already had a long conversation by telephone with Lieutenant Colonel Sutcliffe commanding the Winnipeg Grenadiers. Sutcliffe also felt that the situation was quite hopeless. Wallis told Home "he had always found it best to rest and have a sleep before acting on a big problem *not of any urgency*". With much difficulty "Home was sent to rest. It was clear that he was physically and mentally exhausted," concluded Wallis.

On the 22nd the enemy increased their activity against the defenders on Stone Hill and Stanley Mound, while accurate artillery and mortar fire started pounding Stanley Peninsula.

At 10.30 a.m. Wallis told Maltby that Home had woken up without changing his mind. Wallis added that he hoped to keep the Royal Rifles "going somehow but it was impossible to make them operate offensively". They agreed that 'Stanley Force', as the Brigade was now called, would fight on so long as ammunition, food and water were obtainable. The water supply from the Tytam Pumping Station to Stanley had already stopped, making it necessary to start using reserves.

During the afternoon the enemy attacked Stanley Mound and Stone Hill, which the Royal Rifles were holding with difficulty. With no 3-inch or 2-inch mortars left, the Canadians could give no effective reply. A lack of signals resources prevented the forward artillery observation post being effective. Home was still "anxious to withdraw and was reiterating that further fighting was merely causing useless casualties which could not stave off final defeat," recorded the Brigade War Diary. Home was presumably unaware that Churchill had signalled the Governor telling him to fight on.

Wallis gave orders "for a strong counter-attack, supported by all the fire available, to recapture all Stone Hill and Stanley Mound". It took place at dawn on the 23rd and was successful, with the Royal Rifles reoccupying their forward positions but in smaller numbers. Captain Weedon's Middlesex machine guns' support was most effective, as was the artillery fire.

Almost two hours later, Wallis told Maltby that the Royal Rifles had been driven off the position and that Home had stated that his Battalion had lost by now 18 officers killed, wounded or missing and he had only 350 men left (less A Company, believed to be at Repulse Bay). Home insisted that his unit must fall back as the men were exhausted and would fight better on the flatter ground around Stanley village. Orders were accordingly issued to move back after dark.

After the withdrawal, Wallis spent considerable time that night trying to encourage Home to keep going.

The following morning, Christmas Eve, Wallis attended a conference at the Royal Rifles' HQ. He found the senior officers gathered there. Home announced that "it was the considered opinion of the Battalion as a whole that fighting should cease". Wallis rejected this "and told the Canadians they must either fight or march out under a white flag to Repulse Bay. The Royal Rifles refused to surrender alone," continues the Brigade War Diary. Wallis decided "to temporarily withdraw the

Canadians to Stanley Fort on the southern tip of the Peninsula so that they could rest and reorganise leaving the defence of the Peninsula to more reliable troops."

Was Lieutenant Colonel Home right to seek to surrender? Wasn't the situation quite hopeless? Was Home acting in the best interests of his Canadians, endeavouring to save their lives thereby? Should Wallis have removed him and appointed the Second in Command with categorical orders to hold the front line, instead of the equally exhausted, over-extended, composite, ad hoc group of Middlesex, Volunteers, Gunners and others? Are there precedents in the British Army in war for the sacking of senior officers who refused to attack? Then, a crucial point, can the Brigade War Diary quoted above be trusted? It was largely compiled by Brigadier Wallis himself.

These questions will be briefly addressed in the next two chapters. Certainly none of those in Stanley on Christmas Eve could anticipate the catastrophic events which were about to occur there.

Notes

1. Letter from Brig. A Peffers to Brig. W H S Macklin, 22.9.45 (NDHQ).
2. Guest, Freddie, *Escape from the Bloodied Sun*, Norwich: Jarrolds, 1956, p. 13.
3. Letter Man to author.
4. War Diary of Chief Signal Officer China Command, Hong Kong, 1941, and POW diary of Chief Signal Officer.
5. Beevor, Antony, *Berlin*, London: Viking, 2002, p. 299.
6. War Diary and Narrative of East Infantry Brigade and advanced troops, pp. 123–4.
7. Letter Templer to author.

CHAPTER 14

The Surrender of Hong Kong: Christmas Day 1941

"Christmas greetings to you all," signalled Churchill. "Let this day be historical in the proud annals of our Empire. The order of the day is hold fast."

Sir Mark Young's message read: "In pride and admiration I send my greetings this Christmas Day to all who are fighting and all who are working so nobly and so well to sustain Hong Kong against the assault of the enemy. Fight on. Hold fast for King and Empire."

The Governor was remarkable in at least one respect: during the campaign, quite regardless of the enemy snipers, the shelling and bombing, he was invariably 'out and about' encouraging people, whether it be in an Advanced Dressing Station, a distant unit or a Headquarters. Captain Iain MacGregor, the General's ADC, had just emerged from Fortress HQ on Christmas Day and was waiting for a temporary lull in the heavy bombardment before making a dash for Flagstaff House. He suddenly saw Sir Mark strolling towards him in a beautifully cut, lightweight suit, grey Homburg hat and highly polished shoes. "He was unconcernedly swinging a Malacca walking stick, as if he was playing truant from the Colonial Office and taking a quiet walk in the sunshine of St James's Park," recalls Captain MacGregor. "I called out, 'It's getting a bit hot along there, sir; better take cover.' He smiled and said, 'Hullo MacGregor! Lovely day, isn't it?' and strolled on, neither slackening nor quickening his pace, completely composed and apparently without a care in the world. He walked straight through the shelling, leaving a very red-faced ADC in his wake." [1]

Behind the facade, Sir Mark Young was acutely conscious of what the people in Hong Kong were suffering. Four days earlier he had forewarned London and Ottawa of the extreme gravity of the situation: "Enemy hold key position on hills, and GOC advised that we are rapidly approaching the point at which only remaining resistance open to us will be to hold for a short time only a small pocket of City, leaving bulk of population to be overrun. I feel it will be my duty to ask for terms before this position is reached..."

As the Governor's signal was being transmitted to the Colonial Office, the Director of Military Operations, Major General J N Kennedy, was briefing the CGS. (He had earlier disagreed with Grassett that Hong Kong should be reinforced.) "Resistance could probably not be counted on for more than a few days and it would be on a small scale," Kennedy told Alanbrooke. "Therefore it would have practically no direct influence on operations in the Far East in the way of tying up Japanese forces which might be released for operations elsewhere, but if we fought to the last round and the last man at Hong Kong, we should gain an indirect military advantage in that the Japanese would judge our resistance in Malaya and elsewhere by the same standard... "[2]

The Christmas Day issue of Hong Kong's *South China Morning Post* was as optimistic and irrelevant as usual. "Day of Good Cheer" read the headline. "Hong Kong is observing the strangest and most sober Christmas in its century-old history... All are cheerful in the knowledge that, for all the hardships, they would not go either hungry or thirsty this Christmas... "

Greetings came from an unexpected quarter: the Japanese were keeping up their propaganda broadcasts from Kowloon. "A merry Christmas to the gallant British soldiers," many heard. "You have fought a good fight, but you are outnumbered. Now is the time to surrender. If you don't, within 24 hours we will give you all that we've got. A merry Christmas to the gallant British soldiers... "

The Japanese were certainly giving all that they had to the troops defending the Island. The Royal Scots were in the area of Mount Cameron and to the north. On Christmas Eve D Company had suffered particularly heavy casualties. The effective strength of the Battalion was down to 175 all ranks, although there were a number of missing sub-units which had been cut off but were still fighting with others. Very early on Christmas Day the enemy attacked the Royal Scots again but failed to penetrate any of the positions.

At 7.00 a.m. anti-tank mines were laid on the main Japanese approaches to Wanchai. The defenders were still holding the eastern approaches to Bennetts Hill.

Two hours later two British civilians came through the Japanese lines carrying a white flag. They were A L Shields, a member of the Hong Kong Legislative Council, and Major C M Manners, Manager of the Kowloon Dockyard. Both had been captured at Repulse Bay and persuaded to ask Sir Mark Young to surrender. Not much persuasion was necessary as they had seen the terrible suffering of the seriously wounded abandoned on the hillsides, and the abundance of Japanese troops, artillery and equipment. A bullying Lieutenant had started pushing Shields around. So Shields made a formal protest to the Japanese Commanding Officer, who was so anxious that the fighting be stopped he gave Shields some tea, after ordering the Lieutenant to take off his shoes and stand in his stocking feet as a humiliating punishment.

Shields and Manners told Maltby all they had seen and emphasised the uselessness of continuing the unequal struggle.

"A special defence meeting was immediately called, where it was decided that there could be no talk of surrender," recorded Maltby. "The Japanese sent one message – that their forces would not initiate active hostilities for three hours. I conformed… This impromptu 'truce' was difficult to stage for Japanese planes, operating from Canton, did not conform and bombed Stanley, Aberdeen and Mount Gough… At midday Japanese artillery opened up punctually on a large scale and later hand-to-hand fighting was reported by 5/7 Rajputs on Mount Parish… which fell into enemy hands and an advance along Kennedy Road was threatened. This put Fortress HQ area, which had a garrison of only one Punjabi platoon, in jeopardy… Communications were increasingly difficult to maintain… There were at noon only six guns of the mobile artillery left in action… very heavy dive-bombing attacks were made in the Wanchai Gap… which was reported lost… Captain C M M Man, commanding the Middlesex Z Company, had telephoned 'the line is breaking'. This advance by the enemy along the line of Gaps, the isolation of the forces at Stanley, the deployment by the enemy of such superior forces and armament, the exhaustion after 16 days of continuous battle with no relief for any individual, our vulnerability to unlimited air attack, the impossibility of obtaining more ammunition for the few mobile guns I had remaining, the serious water famine immediately impending – these were the factors which led to the inevitable conclusion, namely, that further fighting meant the useless slaughter of the remainder of the garrison, risked severe retaliation on the large civilian population and could not affect the final outcome. The enemy drive along the north shore was decisive," continued Maltby. "I asked Lieutenant Colonel H W M Stewart OBE MC commanding the Middlesex how much longer the men could hold the line. He replied 'one hour'. The Commodore agreed with my conclusion. At 15.15 hours I advised HE the Governor and C-in-C that no further useful military resistance was possible and I then ordered all Commanding Officers to break off the fighting and to capitulate to the nearest Japanese Commander, as and when the enemy advanced and opportunity offered." That concluded Maltby's despatch.

A Japanese newsreel unit subsequently filmed Maltby and his principal staff meeting the senior Japanese officers outside Fortress HQ. The film shows that there were smiles, salutes and handshakes all round.

* * * * *

A Bloodless Mutiny

There were certainly no smiles at Stanley where Brigadier Wallis, out of touch with events elsewhere, seemed determined to fight on to 'the last man and last round'.

As we have seen, Wallis had decided to withdraw the Royal Rifles to Stanley Fort because he felt it "imperative to clear the battlefield of disaffected troops liable to jeopardise the defence," continues the Brigadier. Then, referring to himself in the third person, he writes, "The Brigade Commander stated *he had also considered arresting or shooting* Lt Col. Home and placing Maj. Price (2nd in C) in command. He had however refrained from doing so as he had come to the conclusion that many officers would require shooting – that it was in fact a bloodless mutiny."[3]

Wallis wrote the above within nine months of the events. It seems apparent from his reference to shooting Canadian officers that he must have become seriously mentally unbalanced. Worse was to follow.

* * * * *

There are few, if any, examples in regimental histories of senior officers being suddenly removed from their commands. Letters found in Scotland, published recently in *The Guards Magazine, the Journal of the Household Division*, reveal one such case, although the official history of the Grenadier Guards does not refer to it. Brigadier R B R Colvin, commanding 24th Guards Brigade, was a highly experienced and capable Grenadier Guards officer who had been wounded at Dunkirk. In April 1943 his Divisional Commander, believing a German position at the Bou in North Africa to be lightly held, ordered him to advance his Brigade at once, although there was no tank support. Colvin protested and was told his attack must take place in daylight the next day. He reluctantly agreed, stipulating that they must start at 6.30 p.m., close to dusk, because there was so much open ground to cover. At noon on the appointed day the Divisional Commander said the attack must be brought forward to 4.00 p.m., which meant there would be no time for a reconnaissance or for briefing the Guardsmen; the attack would have to be carried out in the heat of an African afternoon although the men were still in their heavy battledress (as were the Canadians at Stanley); and at no stage of the attack would they have the advantage of surprise or the cover of darkness (again, like the Canadians at Stanley on Christmas Day).

Colvin refused to carry out these orders on the grounds that there would be unnecessary casualties. He was absolutely right. Yet he was immediately sacked and reduced in rank. The daylight attack, without him, proved extremely costly. In 1987 a Guards battlefield tour visited the Bou at exactly the same hour and date of the attack; the light was incredibly clear and it was obvious that the very strong German position of 1943 would have started killing the advancing Guardsmen at 1,000 yards.[4]

After some unhappy months commanding a reinforcement camp, Colvin was appointed Brigade Commander in Italy, was wounded at Monte Cassino and won the DSO.

* * * * *

Home refused to obey certain orders in Hong Kong, having no confidence in the judgement of his senior officer – Wallis. Colvin did the same, quite rightly, in North Africa. They had one other matter in common: Home was also eventually promoted to Brigadier.

* * * * *

In the absence of the Canadians at Stanley Fort, Wallis reorganised his defences in three zones. The first line consisted of the Middlesex, Royal Artillery Gunners fighting as infantry, Volunteers, and staff from Stanley prison. Wallis had nothing but praise for them, being particularly impressed by the Middlesex and No. 2 (Scottish) Company of the Volunteers which was commanded by Major H R Forsyth. He had been a Gunner in the First World War and a peacetime chartered accountant. Wallis greatly admired his "fine leadership, courage and devotion to duty. This brave officer though mortally wounded refused to leave his post in Stanley. He stayed with his men to the last."

Another whose gallantry was remarkable was a disgraced regular officer who had been imprisoned at Stanley just before the invasion. Sir Mark Young approved his release and Wallis wrote that the Captain was invariably where the fighting was thickest and that "he did the best any man can do to make up for his former shortcomings by his conduct in the face of the enemy".

At 6.00 p.m. on Christmas Eve, the enemy opened a one-hour intense artillery and mortar bombardment on the forward and support positions before launching a major assault with strong bodies of infantry. The enemy were using light tanks, light machine guns, mortars and grenades. Even so, their attempts to filter forward were largely unsuccessful. That night Brigadier Wallis learned with astonishment that some European nurses were at St Stephen's College, a few hundred yards northeast of the police station, in Japanese hands. He thought the hospital had been evacuated; an ambulance was sent to try to rescue them. At 7.00 a.m. Captain Weedon led a well-planned counter-attack and the enemy was beaten back, but not for long.

Brigadier Wallis explained the situation to Lieutenant Colonel Home and said the Royal Rifles must attack. "Home demurred and said his unit had not had enough rest. The Brigade Commander replied that nobody else had had *any* rest at all. That we could not sit inactive and watch the Middlesex, Gunners and Volunteers fight a battle as infantry, when much of the Royal Rifles, probably still the largest unit intact on the Island, was available," reported the Brigade War Diary. "The Brigade Commander insisted and Major Parker was detailed by Lt Col. Home to collect and launch a strong attack." Orders were issued to him at 8.30 a.m. No artillery support was available due to the configuration of the ground.

Fortress HQ told Wallis that "there would be a stand-fast for three hours from 10.00 hours while a white flag party of women and children were being moved from Repulse Bay Hotel". Despite this 'truce', Wallis ensured that Major Parker's attack continued. His D company left the fort at 11.30 a.m. and then departed for the assembly area for the attack between 1.30 and 2.00 p.m. Wallis watched them, recording that "the men were in bunches about shoulder to shoulder as if they found greater courage by this method. They were shouting and yelling as they advanced. On reaching the northwest of the cemetery [which lay just to the northwest of the prison] they were met by heavy fire from St Stephen's and its bungalows and suffered numerous casualties. After some 15 minutes the disorganised Company withdrew right back to Stanley Fort in a broken manner and suffered more casualties in once more crossing the open ground near the prison."[5]

Sergeant G S MacDonell commanded one of the Royal Rifle platoons; he saw it differently: "Since the enemy had a much superior position on higher ground above us and had good cover, I decided we must close quickly or suffer... Accordingly I ordered the men to fix bayonets and charge which they did with fearful war-whoops. Within seconds we were upon the enemy – which led to a confused mêlée of hand to hand fighting which lasted no more than three or four minutes – We then carried on and, driving the remnants of the enemy before us, entered into the houses on the high ground. Another close scrap took place as the Japanese stubbornly refused to be evicted... We continued on until we ran into a platoon of Japanese... we fired first and literally wiped out the enemy platoon as it stood... Heavy fire was now directed at us and casualties began to mount; we therefore returned to the houses to regroup... and began to repel the Japanese counter-attack which now developed in some strength. Shells began to explode through the roof and walls. With ammunition running low and the houses literally being shot to pieces around us, I received an order to pull back as we were in danger of being cut off."[6]

Another British officer also saw the charge. (He was possibly 2nd Lieutenant R H Challoner of the Hong Kong and Singapore Royal Artillery.) He recalled "the last glorious charge of the Canadians, up through the graveyard and into the windows of the bungalows up at the top. We saw the Japanese escaping through the back of the houses, and then return with grenades which they lobbed among the Canadians in occupation. Very few of the Canadians survived that gallant charge."

Twenty-six Canadians were killed and 75 wounded in that attack; fewer than a dozen came back unharmed. The company had been virtually wiped out in an attack that was doomed to fail, states their Regimental and other histories.

"Meanwhile, Wallis – who really seems to have lost his senses by this point and entered into some kind of maniacal frenzy – had ordered Home to send yet another company on yet another counter-attack up through the main road through Stanley village… " states a Canadian historian.[7] They advanced through a heavy artillery barrage which quickly cut down 18 men, six of whom were killed. By now the rest of the garrison in the north had surrendered but Wallis was unaware of this. At this point he was "considering blowing up the fort by detonating the magazine should the enemy penetrate into the whole fort area. Survivors would, if time permitted, join the wounded elsewhere. This matter was a last resort and kept secret," states the War Diary.

The end of the slaughter then occurred. At about 8.00 p.m. a car arrived at Stanley Fort carrying a white flag. It contained Lieutenant Colonel R G Lamb from the Royal Engineers Fortress HQ staff. He was accompanied by Lieutenant J T Prior, King's Own Scottish Borderers, from the operations branch. Wallis knew Lamb and had spoken on the telephone to him over the last three days.

Lamb and Prior informed Wallis that General Maltby had told the Governor that further resistance was impossible, "that H.E. the Governor, the GOC and several senior officers had gone to Japanese HQs to negotiate. They said my orders were to surrender and hand over all arms and equipment without destruction."

This surely was the moment for Wallis to do just that. He knew that hundreds of men were scattered over the countryside dying of their wounds and thirst. He knew that women and children had been abandoned at the Repulse Bay Hotel and were unaccounted for. He knew that nurses and medical staff were close by at St Stephen's College and were extremely vulnerable. (In fact, four Chinese nurses and three British had already been raped and murdered there early that morning; many wounded soldiers in bed had been bayoneted and the British doctors shot and "bayoneted dozens of times as they lay on the ground".)

Those defending Stanley Fort, Wallis knew, were short of ammunition and had been on short rations of food for several days; water was minimal and everyone was exhausted.

Yet what was Wallis's reaction to General Maltby's categorical order, relayed verbally by Lamb, to surrender? "After careful consideration, I decided I could not surrender when this action seemed to me to be locally unwarranted, without written confirmation," wrote Wallis, who sent his Brigade Major, H Harland, to obtain the orders to surrender in writing. The Japanese resumed shelling the fort at point blank range and fired machine guns at the defences.

At last, at 2.30 a.m. on 26th December, Major Harland returned with the orders in writing. Wallis at last ordered the white flag to be hoisted and the cease-fire. For many of the wounded, amidst the hills and gulleys, it was too late. The 'missing in action' columns in the military cemeteries testify to that.

* * * * *

In 1977, 36 years after the above events, I asked Brigadier Wallis why he did not surrender earlier. He replied that waiting for reliable orders "delayed the enemy an extra day and delayed the departure for Malaya of quite a number of enemy troops".

We can see how ludicrous this explanation is. As Major General J N Kennedy, the Director of Military Operations in the War Office, had pointed out to Alanbrooke, resistance in Hong Kong would not prevent concurrent Japanese advances elsewhere. (Moreover the Japanese involved were destined for the south and not for Malaya.)

The crucial point is that the slaughter of many fine Canadian soldiers could not possibly be justified in such circumstances. Dying to capture a few bungalows at Stanley, in the final moments of the fall of Hong Kong, is the ultimate disaster of the short campaign.

Notes

1. Letter MacGregor to author.
2. File 106/2420 A (PRO).
3. War Diary, p. 68.
4. Montagu-Douglas-Scott, C A, 'Tunisia 1943: A Battalion Commander's Viewpoint' in *The Guards Magazine*, Winter 2004/5, p. 237.
5. War Diary, p. 84.
6. *The Royal Rifles of Canada in Hong Kong*, Quebec: Hong Kong Veterans' Association of Canada, 1980, p. 85.
7. Greenhous, B, *"C" Force to Hong Kong: A Canadian Catastrophe 1941–1945*, Canadian War Museum Historical Publication No. 30, 1997, p. 96.

1. The Officers of the 2nd Battalion Royal Scots at a Beating Retreat, Hong Kong, September 1941. This remarkable photograph shows most of those who were to be the key players in the Mainland battle. From left to right: Second Lieutenant Thomson (patrol commander at the Redoubt), Lieutenant Millar, Mrs Millar, Captain Ford (Signals Officer), Captain Pinkerton (Officer Commanding D Company), an officer of 5/7 Rajputs, Major Burn (Second in Command), Captain Duke, Lieutenant Colonel White (Commanding Officer), Lieutenant Colonel McDougall (previous Commanding Officer), Mrs White, Major Walker, Lieutenant Hunter, Miss Peggy Scotcher (Lieutenant Hunter's fiancée who was a volunteer nurse. They were married on Christmas Day, one hour after the surrender, in the hospital where Lieutenant Hunter was lying wounded), Second Lieutenant Slater Brown and Captain Jones (Officer Commanding A Company and the Shingmun Redoubt).

2. Major General C M Maltby (left), the General Officer Commanding the Allies in Hong Kong, meets Brigadier John Lawson who commanded the ill-fated Canadian Brigade.

9. Colonel Tanaka above Repulse Bay. The famous hotel which held out for almost 72 hours lies in the centre foreground.

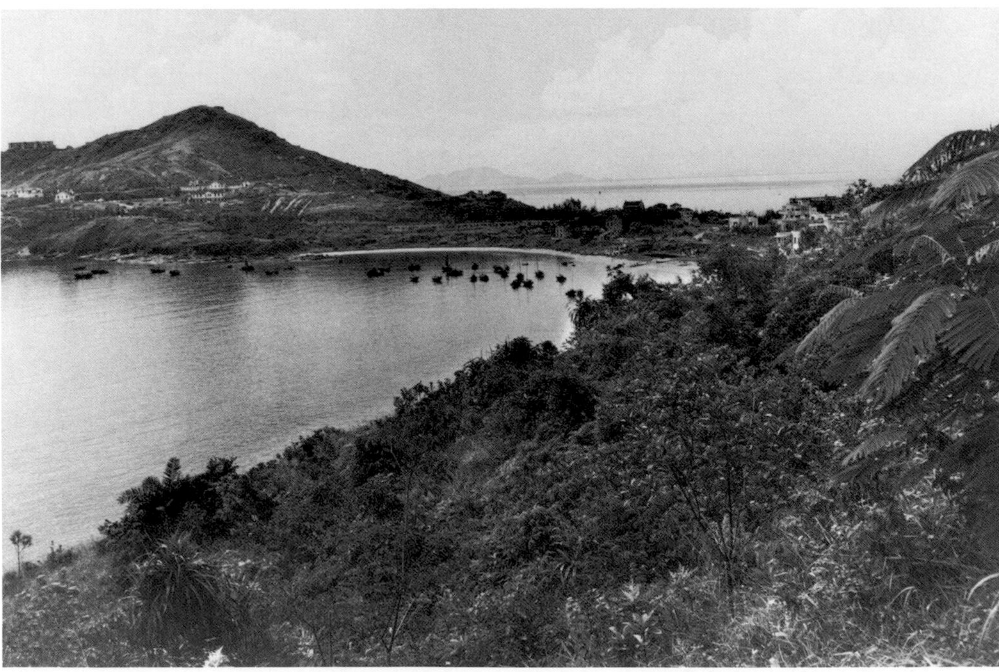

10. Stanley Peninsula (far left), the scene of the Allies' last stand.

11. At 7.00 p.m. on Christmas Day 1941 Major General C M Maltby, seated at the table second left, signed the instrument of surrender. (He may well be looking at Sir Mark Young to the left out of the picture.)

12. Japanese troops enter Hong Kong headed by Lieutenant General Sakai and Vice Admiral Niimi on 28th December.

Four of the five posthumous winners of the George Cross who gathered important intelligence for British Army Aid Group in China. They refused to betray their comrades under torture.

13. Colonel L A Newnham, The Middlesex Regiment.

14. Captain Douglas Ford, The Royal Scots.

15. Captain M Ansari, 5/7 Rajputs.

16. Flight Lieutenant H B Gray, Royal Air Force.

17. *Left:* Sir Mark Young, Governor of Hong Kong.

18. *Above:* Brigadier C Wallis, who refused to surrender.

19. A Japanese fighter (left centre) turns in to attack American bombers above the north shore of Hong Kong Island (looking towards Kowloon and China) 16th October 1944. Smoke billows from Kowloon docks and (to the left) two Japanese ships spout flames.

20. *Above left:* Allied POWs working as slave labour in a Japanese coal yard. Each car contains one and a half tons of coal.

21. *Above right:* Plays maintained morale. These two (male!) POWs put on a sketch.

22. The daily roll call parade at Argyle Street POW camp.

23. Argyle Street POW camp.

24. Beyond the barbed wire at Shamshuipo the POWs could see the patrolling Japanese sentries and the junks. A POW on the right is wearing a *pandochi* to save his shorts for muster parades.

25. Talks were given in the POW camps to fight depression and keep minds occupied.

36. Limbless but cheerful, repatriated POWs on board HM hospital ship *Oxfordshire* as she left Hong Kong for the UK.

37. Major General Umetichi Odada signs the surrender document watched by British, American, Canadian and Chinese officers in Government House, 16th September 1945.

38. The Victory Parade at the Cenotaph in September 1945. The New Territories can be seen in the distance.

39. Sir Mark Young inspects a Guard of Honour on his return to Hong Kong.

40. John Harris (centre-left) presenting a gold key to Sheikh Ali at the opening of the State Hospital in Doha in 1957.

41. Tuen Mun Hospital, Castle Peak, Hong Kong (1,600 beds). Architect John R Harris, 1981.

CHAPTER 15

Truth is the First Casualty in War

To anticipate events, on 18th April 1942, almost five months after the surrender, most British officers were moved into the Argyle Street prisoner of war camp on the Mainland.

Compiling an official account of the units' performance in the war became all important. Bill Wiseman, the Royal Army Service Corps Captain who had lost his leg when a schoolboy, wrote: "When I arrived, there seemed to be a tremendous amount of scribbling and typing going on. It appeared that the General wanted to write his dispatch and had called for War Diaries. Before long I even got involved, having to write an account of the Island Vehicle Collecting Centre, and then to re-write it to comply with Commander RASC's ideas on how it ought to have been operated! All this near history bred so much ill will and bad blood that General Maltby decided to clear the air by expounding his views on the fighting in the Commodore's 'garden'.

"I went with Charles Boxer who had recently been transferred from Bowen Road Hospital. The place was overflowing and the crowd had attracted quite a few Nips including several NCOs. Charles nearly had a fit when the General started 'At 4.45 a.m. on 8th December when Major Boxer had decoded...'"

* * * * *

Three questions were posed at the beginning of Chapter 8 – first, was it appropriate that the Canadians should be so severely criticised in the first draft of the Official History? Montgomery had to intervene to remove much of the criticism. Secondly, can credible new evidence be produced, 64 years after the battle, to convince the reader of this book, however sceptical, that grave injustices on soldiers' reputations have been committed? And thirdly, was it fair that one of the two British Regiments should be denied the coveted Battle Honour 'Hong Kong'?

* * * * *

A retired officer, who was the editor of a distinguished Corps' regimental journal, told a meeting of other Service editors in London in the early 1990s that "discretion and sensitivity is the order of the day; nothing derogatory should be published; our job is to be the guardians of our units' reputations…" I told him that such a view is rubbish. Just as truth is the first casualty in war, so most Service editors prefer to see their role as being to present facts, not tactful fiction.

How is a Regimental History, written in recent years, best tackled? Regimental Trustees may start by appointing an elderly military historian who never served in the Regiment. He laboriously copies out bits and pieces, seldom having the energy to tour the country to interview sufficient people. The Trustees may well reject his manuscript as an expensive failure and appoint a serving or recently retired regimental officer instead – to be overseen by a group of senior, elderly retired officers. They meet infrequently over gin and tonics; each in turn may demand in all perhaps 50 cuts. "Oh, of course it's true, yes," they will agree, "but we can't have the press knowing about *that*, can we?" In Britain, a serving or retired serviceman or woman signs a certificate, on retiring from the Forces, stating that he or she will first clear with the MOD anything written on Service matters. The MOD may end up by asking for another 50 changes (some, but certainly not all, with good reason).

By now the author is beside himself with frustration. One was so angry with the cuts that he refused to have his name associated with his work, because a 'squeaky-clean, second to none' type regimental history is extraordinarily boring; it will not catch the eye of reviewers; few outside the regimental circle will know or care that the book exists. The Regimental Trustees may decide instead on an admirable, flashy, coffee-table type history with lots of photographs, a few good captions and very little else because 300 years have to be squeezed into 200 pages.

There are, of course, exceptions. To give two examples, the Regimental History of the Royal Scots, published in 2001, is certainly a much welcomed 'warts and all' type history. It is of interest that A Muir, writing the 1961 version, did not include embarrassing detail – for example the account of Private Wyllie locking three of his officers in the observation post at the climax of the battle at the Shingmun Redoubt.

Another exception is the post-war 1945–1995 history of the Grenadier Guards. Detail is included on 40 reservists who marched on the Officers' Mess in Malta in 1956 to protest; and a few years earlier in North Africa three other reservists purposely dropped their rifles on a parade, also as a form of protest – all because they wanted to go home! I am conscious of making quite a few references to the Grenadier Guards: I do so because I am familiar with the facts, having served with them for 35 years. (Moreover, the Winnipeg Grenadiers before the war had some things in common with the Regiment.)

* * * * *

Newly released files show how Whitehall vetoed former Prime Minister Harold Macmillan's proposed memoirs, the April 2005 edition of *History Magazine* reveals. The passage, written in 1970, which most disturbed the Ministry of Defence was the negotiation of an Anglo-American agreement jointly to defend Hong Kong in the event of a Chinese attack. Macmillan reluctantly 'modified' his memoirs, omitting this and other important passages.

Will the Freedom of Information Act enable the truth to be known about important political or military matters which hitherto have been kept secret, quite needlessly? Apparently Government departments have been shredding record numbers of official files in the months leading up to the enforcement of the Act, which empowers any member of the public to apply to see secret files. The increase in the destruction rates in one department is 500 per cent. A culture of evasion leads to the destruction of evidence, to avoid coping with an era of openness.

Then there's another problem: "Up to 10 million pages of vital military secrets have been rendered unusable by exposure to asbestos," states a report. "The contamination threatens the operation of the Act. The 63,000 files include the official versions of events such as the sinking of the *Belgrano* in 1982 and the killing of IRA terrorists in Gibraltar by the SAS in 1988." According to Professor Matthew Jones of Nottingham University, "These files are irreplaceable records of this nation's defence and foreign policy during the 20th century."

Incidentally, on the subject of the *Belgrano*, immediately after the Falklands War a small group, led by an Under Secretary of State, was sent to Australia and New Zealand to lecture the Governments' Cabinets and senior officers on lessons learnt during the war. We took considerable trouble to clear scripts with the three Services to ensure they were true. Yet we were fed at least one factual error; for example I was astonished to discover years later that the *Belgrano* had been sailing *away* from the Falklands exclusion zone, and not towards it as we had said.

I fear that the first book I wrote in 1978 contained some factual errors and wrong inferences, partly because I was then relying on a very elderly and prejudiced veteran's memory.

* * * * *

In 1942 officers in Hong Kong were inevitably and understandably anxious that their regiments and corps would be shown in the best possible light. Eventual promotion, decorations and certainly their reputations might depend upon it. They had, after all, plenty of time in the POW camps to write and rewrite their accounts. Most if not all the War Diaries, like the ciphers, had been destroyed in the final days before the surrender, to prevent the Japanese capturing them. The memory of some people, exhausted during the fighting, had to form the basis for their memories on "uncertain recollections of those who survived, some assembled during a malevolent captivity, some in the immediate aftermath of war, others long afterwards from memories embittered by injustice, embellished by time, or embroidered by both," as Brereton Greenhous put it so admirably.[1] Japanese records are not much help. Much of their original documentation stored in Tokyo was destroyed by bombing later in the war.

So how accurate is Maltby's Official Report? "Have finished first draft of story of war in Hong Kong – great labour – much counter checking still to be done though, and gaps filled," wrote Colonel Newnham, the General's principal operations officer on 24th March 1942 in tiny writing on tissue paper. By 10th May the Report was finished.

It may seem extraordinary, but Maltby and Newnham had to compile the Report without consulting either of the two Brigade Commanders – Lawson had been killed in action; Wallis had been in Bowen Road Hospital for skin grafts as he was injured while on a forward reconnaissance towards Repulse Bay and the wound would not heal. When discharged from hospital on 11th April to Shamshuipo Camp and then a week later to Argyle Street, Wallis shared a room with both Maltby and Newnham. He felt "that the General and staff felt *they* knew all that there was worth knowing and that any account I might have was not needed to complete the picture. They also knew I was writing the War Diaries as I had many visits from various Commanding Officers and I told them both what I was doing. I gave my completed diaries to Newnham for perusal and to Maltby for information. I don't think either read them; Maltby was unprepared to amend his own account."

The General's official record of the war was buried in the camp's grounds to prevent the Japanese finding it. It was recovered after the war.

How reliable were Wallis's War Diaries? The Canadians had moved to North Point Camp and so he was not able to consult them. Moreover, during the fighting on the Mainland all his dealings with the Royal Scots were by telephone, before he moved from his Headquarters northeast of Kowloon to Devil's Peak in the southeast.

Wallis carried with him his two War Diaries throughout his imprisonment. They amounted to over 220 pages of manuscript. He hid them in the false bottom of a wooden box which he made for that purpose. He kept "personal clothing (rags?!) on top. I always saw to it that at its apparent bottom, the Japs would find a map, some foreign currency or a tool, or something that I was not supposed to have. Once they spotted any such item, I got them engaged in a big argument and sometimes got my face slapped and they would confiscate the offending item and not search further."

It is possible that Wallis did not hand his diaries in to the War Office until July 1948. They seem to have attracted some attention then, because the Colonel of the Middlesex Regiment wrote to him asking for evidence of how well his Battalion had done. Maltby's Report, published in January 1948, did not make any reference to Wallis's account and so obviously did not mention, to Wallis's anger, that he had held out at Stanley for 11 hours after the General's surrender.

In any event, regrettably, no attention seems to have been paid to Wallis's recommendations for decorations. He had written a citation in the War Diary strongly recommending a Victoria Cross for Major H R Forsyth of the Volunteers, but Forsyth ended up with nothing, not even a posthumous Mention in Despatches.

Long after the war, Wallis was living in Vancouver and wanted Canadian citizenship and so kept a low profile on his highly critical report on the Canadians for fear of not getting both citizenship and a Canadian pension.

Despite doubts on the reliability of both Maltby's and Wallis's Reports and Diaries, some references in the latter stand out – particularly Wallis's writing about shooting the Canadian officers who wished to surrender – clearly indicating his mental instability at that time. Such references have never been quoted before, although 64 years have elapsed in the meantime.

Neither the Royal Scots nor, very clearly, the Canadians trusted his judgement. We should respect their views: their reputations were tragically maligned.

Maltby submitted his Report to the War Office in November 1945 – to be published in the official *London Gazette* in early 1946. But Canadians protested over its critical comments. Field Marshal Montgomery intervened and had the offending paragraphs removed; the Report, as already stated, was not published until 29th January 1948. Maltby, to do him justice, admitted that "memory is a fickle jade" and his Report could be faulty. Moreover, he had not seen Wallis's War Diaries or expressed interest in them; nor had he ever seen the Canadians or Royal Scots in action throughout the fighting.

* * * * *

The views of the Canadian author, Carl Vincent, should be briefly examined. In his book *No Reason Why* he states: "It is a very conservative estimate to say that *at least half the Japanese casualties were incurred in battles against Canadian troops*... the Royal Rifles *executed more counter-attacks at company level or above than the British and Indian battalions combined*... Maltby's staff suffered heavy casualties during the battle, largely because of this incredible lack of caution... "[2]

The reader can judge for himself the fairness or otherwise of these statements. Taking his comments in (my) italics, it is not in dispute that the Japanese suffered considerable casualties on the Mainland from Allied artillery, mortars, HMS *Thracian* and the three forward battalions, in particular the Royal Scots. No Canadian actually participated in the fighting there. When the Royal Rifles were withdrawn to Stanley Fort, at their officers' request to surrender, the front line was held by others. And so the statement that Canadians caused half the overall Japanese casualties is highly suspect.

Soldiers will find Vincent's rather contemptuous criticism of British staff officers, who became casualties "through lack of caution", quite extraordinary. Instead, the 1941 officers concerned should be commended for fighting the enemy so courageously in the front line, rather than keeping safe in the underground Fortress HQ.

Some other authors try to stir up controversy to sell their books – for example, James Rusbridger and Eric Nave claim in their book *Betrayal at Pearl Harbour*[3] that Churchill lured Roosevelt into the Second World War. More recently we have equally ludicrous suggestions that the terrorists' attack on the Twin Towers in New York was all the work of the CIA.

There are also the deliberately deceitful. In 1977 I came across an academic from Britain who had emigrated to Canada. He deliberately misquoted Captain C M M Man as saying that, on seeing the Canadians arrive in Hong Kong, they looked "... *confident* ...". The academic was unaware that Man (later a Major General) had copied his reminiscences to others who could see that Man had written "*overconfident*". The author altered other more significant material to suit his purpose. I passed the evidence to Brereton Greenhous who ensured the man was sidelined.

* * * * *

Finally, we come to the controversy that only the Middlesex Regiment should have the Battle Honour 'Hong Kong', which was denied to the Royal Scots. It is invidious to compare the fighting ability of each Battalion, but I believe a grave injustice was done to the Royal Scots. The best part of a Japanese brigade swept down upon their new, malarial, three-mile front. No unit could have held such an enemy on such unfavourable ground for long. On the Island, the counterattacks fought by the decimated Royal Scots against two Japanese battalions at the Wong Nei Chong Gap are what legends are made of.

Twenty-seven of their 35 officers became casualties, 12 being killed: there was no lack of determined leadership. Although the Regiment has few men alive today who fought in Hong Kong, a campaign should be launched in Scotland to get them the Battle Honour they so definitely deserve.

Shortly after my return from two years' soldiering in Ottawa, I gave a lecture to the Regiment in Edinburgh before their annual dinner. After showing them the Japanese propaganda 1941 newsreel on the fall of Hong Kong and innumerable slides, I was asked the question: "Why did the Middlesex Regiment get the Battle Honour and not us?" It might have appeared a difficult question for a person from a very different regiment in the face of a distinguished audience, but I simply replied that it was a matter of a clash of personalities – between Wallis and the Battalion – just as, in my judgement, unfair criticism was levelled, again by Wallis, against the Royal Rifles, who did their best to overcome their shocking lack of training, in appalling circumstances.

The truth seems to have been obscured by Wallis and others. As Churchill put it in Volume 5 of *The Second World War*, "in wartime… truth is so precious that she should always be attended by a bodyguard of lies".

There are inevitably controversies in war – whether they be politicians claiming in the Spring of 2003 that Saddam Hussein had Weapons of Mass Destruction, or an unbalanced Rajput Brigadier in Hong Kong suggesting that certain battalions were ineffective. Oscar Wilde's "The truth is rarely pure, and never simple" may strike a chord.

Notes

1. Greenhous, B, *"C" Force to Hong Kong: A Canadian Catastrophe 1941–1945*, Canadian War Museum Historical Publication No. 30, 1997, p. 72.
2. Vincent, Carl, *No Reason Why: The Canadian Hong Kong Tragedy: an examination*, Ontario: Canada's Wings, 1981, pp. 201–4.
3. Alden, D, *Charles R Boxer*, Lisbon: Fundação Oriente, 2001, p. 110, Note 39.

Part 4

HOSTAGE TO FORTUNE

With memories by John R Harris

Edited by Oliver Lindsay

CHAPTER 16

Shamshuipo POW Camp and the Escapes

John R Harris continues his memoirs

By Christmas Day 1941 we were absolutely exhausted and extremely hungry. The shelling to the east of us intensified.

Unexpectedly at midday a nun dressed in white opened a small door in the high stone wall of her convent near the Dairy Farm. She beckoned a group of us to come in and the nuns gave us Christmas lunch. The dozen of us Sappers ate roast chicken and apple pie. It was our last good meal for nearly four years. The nuns were Italian: and so theoretically they were the enemy! After the war I went back to thank them but they had all gone – to where I could never discover.

The next day, following the surrender, my platoon was ordered to go to Murray Barracks in Victoria. We drove in my Morris car, passing a Japanese soldier directing the traffic. Colonel E H Clifford, the senior Royal Engineer officer, met us there. I was told to join a Royal Army Service Corps officer in breaking bottles of champagne so that the Japanese wouldn't go berserk with drink and commit more atrocities. The same thing happened in Singapore. I don't expect to see champagne running down a gutter again.

The Japanese quickly closed in on the barracks and took everything they wanted, including our weapons. That afternoon I took my father's large binoculars in a leather case and threw them into the harbour; there is now a 60-storey office development on the site! The field glasses had been carried by my father (a Gunner) throughout the First World War: he had given them to me when I left Surrey in July 1940. It gave me some satisfaction that no Japanese would possess them.

I sought out my two closest friends with whom I had done my officer training in Aldershot. I had travelled with them to Hong Kong in the

Viceroy of India and then we had shared a flat together on May Road – Dickie Arundell and Micky Holliday. Where were they, I asked? Both had joined Sapper Field Squadrons.

Dickie, I discovered, on Christmas Eve had led a section of Royal Engineers from General Maltby's battlebox headquarters into the street fighting in the Wanchai, moving from pillar to pillar to prevent the enemy infiltrating through the very last defensive lines towards Victoria. He was shot and lay in agony in the street before being dragged into a house by the Japanese. If the surrender had only taken place some 20 hours earlier, Dickie could have survived the war and been alive today to design many fine buildings. He was a good friend and an excellent engineer. It was a terrible shock to me.

Micky Holliday had become engaged in our flat in November to Brenda Morgan, a charming nurse from Nottingham, a really dear person. Five days previously her Dressing Station in Happy Valley had been bombed, although it had red crosses on it. She, together with some other hospital staff and patients, was killed. This tragedy mentally unhinged Micky: he was last seen brandishing a revolver and charging up the Wong Nei Chong Road with several other Sappers, going to their certain deaths.

* * * * *

The top priority was the burial of the dead, for it was too late to find the wounded still alive. This is because the Allies were not allowed to bring in their dead and wounded until the Japanese funeral rites had been completed. This meant they were lying in the open until 29th December when the enemy gave permission for them to be collected. Armed with picks and shovels, our burial parties eventually fanned out in pairs. The dead bodies were ugly: the faces blue and skin purple, with maggots attacking the open wounds. Private R J Wright of the Middlesex Regiment found the body of one of his officers, Captain West, amidst six others. "He had been among the most popular of officers who had inspired that confidence which binds an officer to his men with unbreakable bonds of loyalty," Wright remembers. "It angered me to see how ignorant we were that none of us knew the funeral service when we buried them. We eyed each other uncomfortably. Then, in the gathering twilight, a tall, gaunt, bearded soldier quoted those moving lines: 'If I should die, think only this of me: that there's some corner of a foreign field …'

"We remained with bowed heads long after the last words had been borne away by the breeze. The Japanese sergeant had gathered flowers during the recital and had spread them over the bodies. Then we restored the earth."

Another burial party was approached by two armed Japanese, whose suspicion soon melted. "They showed us pictures of their families," recalls Sergeant C B J Stewart of 8th Coast Regiment. "We compared weapons, for there were plenty of ours lying about. The Japanese expressed sorrow over our task and indicated that they, too, had many dead whom they were dragging into large fires."

The Japanese cremated their dead in large funeral pyres amidst much ceremony. The ashes were removed with long steel chopsticks and placed in small white caskets, each bearing a man's name. All the caskets were sent back to Japan.

There is some disagreement on the casualty figures on both sides. Major General Maltby in his Despatch puts his casualties during the battle at 2,113 killed and missing with 1,332 being seriously wounded. An authoritative estimate of Japanese casualties is 2,654 and some evidence suggests that this figure should be considerably greater, but certainly not as high as the 3,000 killed and 9,000 wounded as claimed by Maltby.[1]

On 30th December we were told to gather on the square beside the Murray Parade Ground. I was lucky as I still had a kit bag which I had kept at the Dairy Farm. Apart from personal possessions, it contained a small box of watercolours and pencils for drawing, and a little Bartholomew atlas, *The Handy Reference Atlas*, with which I tried to follow the progress of the war. It survived and is now in the Imperial War Museum. Also in the kit bag were several favourite books and even my army greatcoat which I still have today! We all owed a debt of gratitude to the Japanese who allowed us to take what we could carry into the POW camps. Without my watercolours I would have been unable to reproduce the sketch on this book's back cover. British POWs in German camps invariably had few, if any, personal possessions when first imprisoned.

Some, including the two Indian Battalions, gathered at the Botanical Gardens close by Murray Barracks. "Jap troops rough and bullying (rifle butts)," recorded a British officer serving with the Punjabis. "Hours just sitting on ground. No food until foraging parties raided former stores. Garden ornamental birds rounded up and eaten. Looted clothing from European houses and Murray Barracks stores."

We began our march to the dockside in the early afternoon, passing a Japanese band which was playing triumphant military music.[2] One sailor asked if the band would play 'There'll always be an England'. The ferries were waiting to take us across the harbour to the camp northwest of Kowloon at Shamshuipo. The barracks there had been built for British battalions before the war.

All the familiar sights were there, but instead of the hustle and bustle of ships, junks in full sail criss-crossing the harbour and motorised sampans darting hither and thither, there was a deathly stillness. The massive Victoria Peak, so magnificent on occasions, now seemed to be frowning upon the desolation spread beneath it. As C H Fairclough, a Lieutenant in 5th Anti Aircraft Regiment, put it, "The ferry passed close to sunken ships and it was difficult to keep my heart from sinking with them. We then moved up Nathan Road to Shamshuipo; it was just a shuffle, an orderly shuffle."

I was not to return to Hong Kong Island for 20 years.

Some apathetic Chinese watched us. Towards the end of our march, I felt faint and dizzy. The world became blurred and my knees felt weak. I knew that it would be a disaster for me if I collapsed and had to abandon my kit bag for I no longer had any other possessions. Alongside our column strode Japanese guards. Extraordinarily, God helped me. Suddenly one of the guards gestured to a Chinese on the pavement, waving him towards me to carry my load for the last half mile. I gave the coolie all the money I had.

Also in my kit bag was a silver flask full of brandy. Later the unlikely request was passed to all POWs, "Does anybody have any brandy for a prisoner who is critically ill?" I gave the doctor my flask that I had kept for two and a half years. Unfortunately the soldier died that night.

Finally, at dusk, we reached Shamshuipo Barracks. I was horrified by the conditions there. Altogether, 5,777 of us were crowded in. Quite apart from being bombed and shelled during the battle on the Mainland, the barracks had been looted of everything portable – doors, windows and their frames, furniture, metal pipes and electrical fittings: most of the huts were just empty shells with concrete floors. There was no food. Only a few weeks before, I had been dining on the veranda of the marvellous Peninsula Hotel in all its glory with Dickie and Micky, overlooking the harbour. Now I had sunk to the bottom of my existence.

I was glad that I had not witnessed the Japanese victory parade which had occurred three days earlier. Over 2,000 men marched through the streets, accompanying Lieutenant General Sano who was on horseback. Europeans were not allowed to watch, while the Chinese were encouraged to line the route and cheer. They were given small flags but they watched with no enthusiasm. The Japanese Imperial Air Force gave a very successful aerobatic display.

* * * * *

On 31st December the survivors from East Brigade at Stanley were marched across the Island to North Point Camp, where conditions were even worse than at Shamshuipo. The camp had originally housed Chinese refugees. During the fighting the Japanese stabled their mules there. The huts had not been cleaned and were swarming with flies. Unburied corpses smelt terrible. At least 200 men were crammed into each hut.

Brigadier Wallis persuaded the Japanese guards to allow him and a few others to take out foraging parties to obtain food, cooking utensils, medical supplies and books. He even obtained a truck to visit a hospital to get news of survivors.

"During the first few days at North Point Camp a small number of Canadian other ranks started saying that now that we were POWs, everyone was equal and that a camp committee should be chosen by them and that officers had nothing more to say," wrote Brigadier Wallis.[3] "But fortunately some measure of discipline was gradually re-established."

Private Wright, the Company Clerk in the Middlesex Regiment, also described the initial days as a POW: "Discipline had vanished. We encountered our superiors only when it was unavoidable; they had lost the respect and authority conferred by rank and uniform. We scrounged, looted and stole, ignoring the respect we owed to each other. We fought and argued over trivial matters and behaved like untutored and inexperienced children."

* * * * *

I am afraid that discipline had collapsed in Shamshuipo Camp as well. People almost preferred to lie down and die. We had neither the knowledge of how to cook rice in such quantities, nor the cooking utensils. Fortunately we had a splendid Royal Engineer officer, Caesar Otway. He designed the cookhouse, in which rice could be cooked, out of oil drums and a barrel. The smell and taste of the rice was awful but, even so, the sensible ones ate it.

Otway had been manning searchlights in the front line at Lei Mun when the Japanese had landed on the Island. He had only just escaped from them and turned up at the Dairy Farm in a terrible condition, cut, bruised and nearly blinded. We cleaned him up with a hose. He had lost his trousers crawling through a drain and on barbed wire. Fortunately I had two pairs and so gave him one – he wore those trousers, much patched, until the war's end.

Seeing the need to maintain discipline, Major General Maltby addressed the POWs from a balcony, giving us all a good 'pep talk'; he emphasised the need for us to maintain our standards if we were to survive, to try to hold sickness at bay by cleanliness and to respect our neighbours. Things improved gradually thereafter but stealing continued. If you queued up for your rice ration, you had to have a friend to guard your blanket otherwise it would have been stolen.

I have always understood that, during the surrender negotiations, General Maltby put one particular request to the Japanese. He asked if he could remain with his men, rather than be sent elsewhere as was Sir Mark Young; he wanted to share all their privations. His request was granted.

Colonel Newnham, whom I got to know very much better than many other POWs, kept the following diary.

Dec. 30 Up Nathan Road. Chinese population all silent. All concentrated in Shamshuipo. No food.

Dec. 31 45 bags grade 3 rice, broken, given by Japs for 5,777 officers and ORs. No cooking utensils. Late at night 30 small pigs arrived.

Jan. 6 Jap band played in camp. Good.

Jan. 8 'Stew' wangled by Boon for evening meal. 17 men run in for looting, i.e. destruction of good buildings for firewood.

Jan. 12 Colonel Royal Artillery to dine with Lt Gen. Kitiyama commanding all troops in HK area.

Jan. 14 Still unburied bodies in Wanchai; oil tanks near Cosmopolitan dock still burning. Weather early Jan. beautiful, gorgeous.

Jan. 17 No news of any identification discs having been collected off our dead.

Jan. 25 Great bitterness of those forced to vacate derelict buildings which they have worked on (and scrounged for) so hard. General morale and discipline of camp is definitely bad. Perhaps better now in future as units all together.

Jan. 26 No news from anywhere. 51 cases of dysentery.

Jan. 29 Degrading sight of British soldiers scrambling in dust for odd cigarettes, thrown by Japs from guardhouse upper veranda onto corner of prison compound.

Feb. 1 Good sermon by Padre Bennett in 'Chapel Hall'.

Feb. 7 From Jap point of view if POW escapes it is shameful desertion especially by an officer. Difficult to get our views across i.e. our duty to escape.

Feb. 8 Two Chinamen shot by Japs just outside our wire, probably for looting or trying to sell food through wire. Japs gave us a piano, palms in pots, 100 brooms for our mess.

Feb. 10 Conditions in camp hospital still appalling – no medicines, no aspirins, no milk or proper food for convalescents ...

* * * * *

Rollcall parades were held daily in Shamshuipo. Some men brought their musical instruments into the camp and so a band was formed, making concerts possible. Some Europeans who had not yet been interned passed food and medicines through the wire to their friends in the camp, as did Chinese. Unfortunately I knew virtually nobody who could bring me such things.

The Japanese guards in the towers around the camp were very cruel. I saw them many times opening fire with machine guns on families, including babies, in sampans who were crossing the harbour collecting food: the rowing stopped, we could hear the cries of the terrified men, women and children, before the sampans drifted lifeless away on the tide. A Chinese man paid with his life when he unwittingly brought a drum of water into the camp when the Commandant was expecting a drum of oil. Every day Japanese sentries would gather some Chinese together, tie tins on their ankles so that they couldn't move without the tins making a noise on the cobbles, and then line them up at the edge of the harbour, before bayoneting them – just as they had done to the POWs at Repulse Bay. I saw their bodies drifting away in the water and other horrible things and can picture them today, just as I can remember seeing and hearing people in my midst who were dying. If you asked me today what my firm was doing 20 years ago, I would have difficulty telling you, but some of the terrible things I witnessed over 60 years ago will be with me forever. The Japanese were indeed a cruel people.

Shamshuipo was really awful: it was almost the worst part of the war for me. I, like others, thought we would never see our parents again; we despaired of ever returning to our homes.

Inevitably, people's minds turned to the possibility of escaping. The most fortunate were the surviving crews of the Motor Torpedo Boats, who evaded capture with the one-legged Admiral Chan Chak; he was one of Chiang Kai-shek's representatives in Hong Kong. After many adventures 62 British reached Kunming before travelling 600 miles to Burma, and on 23rd February 1942 sailing to India, ahead of the rapidly advancing Japanese. The full story is told in Oliver Lindsay's *At the Going Down of the Sun*.[4]

There were a few escapes by very courageous men. All but one took place in the early period of imprisonment when the Japanese were least organised, the POWs' health had not deteriorated, and Maltby's policy of not escaping had not been imposed.

The most significant escape took place in January 1942 from Shamshuipo Camp. Lieutenant Colonel L T Ride, who had fought in France in the First World War, held the post of Dean of the Medical Faculty in Hong Kong Hospital and had commanded the Volunteer Field Ambulance during the Japanese invasion.

"All Colonel Ride's leisure for the past few years had been given freely to public service designed to prepare the Colony against the Japanese attack which he saw as inevitable," read a British report in May 1942. "He set himself the highest standards of citizenship and patriotism; apathy, wishful-thinking and inefficiency he regarded with bitter and outspoken contempt. If our Colonies were populated with Rides, we would run an Empire which would be the marvel of the age."[5]

On the afternoon of Christmas Day, Colonel Ride noticed that the enemy shelled more hospitals than usual for it indicated "that the Japanese fight according to the rules of warfare only as long as it suits them". On 29th December Ride reported to Maltby that he had found the bodies of over 50 Navy, Army and Air Force who had been murdered in one location alone. A week later he told the General that the POWs would soon fall victim to dysentery and cholera because of the primitive medical facilities, the meagre diet and lack of drugs. "I was convinced," recalls Colonel Ride, "that to save the POWs' lives someone must escape and either force the Japanese to alter their policy to look after the prisoners adequately, or to smuggle in medicines into the camps from China. I decided I must escape quickly."[6]

Ride escaped by sampan at night on 9th January with three others – two from the HKRN Volunteer Reserve and Ride's former clerk. They quickly reached China, to start organising help for the POWs with enormous difficulty. General Maltby was unenthusiastic when consulted beforehand on their attempt to escape.

On 10th January the Japanese interrogated Major J N Crawford, the Second in Command of the Field Ambulance: "Where is Ride, the Senior Medical Officer?" they demanded. Crawford replied that he had never heard of such a man and that he, Crawford, was the Senior Medical Officer. The Japanese left thoroughly perplexed: there were no repercussions because they could not establish what had happened.

On 31st January General Maltby sent for Captain A G Hewitt, the Adjutant of the Middlesex Regiment, having heard from his Commanding Officer, H W M Stewart, that he wanted to escape with two others – Captain Douglas Scriven, the Battalion's medical officer and Pilot Officer D Crossley from New Zealand. Maltby listened to his plans and gave him two letters, written beforehand, for the British Embassy in Chungking. He also arranged for Hewitt to have 800 Hong Kong dollars. "It was most encouraging, but the General did not wish me good luck, nor indicate in any way whether he approved of my attempt to escape. Perhaps he did not wish to become involved," concluded Hewitt.[7] That night they escaped successfully under the wire and on to a waiting sampan. I remember well seeing the sampan arrive on which they escaped.

The following night three others also slipped under the wire from Shamshuipo – Major J H Munro, Flying Officer Moore and Captain I B Trevor of the Volunteers. They swam for 40 minutes pushing a small raft they had made themselves from firewood. On it were ten tins of bully beef from friends' treasured secret stocks.

Two Royal Scots Privates, J Gallacher and D Hodges, also slipped past the Japanese sentries, reaching the British in China, who arranged for them to be returned to Britain.

By now the Japanese were seriously concerned at these successful escapes, aware that the POWs who reached China would pass on important information. Moreover the loss of face was intolerable. The Japanese responded by suspending in February the 'parcel day' by which large parcels could be delivered openly to the POW camps. A report from the International Red Cross in July states that the 'parcel days' were not resumed until later that month, and then stopped again until December 1942 due to more escapes.

In early February they arrested four RAF officers – Wing Commanders H G Sullivan and H T Bennett with Flight Lieutenant H B Gray and F Hennesey. They were thrown into an overcrowded cell in Saigon; it was so full of Japanese defaulters that they could not lie down. Sullivan, the senior RAF officer who had fought in Hong Kong, fell seriously ill with amoebic dysentery and was removed to a Japanese military prison where he was given fruit and illustrated papers by friendly Japanese patients who had been wounded in Malaya. "On 9th February 1942 I was given a banana to celebrate the fall of Singapore and on the Emperor's birthday we received seaweed as a great treat," remembers Sullivan. "In July we were returned to Hong Kong in a freighter with a gaping hole in her side where she had been torpedoed."[8] The voyage was remarkable for the kindness of the Japanese crew, soldiers and 'comfort girls' who continuously offered the RAF officers sweets, fruit, whisky and coconuts. "The Japanese were a weird crowd," he concluded.

Major General Maltby had become increasingly concerned that the trickle of POWs who escaped were endangering the lives of the remainder; the health of many was already in serious jeopardy. We have seen how the 'parcel days' had been stopped.

In April 1942 there took place the most controversial escape due to Maltby's policy: the story, well documented, can be told for the first time. It must be remembered that in the British Army, and probably in others, soldiers were encouraged, in principle, to escape: it was their duty to do so.

Three Royal Artillery officers – Captain J D Clague, Lieutenants J L C Pearce and L S White, with Sergeant D I Bosanquet of the Volunteers, had discovered a man-hole giving access to a typhoon drain which ran under the camp for over 50 yards to the sea.

Clague had some reservations on the few escapers who were leaving their families in Hong Kong. He was particularly thinking of Pearce, who had a brother and mother in the Colony; the escapers would have to "bear the consequences and suffer for the remainder of their lives from appalling feelings of personal guilt over what subsequently happened to their loving families," Clague felt. (Sir Douglas Clague Kt CBE, MC, became a man of immense wealth and influence in post-war Hong Kong.)

Major General Maltby's policy, by now, was not to permit escapes "by small parties or even individuals... the general standard of health had reached a very low level," he wrote after the war. "Any escape would have caused severe and immediate repercussions and further privations would have been fatal to many, and further, there was the probability of transfer to Formosa or Japan, from which places there was no escape."[9] Maltby began to consider a mass break-out instead. This extraordinary project will be discussed later.

Clague was told to see Maltby. The General flatly refused to give his assent to Clague's escape. They "were acting irresponsibly and without consideration". Duggie Clague was furious. He saw "Maltby again and said 'we're going in 45 minutes' and he still didn't approve. Duggie was given neither task nor encouragement."

Their disappearance would be discovered by the guards at the morning roll-call. They would therefore have only a 10-hour head start after they had made landfall at Laichikok before a full-scale search would be made for them. Colonel Newnham, Maltby's principal operations officer and a key man in the story which will in due course unfold, agreed with Maltby and tried to discourage the escape, but changed his mind and said "if you've got a plan, put it into effect".

Colonel Newnham got up to leave them. "As he reached the door he turned, undid the top button of his battledress and pulled out a carefully folded piece of paper and said, 'There is a map. I will be back in 20 minutes to collect it,'" wrote David Bosanquet in his memoirs.[10] Much of the next 20 minutes were spent poring over the map memorising what they could.

Some four months later, on 20th August, four brave men of the Winnipeg Grenadiers escaped from North Point Camp. Their sampan sank when they were trying to cross to the Mainland. They were picked up by the Japanese Navy, beaten with a baseball bat and then shot without trial. Two Royal Engineer Other Ranks were also executed after an unsuccessful escape attempt.

Meanwhile, led by Clague, the four from Shamshuipo crawled through the typhoon drain. (I, with others, tapped on the ground above the drain with a pole, using a pre-arranged code to indicate the location of the Japanese guards.) The escapers then swam to some boat-building yards, were helped by friendly Chinese, as were all other escapers from Shamshuipo, and boarded a junk which took them beyond danger.

The Japanese counted us at roll-call the next morning as usual and so discovered their absence. In Nazi POW camps, Allied POWs sometimes managed to fool the Germans into thinking no escape had taken place; but after the first few weeks in Hong Kong's camps, the Japanese roll-calls were very thorough.

On thinking about it now, I feel that Maltby's policy of discouraging individual or small groups escaping was the most appropriate and realistic one. The Japanese authorities had made it abundantly clear that they had no intention of abiding by the rules governing the treatment of prisoners of war as laid down by the Geneva Convention. Our enemy had also made it plain to Maltby and others that POW escapes, whether successful or not, would be met with severe individual and collective punishment, including the drastic reduction or withdrawal of rations and medical supplies, which were already at a critical level. Many men were already beginning to suffer from deficiency diseases.

I would re-emphasise that I held the General in high regard. Ralph Goodwin, an RNZNVR officer, expressed the opinion of many when he wrote that General Maltby "was in an unfortunate position. Left in command of a weakly defended outpost of the Empire which had no hope of prolonged resistance, he then found himself in internal charge of a prison camp under guards who cared nothing for the Geneva Convention. Time and again he was called upon to protest to the Japanese Commandant against the actions of the guards, and he took great risks of personal injury in pressing his demands."

It is true that Clague, Ride and some other escapers were to play a significant part in helping the POWs, as this book will relate, but the consequences for some were to prove truly catastrophic.

We must now return to the early days of our imprisonment as *Guests of the Emperor*, as one ex-POW called his book!

Notes

1. Jason Wordie, in *Ruins of War*, p. 213, gives lower figures for Japanese casualties.
2. Not all POWs agree the date of the march to Shamshuipo Camp. Perhaps the move was spread over several days.
3. Letter Wallis to OL.
4. Lindsay, Oliver, *At the Going Down of the Sun*, London: Hamish Hamilton, 1981, pp. 5–21.
5. Loose Minute 29.5.42, CO 129 590/25 HN 00152.
6. Interview Sir Lindsay Ride with OL.
7. Interview Colonel A G Hewitt with OL.
8. Letter Sullivan to OL.
9. Goodwin, Ralph, *Passport to Eternity*, London: Arthur Barker, 1956, p. 5.
10. Bosanquet, David, *Escape Through China*, Toronto: McClelland & Stewart, 1982, p. 68.

CHAPTER 17

Argyle Street Officers' Camp

In April 1942, most unexpectedly, 336 officers and up to 100 soldiers (ostensibly to act as batmen) were paraded at Shamshuipo. We marched off in an easterly direction, not knowing where we were going. It took six hours to get to the Argyle Street POW camp in Kowloon, after the Japanese had searched and counted us. I was carrying my kit bag.

The camp had been built initially to house Chinese Nationalist troops who had sought refuge in Hong Kong from the Japanese. The enemy used the camp for prisoners of war. Colonel Ride visited it after the surrender and found about 1,200 prisoners there – largely Rajputs and Punjabis. He saw 100 dysentery cases lying on the cold concrete floors. "Pools of blood, mucus and pus lay everywhere, and what was not sucked up by the swarms of eager flies, soaked into the ground," he recalled. Cholera, which was endemic in Kowloon, would certainly slay those whom dysentery had failed to kill.

The Indians and others had then been moved largely to the Mau Tau Chung Camp nearby. It is visible on the back cover of this book. While Argyle Street was briefly empty, the looters, as at Shamshuipo, had systematically stolen everything movable.

I saw immediately that our camp was completely bare. The Japanese had made no preparations to meet us. There was no rice cooker. The first meal, inevitably of rice, had to be sent in. We had to beg the Japanese for equipment and to pool anything useful.

It was inevitable, I suppose, that the Japanese would separate most of the officers from the soldiers who were left in Shamshuipo. Similar events had happened in Singapore when the officers were moved to Changi. On their 17-mile forced march with little food, the "arrogant and brutal behaviour of the Japanese soldier was apparent. This was manifested by the casual shooting of Chinese or Tamils perceived to be obstructing the column's progress in any way."[1]

The Argyle Street Camp was surrounded by high and electrified wire fencing with up to a half a dozen guard towers which were always manned and contained searchlights.

* * * * *

Just before moving from Shamshuipo we were joined on 11th April by Brigadier Wallis who wrote: "I had been sent to the Bowen Road Hospital as my injury would not heal and was getting worse. The Commanding Officer of the Winnipeg Grenadiers, J L R Sutcliffe, died in the bed opposite me on 6th April." His death was attributed to beriberi, dysentery and anaemia "but in the opinion of some of his officers he died from dejection and melancholia caused by critical self-evaluation of his own battle performance," recorded a Canadian historian.[2]

The Japanese let the Protestant Chaplains, together with a number of Canadian officers, attend Sutcliffe's funeral. Tokunaga and other Japanese officials were also there, bringing floral tributes for the Canadians and themselves to lay on the grave.

Another officer in Bowen Road Hospital was Major Charles Boxer, whose optimistic reports on the Japanese immediately before the war so misled Major General Maltby. "He had been in charge of intelligence at Fortress HQ," continues Wallis. "He was a fluent Jap scholar and was given a separate room where he was constantly visited by Jap officers to whom I felt he was inclined to be unnecessarily friendly. He was also visited by a lady who had half Chinese and half American nationality who had not been interned. Boxer made me feel uneasy and suspicious. I was taken aback to see how intimate he was with the Japanese."[3]

Another wounded officer who came to know Boxer well in hospital was the one-legged Captain 'Bill' Wiseman of the Royal Army Service Corps. He saw Boxer being visited by Japanese officers whom he had come to know during his many visits to the frontier. They brought Boxer presents, Wiseman recalls, including canned fruit and a crate of whisky. Wiseman once awoke to see the Japanese bowing towards him (Wiseman) "and making various appreciative noises". Afterwards the curious Wiseman asked Boxer why they had been so respectful. Boxer replied that he had told the Japanese that Wiseman had "acquired his wooden leg while extending his foot in an unsuccessful attempt to stop a German tank at Dunkirk". Some found Boxer's sense of humour, like his behaviour, puzzling.

Brigadier Wallis, while recovering from his injury, was able to leave Bowen Road Hospital several times "by showing an expired Japanese pass which I was given in North Point; it bore a prominent Jap chop (seal). I calculated correctly that most Jap sentries were probably unable to read. I was thus able to visit American consular friends but my luck ran out. There was a chronic shortage of electric light bulbs; the hospital nurses had theirs stolen when they were on duty. So I spotted an old sofa on the veranda and cut out the back cover (where the Japs could not see it) and I sewed some 20 small bags with a string fastener and the girls could carry these with them to keep their own bulb safe.

"The hospital was full of our sick and wounded and there were frequent deaths," continues Wallis. "I was distressed to see a British Other Rank exchange his greatcoat (and Winter was upon us) with a Jap guard for a few cigarettes."

Wallis was sent very briefly to Shamshuipo before moving with Maltby and others to Argyle Street, where he found Maltby "a very distressed and disillusioned man. It took me several months sharing the same room to cheer him up and convince him that, far from our troops not being deserving of honours, as he believed, there often is far greater gallantry in defence than in attack. I eventually got him to see that he was being unfair to many brave men." (Details on those receiving the principal honours and awards for all the 1941–1945 Hong Kong campaign are in the final chapter.)

* * * * *

Colonel Newnham continued to keep up his diary in tiny writing on rice paper:

Apr. 13 Fleas for last 7 weeks – all off blasted dog of the General's. 4 months now and still we have not been allowed to send a letter or pc home or even communicate with families in Hong Kong. Against the Geneva Convention. News of Colonel Sutcliffe's death. Permission refused for GOC and staff to go to funeral.

Apr. 21 We now have 550 all ranks in Camp measuring 180 x 140.

The Japanese started to pay officers but not the soldiers. Virtually all the officers agreed to take only part of their pay, the remainder going into a pool for the men or for the purchase of medical necessities and luxuries such as eggs for the hospital. Unfortunately the yen depreciated so quickly I could barely afford to buy anything.

On 23rd May 1942 the Japanese started to insist that each POW, internee and patient in hospital must sign a form written in English and Japanese stating that he or she would not escape. There is a certificate in the Imperial War Museum: it states "I hereby swear that I shall not make any attempt to escape while I am a prisoner of the Imperial Japanese Army", followed by a date and place for a signature. The requirement was sanctioned by Japanese military law. Those who violated it faced death, as had the four Winnipeg Grenadiers, or a long prison sentence.

The very unpleasant Colonel Tokunaga, of whom more later, insisted that since the surrender had been unconditional, everyone must sign it. He told the Canadians at North Point that failure to do so would signify "mutiny for which death was the obvious outcome".

Among those who refused to sign was a Canadian, Lance Corporal J Porter. A Japanese officer spent several hours begging him to sign the pledge. He was given two helpings of beef stew, cups of tea filled with sugar and invited to help himself from a silver cigarette case. The following day he was taken to an even more senior officer who expressed astonishment that Porter had volunteered for the war. The officer commented on Porter's bravery in refusing to sign and added that he wished the Japanese behaved in such a way. "I replied that I was not doing it because I was brave, but that I was doing it for my King. The interpreter then slapped my face hard," recalls Porter.[4] He was taken to Stanley Prison with six others; the conditions there were foul. They were shaken awake every hour throughout each night, beaten with truncheons and urged to sign.

"On 31st May our food and water was stopped. Several of my fellow prisoners were suffering from dysentery; no toilet paper was supplied and the mess in the cells was frightful. Their sufferings became so acute that on 4th June we decided to sign the form," reported Porter.

The patients in the Bowen Road Hospital were equally reluctant to sign. The senior officers there advised against doing so. On 26th May all ambulatory patients and the hospital staff were crammed into the hospital's tennis courts and left there under a hot sun. Later in the day an officer from Argyle Street arrived to tell the men that General Maltby felt they should comply; most did so. (Three years later, after the hospital had moved to Kowloon, the staff and patients had to sign the same documents again but with the original date.)

Charles Boxer and two other officers still refused to sign the form in late May 1942, possibly because they believed that they were answerable to the King, not to the Japanese. As a result Boxer's future wife, Emily Hahn, was not allowed to see him. She had not been interned, thanks to his influence and uncertainty about her nationality because of her previous relationship with the Chinese Sinmay Zau. One day she went to Boxer to discover that he had been moved she knew not where. Nevertheless, according to one source she continued to deliver parcels to the patients, and also to friends interned in Stanley Camp. Together with others, whom she called "the army of basket bringers", parcels were also taken on a regular basis to Shamshuipo and Argyle Street where she found Boxer once more. She claimed to have spent four days a week on such deliveries, receiving funding probably from Doctor P S Selwyn-Clarke. The International Red Cross, however, reported all 'parcel days' had been stopped.

Suddenly the camp was struck by illness, frighteningly similar to cholera. One victim, a Volunteer, had succeeded in concealing the fact that he was completely bald, having hung on to his toupee, his dearest possession. But when he was carried on a stretcher to the hospital it fell off. Several brother officers were horrified – commenting on the gravity of the symptoms which had apparently suddenly deprived him of his hair.

What was not so funny was an "explosive" outbreak of diphtheria. Eighteen critically ill were admitted to Bowen Road Hospital in August 1942 and no fewer than 59 in September. Twelve of them died that month and seven more later. In a number of these cases there was extensive skin ulceration mainly affecting the scrotum and the perineum, while the nose and face were also sometimes affected.[5] The Canadians at North Point and Shamshuipo were the worst hit because they had not been inoculated in Canada beforehand. Between June 1942 and February 1943 there were 714 recorded cases, of whom 112 Canadians died. The Japanese chief medical officer, Doctor Saito Shunkichi, was accused of withholding vital serum.

One day at dawn I realised I was seriously ill. We had military doctors in the camp but virtually no medical equipment. We had to make an operating table out of planks: it was a pretty grim affair.

I had a sore throat which gradually produced a film across it. I had diphtheria. At that time there was almost a daily procession from Shamshuipo Camp bearing those who had died of it. A bugler blew the Last Post and all of us stood to attention.

At the 10.00 a.m. roll call parade, I was too weak to get up; the Japanese guard came round to count me, still in bed. I was then taken to a small isolated hut, the 'hospital' in the far corner of the camp. There were three others already there, one of whom was Roger Lamble. Although we were very ill, we largely had to look after ourselves. Rice was passed to us through a small hatch.

Suddenly, after a few days, I became much worse. One of the doctors gave me an injection of the vital serum, of which there was a desperate shortage. Two days later he returned again to give me another one. The next night, I remember, I yelled out as a film developed across my throat which I think was the standard diphtheria taking its course. Instead of my losing consciousness and dying, as many did, the film broke and within about ten days I had recovered, although I was still very weak.

After the war I came to hear of the work of Dr P S Selwyn-Clarke, the former Director of Medical Services in Hong Kong. He had persuaded the Japanese, who were themselves very nervous of catching any disease, that he should not be interned. He was allowed only the minimum of staff but, despite Japanese obstruction, he sent medicines into the various camps and looked after the dependants of the Volunteers and families of the other emergency services.

There was another possible source for the serum which saved my life: it could have come from the British Military Hospital at Bowen Road which was run by Dr Donald Bowie, who wrote in his memoirs: "I want to record my personal admiration for the courage of doctors and Royal Army Medical Corps and Royal Army Dental Corps soldiers who nursed these diphtheria cases. Everyone knew of the shortage of serum and of the risks of infection. No one shirked the close contacts involved in the treatment of these patients and this to my mind was an outstanding example of cold and sustained courage in a situation where staff were at risk for at least five months. The work of these men cannot be praised too highly and the story deserves to be cherished in the annals of the Corps.

"Since serum was in such short supply Major G C F Harrison RAMC, after anxious consultation, gave transfusions of blood from patients who had recovered from diphtheria to four patients suffering from the disease in an acute form. Two of these recovered," concluded Bowie.

* * * * *

The superintendent of all the camps in Hong Kong was Colonel Tokunaga Isao, nicknamed 'Fat Pig' because he was so obese. He had been a regular soldier for 30 years and lived in Kowloon with his Chinese mistress. He had a violent temper, and was totally unscrupulous as well as a thief.

We also had to put up with the Japanese interpreters. Nimori Genichiro, nicknamed 'Panama Pete', was a smallish Japanese-American who had pointed ears and wore military boots and a khaki cloak. He had spent most of his life in Chicago, was dapper, diminutive and addressed everyone as "Youse guys". We particularly disliked Inouye Kanao, nicknamed 'Slap Happy' or 'Shat in Pants'. He was swarthy, usually unshaven and had eyes set closely together. He was a Japanese-Canadian whose uniform was so ill-fitting that the seat of his trousers hung in a pendulous kind of bag. He had a grudge against everyone and Canadians in particular.

Kyoshi Watanabe, another interpreter, was quite different. He had been a Lutheran Minister; he certainly succeeded in combining Christian charity with his duties. The other guards became aware of his unobtrusive acts of kindness and so he was transferred elsewhere, to our disappointment. Another helpful interpreter was the stocky, bandy-legged 'Cardiff Joe' who was reputed to have money still in Cardiff, to where he seemed anxious to return. Finally there was the lanky, short-sighted tubercular youth named Katayama; he was such a negative character that he was never given a nickname.

Apparently up to 400 Indians, some former soldiers, served in Hong Kong's camps as sentries and in other jobs. No doubt some of them were pressurised to do so. Formosans (Taiwanese) were also guarding us at times. A few of them were humane and helpful but most were cruel and exploited the prisoners, especially the females at Stanley, I read after the war.

I should emphasise that in 1942 it was almost impossible to discover what was going on in the internment camp at Stanley or in the other POW camps, nor what was happening outside Hong Kong. This was particularly distressing for families who could not learn if their loved ones were alive.

Taking the Royal Scots, for example, all but three of the 43 wives had been evacuated from Hong Kong to Australia in June 1940 on the orders of the Governor. The exceptions were Mrs S E H E White, the Commanding Officer's wife and 'Quartermaster' of the Volunteers Nursing Detachment. Mrs H A W Millar was also a nurse, as was Peggie Scotcher who married Lieutenant T D Hunter, the Battalion's Intelligence Officer, on Christmas Day, one hour after the surrender, in the hospital where he was lying wounded. It was not possible to find out where they were, or under what circumstances they were living – or indeed if they were still alive – until far too long. In fact, all three endured the same privations as the men in the Stanley Internment Camp and all did survive.

On 3rd July 1942 two representatives of the International Red Cross made their first visit to Hong Kong. They were Rudolf Zindel, a successful Swiss businessman who had lived in Hong Kong before the war, and Edward Egle, an IRC official based in Shanghai. In one day they visited the camps at Argyle Street, North Point and Shamshuipo, together with Bowen Road and St Theresa hospitals.

Their report on our Argyle Street Camp read as follows: "This camp, built on raised ground prior to the outbreak of the Pacific War housed from 600 to 800 interned Chinese soldiers which were forced over the Hong Kong Border during the Sino-Japanese fighting in October 1938. The camp is exceptionally well drained; the barracks are built of wood, log-cabin style, and give a neat impression; open space is somewhat limited, but appears adequate.

"On the day of our visit, the Camp contained the following Prisoners of War:-

	474	Officers (including Major General Maltby)
	19	N.C. Officers
	93	Batmen (Orderlies)
TOTAL	586	Officers and men – from Regular Army Units, the Royal Navy and Hong Kong Volunteers

"A 'bakery' had only just been started, previous to which 'dough-cakes', cooked in water, were served. A 'Canteen' was available, which was being supplied with fresh stocks about every ten days, but was usually quickly sold out. No facilities for religious services.

"There was no 'parcel-service' in the Camp, since February, but an early resumption is promised. (Note: the 'parcel service' actually recommenced middle July 1942 and has been maintained once per week, ever since.)"[6]

Zindel and Egle made equally reassuring comments about North Point Camp which contained 1,577 Canadians and 28 Dutch Seamen, and Shamshuipo, where 4,404 officers and men of the Royal Navy, Army and Volunteers were housed. Their remarks on Shamshuipo, for example, included the comment: "Food said to be sometimes better, sometimes worse, with meat rare, but, generally speaking, no cause for complaint. The officers consulted assured us that the treatment accorded to them and their men was good."

Why didn't Zindel and Egle have the guts to report the truth? They saw that the POWs looked haggard and ill. They heard Captain K M A Barnett say first in French and then in English, "We are dying of hunger." They saw that he was immediately knocked to the ground.

Zindel met a POW named R Egal, a Free French who had been fighting with the British. "Pretending to know me, he heartily shook hands in the presence of the Japanese," wrote Zindel. "While doing so, he slipped into my hand a small object which I succeeded in getting into my trouser pocket without arousing suspicion. Later, in my house, I inspected the object which turned out to be a small cutting of a bamboo branch. It had been hollowed out, but stopped at both ends with a little straw. Inside the tube I found a note, written in ink, in exceptionally fine but clear writing, which gave valuable information concerning the Argyle Street and Shamshuipo Camps."

What explanation had Zindel for sending totally misleading reports which were cheerfully circulated by the International Red Cross in Geneva? "Through a contact which I had in the censor's office in Hong Kong," he wrote later, "I learned that all my Delegation mail and cables were strictly censored. My first full reports to Geneva never arrived. At least one was given by a Japanese censor to his girlfriend, who in turn boastfully reported the matter to me. She was able to quote extracts from the report." One report which eventually passed the Hong Kong censor after satisfactory explanations was returned to Hong Kong by the censor in Tokyo three months later.

"International Red Cross delegates report that the general state of health of the prisoners in Hong Kong is good," reported *The Times* on 27th October 1942, "and that they are satisfied with administrative arrangements." The Commander in Chief India cabled two days later stating that this report was in direct contradiction of the facts, for there were a minimum of three diphtheria deaths daily in Shamshuipo. The Foreign Office and Colonial Office initially sat back and accepted the favourable reports, although there was every likelihood that the contrary reports from Chungking on Japanese brutalities were quite likely to be true.

I saw Zindel's visit. We were terribly disappointed that he was "whisked past us at twice the speed of light", as one of my friends put it.

Couldn't Egle back in Shanghai have sent a true report through his channels? Apparently not. Indeed, according to one author, "he praised their operation so lavishly that the Japanese expressed their gratitude to him by hosting a banquet in his honour at Shanghai's Cathay Hotel."[7]

Zindel headed a staff of 30 to distribute financial aid amounting to £10,000 per month that the British Government regularly dispatched to the civilian internees at Stanley. In 1945 it was learnt that the Japanese government "siphoned off a large part of those funds to exchange for gold in neutral countries so that it could purchase critical war supplies".[8]

Behind the scenes, Zindel may have helped us more than we then knew. For example, he arranged for 1,450 books from a library in Victoria to be transferred to us in Argyle Street. At least a third of them were in continuous circulation. Moreover, Zindel sensibly used what remained of the £10,000 to help us POWs, to the dismay of the War Office which believed that "proper care and maintenance of the POWs is the duty of the capturing power". The monthly allocation, due in part to Canadian pressure, was later increased to £60,000.

Within two years Zindel's ability to do anything constructive seems to have deteriorated. "Zindel is working under a great mental and nervous strain," wrote the Red Cross delegate in Chungking to Geneva in August 1944. "His office and flat have been searched by the Jap police who call weekly and look into everything. It is doubtful whether Zindel is allowed or would dare to send you reports stating the true facts."

* * * * *

Quite unexpectedly we had our hopes raised most dramatically.

On 24th October 1942 China-based aircraft of the American 14th Air Force bombed selected targets, returning the two following days to drop incendiary bombs. This was tangible evidence that the tide was turning. Our morale soared.

The leading American bomber carried B A Proulx, a Canadian who had escaped through a sewer from North Point Camp. He had made contact with General C L Chennault and briefed the American pilots on the location of the POW camps. We did not know that the next raid would not be for another 10 months, after which they averaged almost one a month. We were not allowed to dig air-raid shelters. In Shamshuipo Camp we knew that some oil drums containing high-grade aviation gasoline were stored in pits within the camp's perimeter. The Japanese optimistically left the drums there, confident that the Allies would not bomb their own men.

The excitement of the bombing raid had not diminished when a small miracle occurred. On 1st November 1942 Red Cross parcels were delivered to the camps. "Oh brother!" wrote G White of the Royal Army Service Corps. "We all went crazy – talk about kids at a Christmas tree, nothing to the way we danced round here."

As another POW put it in November: "We were amazed to receive the shipment of foodstuffs. Bully beef, cigarettes, jam, meat and vegetable rations, cocoa, dried fruit, sugar and clothing. This changed the whole picture. We now had reason to hope that these shipments might be repeated and that we stood a good chance of surviving. We did not allow our optimism to govern our judgement and we doled out the foodstuffs very carefully, enough to bring the calorific value up to about 2,800 calories, with a protein content from all sources of about 70 grammes. In this way we managed to spin out this supply of food for some 15 months. It was just as well that we did for never again did we get such a shipment."

According to Captain J L Flynn, working parties were very occasionally provided with a lorry enabling the POWs to loot warehouses and the private houses formerly occupied by Europeans.

As Christmas 1942 and the first anniversary of our imprisonment approached, it would be silly to pretend we had anything other than deep forebodings as to the future. The Japanese had told us of endless British and American defeats: the loss of the bases in the Far East, nasty setbacks in the Middle East including North Africa and the fall of Tobruk, the Mediterranean largely closed to us, the Germans having the Russians on the run – naturally we didn't know what to believe.

We undoubtedly had traitors in our midst. Maltby and Wallis discussed what to do with one suspect who was believed to be informing the Japanese on us. "We considered whether I should walk round the camp with him on the exercise circuit and accidentally see to it that he fell into the live wires," wrote Brigadier Wallis. A doctor planned a more sinister death for the traitor. "We decided against any such action, feeling that in the end God would bring him to his just deserts."[9]

Lieutenant Tanaka Hitoshi, a guard at Shamshuipo, received a message from a POW that a certain hut should be watched as a particular officer was planning to escape. The message had been attached to a slate and hung in the guard's office. The Japanese watched the hut before accusing Lieutenant Hyland of being the potential escaper; he admitted that this had been the case and agreed not to do so. This incident was related at the trial of Colonel Tokunaga in January 1947.

Suddenly the Japanese started sending shiploads of us to Japan to work, we assumed correctly, as slave labour in conditions which were doubtless even worse than those which were killing some of us in Hong Kong.

Notes

1. Interview Lt Col. P K Betty/Brig. C Bullock, 11.3.04, quoted in *The Simouree*, Winter 2004/5, p. 48.
2. Greenhous, B, *"C" Force to Hong Kong: A Canadian Catastrophe 1941–1945*, Canadian War Museum Historical Publication No. 30, 1997, p. 122.
3. Letter Wallis to OL.
4. *Townsville Sun*, November 1976.
5. Bowie, D C, 'Captive Surgeon in Hong Kong', *Journal of the HK Branch of the Royal Asiatic Society*, March 1977, Vol. 15, p. 173.
6. FO 9/6 761 HN 00649.
7. *The Hong Kong News*, 15.7.42, 4.9.42 and 28.10.42.
8. *South China Morning Post*, 17.9.45, interview with C D W Man.
9. Letter Wallis to OL.

CHAPTER 18

The Sinking of the *Lisbon Maru*

"In September 1942 Japanese soldiers arrived in Shamshuipo Camp, leant their rifles against a wall, donned white coats and medically examined us," recalls Lance Corporal A J Taylor of the Hong Kong Signal Company. "They wanted to be sure that no disease should be carried to the graceful land of the rising sun. Each POW was inoculated and his anus probed with a glass tube. It was rumoured that the inoculations were to sterilise one, and so some avoided the draft, leaving others who were less fit to make up the numbers."[1]

The first draft of 700 POWs left for Japan in early September. On 25th September POWs were paraded in Shamshuipo and Argyle Street to be selected or otherwise for the second draft. Men on my immediate left and right were called forward. Why wasn't I chosen, I wondered? Perhaps because I looked a bit weedy in those days? The Japanese would give no indication of the draft's destination; there was just a vague promise that the climate would be better.

Two days later 1,816 British POWs left Hong Kong in a 7,000-ton freighter, the *Lisbon Maru*. Lieutenant Colonel H W M Stewart OBE MC, the Commanding Officer of 1st Battalion the Middlesex Regiment, commanded the POWs despite being sick with pellagra and malnutrition. His batman carried a wooden box-like stool. Rumour had it that a wireless set was in the box, which was the only object never searched.

The Royal Navy POWs were squeezed into hold No. 1 nearest the bows, the Middlesex and Royal Scots in the middle hold No. 2, and the Royal Artillery in the stern in No 3. The ship also carried 800 Japanese troops. She had only four lifeboats and six life rafts, two of which were for the POWs. Half the POWs had life jackets.

Food was good by Shamshuipo standards, from where most of the POWs had been chosen. The sun shone and the nights were warm. Prisoners were sometimes allowed on deck for fresh air and exercise; those who resembled prematurely old men began to get a touch of colour in their cheeks. But the filth and slime in the holds from those who were too weak to get up and wash themselves was terrible.

Dr Selwyn-Clarke had warned the British Consul in Macao that POWs were on the *Lisbon Maru,* which carried no markings indicating that they were on board. Almost 12 weeks earlier, on 1st July 1942, the American submarine USS *Sturgeon* had sunk the Japanese *Montevideo Maru*. Of the 1,053 Australian soldiers and 200 civilians battened down below decks, none survived.

At 7.04 a.m. on 1st October USS *Grouper* of the Pacific Fleet Submarine Force began her approach off the coast of Shanghai to the *Lisbon Maru*. Her first three torpedoes, fired at 3,200 yards, missed. The fourth led to a loud explosion. There were no casualties on the ship and some POWs assumed there had been an internal explosion in the engine room. *Grouper* was commanded by Lieutenant Commander Rob Roy McGregor. The submarine came under fire: "Sharp explosions all around us," noted the Commanding Officer, whose last two torpedoes, fired at 1,000 yards, also missed.[2] The American torpedoes early in the war malfunctioned; the heavier operational warheads ran well below the depth of the training heads. The faults were not fully recognised for a further year.

The POWs listened to the explosion of depth charges and a Japanese light bomber patrolling overhead. It was the beginning of a long and increasingly anxious day because the ship was slowly listing. The Japanese pulled heavy tarpaulins over the hatches, thereby sealing the POWs down and preventing fresh air reaching them.

Colonel Stewart shouted to everyone in his middle hold to be quiet. He told them what he thought had happened and asked for silence so he could appeal to the Japanese. The stench of those who could no longer use the wooden latrines on deck was asphyxiating.

Tapping on the bulkhead from No. 1 hold indicated that two diphtheria patients had died and there was no way of escaping. Meanwhile the sea was entering the third hold. Gunners working on the pumps quickly lost consciousness owing to the heat and lack of air. At 5.00 p.m. the Japanese destroyer *Kure* took off the 800 Japanese troops, leaving only the crew and 25 guards under Lieutenant Wada, and the ship's Captain, Kyoda Shigeru, who pointed out that the POWs were likely to drown. Wada replied that the Master of the ship had no authority to interfere. At 9.00 p.m. the heavy hatches were closed over the holds. Attempts were made to tow the *Lisbon Maru* towards Shanghai but the towline was heard to snap.

The heat in the holds was terrific. The night was made more hideous by the curses and the moans of the sick, some of whom were calling for the padre. Everyone was told to lie quietly, stop talking and try to sleep to conserve air and strength.

By 9.00 a.m. on 2nd October, over 24 hours after the torpedoing, the air in the holds was dangerously foul; it was obvious that the men could not survive much longer. Captain Kyoda Shigeru knew that the ship was in imminent danger of sinking. All the Japanese, less five guards, were taken off leaving the POWs to drown.

Colonel Stewart ordered Lieutenant W M Howell, Royal Army Service Corps, to make a second attempt to make a hole in the hatch covers, using a long butcher's knife which Private Speight HKVDC had smuggled into the ship.[3] With a great effort, he forced his knife between the baulks of timber, slit the tarpaulin, forced up one of the timbers and climbed through the gap. He and Lieutenant Potter who followed him saw POWs from No. 3 hold struggling to get out through the portholes on the well deck. Howell opened the bulkhead to release them.

The Japanese guards on the bridge opened fire at the hole in the hatch, killing one man who was just emerging. Potter was also killed.

The *Lisbon Maru* suddenly gave a fearful lurch; water gushed in through the first opening in the hatch. "Wild panic ensued," remembers Lance Corporal Taylor. "Within seconds the ladders to the second deck were a mass of writhing, struggling bodies." Order was quickly restored and the men formed up into long queues at the stairway and ladders. Water poured into No. 2 hold; there seemed little hope of getting out in time. In the dim light which filtered through, Captain N H Cuthbertson, Adjutant of the Royal Scots, carefully put on his glengarry: he said that he preferred to meet his God properly dressed.

The ship went down by the stern but by good fortune the water was shallow and the stern rested on a sandbank while the bows remained clear of the water. Many of those in No. 3 hold drowned before they could get out.[4]

Hundreds of men took to the sea; a swift current was running westwards towards some islands four miles away; they looked rocky and dangerous. Four Japanese auxiliary transport boats were slowly circling the *Lisbon Maru* shooting at the POWs in the water. Taylor, still on deck, made two rafts from ammunition boxes and planks for the non-swimmers. Just as he was wondering how to launch them, there was a muffled explosion and the ship sank instantly, sucking many down with her.

The Japanese at last started to pick up survivors, possibly because some POWs were seen to have reached the Islands and might live to say what had happened. Indeed Howell was among the first to do so. The Sing Pang Islands are in the Chusan Archipelago off the Chekiang province. Howell spoke a Shanghai dialect and explained to the villagers that the numerous heads in the water were British prisoners and not Japanese, whose fate the Chinese villagers had been cheerfully contemplating. The villagers immediately set off in junks and sampans and rescued about 200. Many other POWs were unable to obtain a footing and were swept past the Islands before drowning.

The Chinese fed and clothed the POWs before the Japanese landed on the Islands the following morning. The Chinese males then put on their militia uniforms of the Wang Chai Wan, Japan's puppet leader in the territory conquered by Japan.

Japanese Marines rounded up the POWs, making them return most of the clothing given to them by the villagers. On board one of the Japanese ships, the body of a POW who died was tossed overboard without a hint of humanity, while on another ship Company Sergeant Major E J Soden of the Middlesex remembers that they were treated very well. "The Japanese said that they had been trained by our Navy and fed us well, giving full military honours to those who died."[5]

The survivors of the *Lisbon Maru* reached Shanghai on 5th October. Out of 1,816 POWs, 843 had been shot in the water or drowned. Two weeks later the *Japan Times Weekly* claimed the Japanese had done their utmost to save the POWs following the sinking of the ship by the Americans.

The dependants in Britain and Australia of those who had died quickly received a lower scale of allowance as their husbands were missing. The internees at Stanley learnt of the "atrocities by Americans" but had no information for 18 months about who had died.

Fortunately, thanks to the villagers of Woo Tung-Ling on the Sing Pang Islands, a civilian called A J W Evans, Warrant Officer J C Fallace and W C Johnstone (both of HKRNVR) survived. They were led to

Free China by guerrillas from neighbouring islands; their statements reached the Foreign Office in January 1943.[6] The Swiss Government was asked to communicate the true facts to the Japanese, based on the first-hand evidence of the three escapees. "The treatment of the prisoners amounts to flagrant violation of the customs and usage of war..." read the British Government demand for a full investigation. In November 1943 the Japanese replied that the British should be grateful for 900 prisoners being rescued.

The responsible officers were brought to trial in Hong Kong in 1947, as will be related. However for many POWs it was too late; they were so weakened by their treatment that 244 died during their first year in Japan. Among the dead was Lieutenant Colonel Stewart. Thus, of the original 1,816 POWs only 724 survived.

* * * * *

A further 2,000 POWs including 1,184 Canadians were sent from Hong Kong in 1943. The Japanese split up the British, American, Australian, Dutch and Canadian POWs in Japan among 120 camps, making them work in shipyards, docks, mines, quarries and factories. There were 250 more POW camps in Burma, Malaya, Borneo and the Dutch East Indies, Singapore, Thailand, Indo-China, the Philippines and Hong Kong.

Conditions in the camps varied considerably. Some POWs were treated as slave labour, just as the Germans treated some of their captives in Nazi Germany in 1941–1945.

The POWs who worked in semi-darkness in mines faced a constant danger of being entombed by landslides. The more fortunate worked in the docks; they suffered less, partly thanks to their ingenuity in stealing food.

CSM E J Soden was sent to Kobe near Osaka, where many died through lack of proper medical treatment – so many that the bodies were squeezed into an apple barrel before they were cremated. "I still get a lump in my throat when I hear the song *Roll out the Barrel*. After a few months I was sent in groups of 20 to work in the docks," he wrote. "It was of paramount importance to steal food, particularly for the sick. When I was unloading from a cold-storage depot, one of the lads hid a large frozen fish between his legs; it was held in place by string. This caused much amusement among the guards who searched him. Feeling the fish, they mistook it for his penis, shouting '*Oki Jimpo*', meaning 'big cock.'" On another occasion the POWs there noticed a Japanese making a hot bran and oat mash for his horse. He left it to cook, and on his return found the container full of water. His bewilderment was watched at a discreet distance by well-satisfied POWs.

The POWs became increasingly vulnerable to American bombers; some were near both Hiroshima and Nagasaki.

At Camp 17 the Japanese displayed a regulation which read:

It is forbid to plot to kill the Commandant.
(Penalty: Shoot-ted to death and life imprison.)

It shall be forbid to steal of Japanese Army.
(Penalty: The heavy punish, life not assured.)

All prisoners shall take care of their health.

* * * * *

Naturally those of us left in Hong Kong had no knowledge of the utter despair faced by some of the POWs sent to Japan. The physical exhaustion from 11 hours per day breaking up pig iron, for example, was a terrible challenge. "But not all the Japanese were cruel and unjust," remembers Corporal H F Linge of the Royal Army Ordnance Corps who recalls seeing at a station near Osaka the strange sight of Japanese women and children dressed in brightly coloured kimonos and wooden clogs watching the prisoners. They showed no animosity.

Notes

1. Interview Taylor with OL.
2. Hamilton, G C, *The Sinking of the* Lisbon Maru, Hong Kong: Green Pagoda Press, 1966.
3. Article in *The Thistle* (Regimental Journal of the Royal Scots), April 1946.
4. RN Archives Adm 199 1286 HN 00493, p. 188.
5. Letter CSM Soden to OL.
6. Report 29.12.42, British Embassy Kukong to Foreign Office, CO 980 67 HN 00649.

CHAPTER 19

Operations Most Secret

In March 1943 I was a member of a working party in Argyle Street POW camp unloading firewood from an old lorry which came into the camp on a regular basis. I was in Hut No. 3 and it was our hut's turn to be on duty to empty it. Suddenly the Chinese driver gave a cough and tossed over his shoulder a crumpled, empty cigarette packet on to the vehicle's floor, immediately behind the driving seat. I swept the packet up with the bark chippings out of the back of the lorry. I had to be very careful as a Jap sentry was only four feet at most from the driver.

Six guards were turned out whenever a supply lorry came into the camp. On one occasion the truck was not promptly unloaded by the POWs and so it immediately drove out again amidst laughter from the Japanese guards. Therefore we had to be on duty awaiting the vehicle's arrival.

After the lorry had left I picked up the cigarette packet very excitedly and took it to the latrines. Behind a screen there, I unfolded the paper but found it blank. I immediately took it to Colonel Newnham, Maltby's principal operations officer. I knew him well. Indeed, I regarded him as a good friend although I was very junior; we regularly played chess together. Newnham was clearly delighted by this unexpected development. We went together to the cookhouse. He held up the paper from the cigarette packet in front of a charcoal fire. We saw a message appear. Colonel Newnham showed no emotion. Apparently he had been waiting for over a year for these messages to reach him in Argyle Street. I did not know that messages had already reached the camp in Shamshuipo.

We were in touch with the world!

Colonel Newnham told me later of the significance of this event. He decided to bring in another Royal Engineer officer – also an architect and a very good friend of mine – Captain Godfrey V Bird from Hut

No. 10. He was one of the Colonel's staff officers from the battlebox. Godfrey had been badly wounded, like others, when he had left the Headquarters to fight the Japanese.

Newnham told the two of us to maintain this contact. And so started an extraordinary chain of events, the key parts of which can be told in full for the first time here. The Colonel stressed the acute dangers involved – not only for us, but also for the Chinese agents who were "an unknown quantity". Both Godfrey and I assured him we would help in any way we could. Newnham had probably chosen Godfrey because they had worked together during the fighting. I appreciated the great danger that I was running into.

I was asked if I would recognise the Chinese driver if he came in again. I said I could not be certain but on the next visit I would try to deliver an outgoing message. This wasn't as easy as it sounds because the vehicle was watched by the Japanese sentry, the guard house 40 feet away and the Japs in the tall watchtowers around the camp. Newnham insisted that my delivery of the note was of secondary importance; security must be the guiding factor at all times, he said.

The next time the lorry came in I waited for the Japanese guard, who sat alongside the Chinese driver, to get out. Then I dropped in the reply note behind the driver under a piece of bark. A few days later I picked up another note which had been delivered in the same way as the first. That was the very beginning of the two-way traffic in messages. I was the first to be involved in this activity in Argyle Street, but I didn't know where it would all lead to, nor what was in the messages. This was kept from me by Newnham in case I was caught. (The actual vehicle delivering the supplies varied somewhat as time went on.)

People were beginning to get suspicious of both Godfrey Bird and me; men in each hut had previously taken it in turns to unload the trucks. There was a roster on who was assigned to this task. Yet Godfrey and I were now always there as well. Others guessed that something strange was happening; a few seemed afraid that they might be implicated. "Why is Harris here again?" people asked. "There's something funny going on."

This disturbing development was overcome by an officer in each hut's working party being made responsible for calling out their men on the arrival of the ration lorry. It was also their job to ensure that outgoing messages were planted and the driver's attention attracted to them. Newnham therefore selected seven others in addition to

Godfrey and me. He explained the procedure, emphasised the danger, gave them an opportunity to think it over and to withdraw their names if they thought the risks too great. No one did pull out and the work proceeded with the newcomers. They were Captain J A Lomax RA, Lieutenant G P Ferguson HKVDC, J Redman HKVDC, J C McDouall HKRNVR, R B Goodwin RNZNVR, Sub-Lieutenant J R Haddock HKRNVR and Flight Lieutenant D S Hill RAF.

In addition, Chris D'Almada and Lieutenant Ian Tamworth HKVDC watched the drivers to receive any messages offered by them by hand and to pass messages when direct hand-to-hand delivery seemed safest.

A vital go-between was now chosen by Newnham – Captain (later Major) J R Flynn. He was one of the seven British regular officers serving with the 2/14 Punjabis and had been commissioned from the Royal Military College Sandhurst in the 1930s.

Beyond the Argyle Street officers' camp and the road which ran between Kai Tak airport and Kowloon was a large vegetable garden which contained in one corner a chicken farm. To the east of it was the cemetery. Beyond lay the Indian POW camp of Mau Tau Chung (spelt Matauchung in some accounts).

Newnham asked Flynn to obtain military intelligence from the Rajput and Punjabi POWs, many of whom were 'employed' over much of Hong Kong and adjacent ports including Swatow, Canton and Hainan, providing escorts, manning police and sentry posts on roads, railways and the airfield, usually under Japanese command. Some Indians also worked in Japanese offices as clerks. In his reminiscences of 153 pages[1] Flynn wrote, "The POWs were in a position to observe and get information from Chinese, Koreans, Formosans and third nationals (e.g. Portuguese, and Indians serving in the Hong Kong police)." Newnham wanted information "on enemy strengths, guns, and number of ships in the harbour etc. *He told me he was passing it on.* I alone made daily contact (verbal, thrown messages, signals, hidden messages, messages passed by Korean guards and Chinese civilians). I alone, except for Maj. G E Grey 2/14, Capt. Hamta Prasad 2/14, Maj. Browne 5/7, was completely bilingual in Hindustani and Punjabi (and some Pushtu). These others were never in contact with the Indians. No Indian ever betrayed me even though I and many of them were interrogated (brutally at times). I suffered a lot of criticism for talking to guards."

Flynn attended classes learning French with General Maltby, who arranged for Flynn to have regular appointments with Newnham to pass on the information, after Flynn had translated the messages when necessary.

Flynn remembers "one particular incident. I got a very long and detailed report from Subedar Major Haider Rehinan Khan 2/14 who was a most honourable, dignified, intelligent and much loved officer, the finest example of the Senior Viceroy Commissioned Officer upon whom the honour of a battalion depends – a tower of strength to the prisoners. He subsequently spent much time in solitary imprisonment for his adamant loyalty to the Crown.

"His report covered accurate (later proven) news of Allied progress in Europe, names of traitors in the Indian camp and Jap enquiries about an Allied 'listening post' some great distance from HK. I discussed it with my CO (Grey) and we agreed only Maltby was to see it because of the danger Newnham might be in. Grey came with me. Brigadier Wallis was there. I objected. (I and my contacts were at risk too.) Wallis maintained he was my Brigade Commander. (2/14 and 5/7 were only brigaded under Wallis's command on the Mainland on the Canadians' arrival; actually Wallis was the senior Indian Army officer as distinct from a British Army Brigade appointment.) I was adamant that Wallis should not be present. Maltby supported me and asked Wallis to withdraw. He did. Livid."

The above report is important for it indicates that Maltby knew precisely what was going on in the smuggling of top secret information on Japanese activities to the British in China. His life was at risk, just as were the rest of us who were most intimately involved. (Flynn had no respect for Wallis, describing him as "plausible, self-inflated; he exercised no brigade control and direction and training; he only ordered withdrawals; he was despised by 2/14...") Flynn, like others, had his prejudices.

Flynn accompanied officer 'working parties' which tended the vegetable garden. "Messages and parcels would be left for me in holes in the ground, marked in various ways (e.g. potato peel, eggshell, stick, dead flower) or thrown over the Indian fences when guards distracted, and, remarkably, at Muslim call to prayer five times daily. A group of Muslims would be near the garden fence and their 'prayers' would be in Hindustani and Pushtu. I had four main contacts, men like Haider Rehinan. They in turn chose suitable Indians to help."

* * * * *

I had no idea of Captain Flynn's involvement because he dealt only with Maltby, Newnham and Grey. Everything was on a very strict 'need to know' basis, nobody being given a single scrap of information on the intelligence set up unless they were vital go-betweens.

Nor did I know to whom in China the messages were being passed, or that Captain Douglas Ford, the former Royal Scots Signals Officer in Shamshuipo Camp, had been gathering information, like Flynn. In October 1942, six months earlier, Chinese POWs from the Volunteers had surreptitiously been given messages while working at Kai Tak airport. Knowledge of this link was initially confined to Captain Ford, Dr R K Valentine HKVDC, D L Prophet, Flight Lieutenant H B Gray RAF and two NCOs – Sergeant R J Hardy and Corporal Bond.

The former Canadian Second in Command of the Royal Rifles was transferred from Argyle Street to Shamshuipo in February 1943. He was John N Price who had now become a Lieutenant Colonel. He was briefed on the secret operations.

Under Newnham's driving force, the smuggling of secret messages rapidly increased to both Shamshuipo and Argyle Street. Drugs, maps, compasses and news items were smuggled in. It all seemed rather too easy. Work proceeded smoothly and patients in the camp hospitals soon felt the benefit of increased supplies of drugs. But passing the messages through the drivers had its dangers. Moreover, the Japanese were becoming more inquisitive; their searches became more frequent. Understandably, Newnham seemed to feel the pressure more than any of us; he lived in a state of nervous tension.

In May 1943 it became apparent that a Japanese officer was watching us through binoculars from a hilltop half a mile to the north. All operations were cancelled. Lieutenant R B Goodwin RNZNVR thought up a new system of passing messages; a note was sent to the outside contacts telling them to fix three nails in a precise position in a dark corner under the floor of the truck, between which messages could be held by rubber bands. He made a small wooden model on which we practised despatching and receiving messages until we were all confident. It took only seconds to move the message between the nails. Goodwin also made a hollow bolt out of wood and this was fitted in the supply lorry. Messages and drugs could be hidden inside the false bolt.

The information being passed, I learnt after the war, was very important to the war effort. To give but one example, operational intelligence was passed to the United States Air Force's 68th Composite

Wing Headquarters at Kweilin, which had no intelligence sources of its own at that time.

* * * * *

What would have happened, one might speculate, if a similar intelligence organisation had been working in a German POW camp in, say, the Portsmouth area where the POWs could gather intelligence from outside working parties – perhaps through Italian POWs who were employed on farms in the countryside? As in Hong Kong, there could easily have been hidden wireless sets in the POW camps. It might also have been possible to construct them so they could transmit to the Germans in France.

The Germans parachuted spies into Britain with wireless sets. Most were 'turned' to work for the Allies, while others were executed. But had one spy established himself or herself in a 'safe house' in the Portsmouth neighbourhood, he or she could have assembled intelligence, just as we in Hong Kong were doing, on ships, aircraft, weapons, troop movements or whatever. The repercussions resulting from such spying activity, particularly in the dark days of 1940 or before the D Day landings in Normandy in June 1944, could have been horrendous.

Fortunately neither the Germans nor the Italians achieved anything similar to what we were up to, but the above scenario serves to emphasise the value the British, American, Chinese and other Allies attached to our intelligence reports.

* * * * *

News began to filter down to a few of us that, with Maltby's blessing, an extraordinarily ambitious plan was being considered for a mass breakout from the POW camps.

"In all three camps the general standard of health had reached a very low level, and any escape would have caused severe and immediate repercussions and further privations that would have been fatal to many," wrote Maltby in 1956. "Therefore our aim, which unfortunately was never to materialise, was that a collection of food, arms and ammunition should be established in the nearby hills, a large diversion should be made by the guerrillas accompanied perhaps by an air raid, and under cover of these there should be simultaneous break-outs from all three camps. One-third of our numbers, owing to their physical state, would have had to be abandoned. Another third we reckon would probably have fallen in the subsequent fighting, but the remainder, we hoped, would be able to make their way to freedom and so continue to participate in the war. Ambitious, perhaps, but that was our aim."[2]

I found it difficult to take such a plan seriously. The guerrillas to whom Maltby refers had helped a few escapers in early 1942, but there seems no chance that they could have set up arms caches near the POW camps. To lose one third of our number – several thousand men – is clearly a price absurdly high. Japan, in 1943, still controlled the land, air and sea in and around Hong Kong and the neighbourhood. Above all, as he says, our health had so deteriorated, we would never have made it over the mountains to the north, and the vast distances thereafter, on foot. Such a plan might look good on paper but, unlike Maltby, I am glad that it did not materialise.

This should not be regarded as criticism of him. Wars are not won by endless defensive measures. He always stood up for us most bravely against the Japanese. As Captain Flynn, who saw him so closely involved in the passing of the most secret intelligence, put it: "Maltby was in a class of his own in dealing with the Japanese and keeping the camps orderly and controlled."

* * * * *

Suddenly disaster struck. In mid June 1943 an SOS came from Lee Hung Hoi. He was one of the very courageous Chinese truck drivers. Naturally we closed the operations down immediately, but it was too late.

On 1st July the lorry drove into the camp as usual, but the driver was now acting under Japanese orders. He suddenly tossed out a piece of paper. I count my blessings that it was not my turn to be on duty that morning. I was there at the beginning. I didn't want to be there at the end! Sub-Lieutenant J R Haddock, by chance, happened to be on duty. He picked up the paper when he felt it was safe to do so and hid it on top of a lavatory cistern before strolling nonchalantly to his hut. Ten minutes later he was sent for by the guards and arrested. Captain Bird retrieved the paper and applied iodine to reveal the secret writing: it was blank. "This made me suspicious that it was a plant," he wrote later. "But I could not connect the plant with Haddock's arrest because I was told that no Japanese had seen him pick it up. I put the paper back on the cistern, and on checking later it had mysteriously been removed."

In Shamshuipo that same morning "during a softball game between the Canadians and the Portuguese prisoners in camp, I noticed Matsuda and two sentries coming in through the main gate," wrote Lieutenant Colonel J N Price, who now commanded the Royal Rifles following Home adopting the rank of Colonel. "I saw them re-emerge with Sergeant R J Ruttledge Royal Canadian Corps of Signals. Realising that our key man had been caught, I remained helplessly watching the game. An hour later Matsuda took away Flight Lieutenant Gray and Sergeant Hardy. This made it certain that our work had been discovered.

"Ford had gone at once to his room and removed as much incriminating evidence as he could. He then went to Gray's room where the old football hung on the wall; it contained maps, war bulletins, and compasses. He was too late! The guards were already searching there. By this time we were well schooled in nonchalance and in a sort of fatalism which helped us to control all emotional expressions. The guards continued searching the room and went out eventually without even glancing at the football. For some days Ford, I and others lived under a terrible strain and anxiety. On 10th July Captain Ford was taken out. I made disposition of my effects as it seemed certain that I would be the next victim," concluded Price.[3]

On that same day "I saw Colonel Newnham being taken away," remembers Captain Bird, "and I went to the underground hiding place outside the window in which a precis of all messages was kept. General Maltby decided to burn them together with the maps. I kept only six front collar studs; they concealed compasses which had been sent to us".[4]

The last few messages sent from Argyle Street could not have been more incriminating if intercepted by the Japanese, as they probably were. They had dealt with the possibility of a guerrilla raid on the perimeter fence to free the POWs.

About two weeks after Colonel Newnham had been arrested, Major Charles Boxer summoned those of us who were left. He told me and the other 'operators' nothing about what was happening but said it was just possible the messages would start again using the ration lorry. He wanted only volunteers as the work would be extremely dangerous. We agreed to continue as before, but, on resuming unloading the vehicles, nothing was ever passed to us.

Boxer had ended the meeting with us by saying: "If any of you get through alive, I will see your name is put forward at the end of the war."

This never happened, certainly in my case. I was sad the others and I never received any recognition. I am now the only one still alive!

Although they were constantly in my thoughts, I did not learn of the fate of Colonel Newnham and some of the others until the Japanese surrender. We knew that they would be tortured most dreadfully, going through the most appalling experiences. For 25 months I had to live with the possibility that I might be arrested. General Maltby, too, must have had a very stressful time waiting to see if he would be incriminated. He had protested strongly at the arrests, but, as usual, the Japanese refused to tell him anything. Instead, Maltby, Wallis and 13 other senior British officers were put in a special inner perimeter within Argyle Street; on 4th August they were sent to Formosa.

Prior to the mass arrests, Lieutenant H C Dixon, a young New Zealander in the RNZNVR, had found pieces of a wireless set in a bombed house while on a working party. He was a radio technician and when in July 1943 some valves were stolen from a Japanese set, key POWs were able to listen to broadcasts for about four days a week from London, San Francisco, New Delhi, Sydney and Chungking. The wireless also picked up a considerable amount of operational transmissions from American China-based aircraft, thereby enabling those listening to become familiar with their wave-lengths and methods of operating.

The four most involved were Dixon, Commander R S Young RN, formerly head of the Stonecutter Island Radio Intercept Station, Commander D H S Craven RN, a survivor of the ill-fated Norwegian operation at Narvik, and Major Boxer who mixed the wireless news items with local newspaper reports for the Camp's daily war bulletins.

The wireless set was potentially of the utmost importance, for Dixon had constructed it so that it could transmit to report on, for example, Japanese troop movement, aircraft and shipping. Argyle Street was close to both Kai Tak airport and the harbour where we could see occasional activity, "I could never feel happy about the set," wrote Craven "and I only hoped that we should not be betrayed."[5] The wireless was hidden in a biscuit box, which was usually buried.

The blow fell on 21st September 1943. During an extended four-hour morning parade, the Japanese Military Police went without hesitation to the spot where the set was hidden.

"At 7.00 p.m. Young was arrested, which confirmed in my mind that we had been given away. I was arrested at 10.00 p.m. and Dixon an hour later," wrote Craven. Boxer was apprehended six days later, joining nine in all who were being held. Two of them had nothing to do with the wireless but had beds on each side of Dixon.

The interrogators said they knew all about Colonel Newnham's case and claimed that the wireless could transmit, which was vigorously denied. Each of the prisoners was beaten, starved and deprived of water for many hours. Craven described the constant questioning as "devastatingly unnerving".

"The Japanese system of justice is that all possible information is extracted from POWs; severe and intolerable torture is resorted to as necessary. Prisoners frequently die and are sometimes deliberately killed in a most brutal manner as a punishment for withholding the truth; the Gestapo treated their prisoners in a similar fashion.

"When the information has been wrung out of all those implicated, it is pooled, and out of the pool are produced 'statements' alleged to have been made by each prisoner. Though this is instantly recognised as not being one's own work, it contains the true picture. After this, the court martial which follows months later is mere formality. There is no question of pleading guilty or not guilty, and there is no defence; the prosecutor demands a specific sentence from the President of the Court, and the proceedings are closed," recalls a POW.

On 21st October Boxer, Young, Dixon and Craven were charged at the Military Police Headquarters with constructing a short-wave radio, using it to obtain enemy broadcasts and publishing this as news to POWs. "We all pleaded guilty and were then transferred to Stanley Prison," wrote Craven. "I had developed beriberi, the vitamin deficiency disease, and become completely paralysed. I being helpless had to be carried. We anticipated a few weeks' imprisonment, but we were told by an NCO that we were going to have our heads chopped off."

Boxer was able to conduct several whispered conversations with Colonel Newnham and Captain Ford during exercise periods at the prison. He learned how they had protected those of us who had planted and received the secret information from the ration trucks, despite the most strenuous efforts of the Japanese to get them to divulge our identities.

Boxer in a cell nearby reported that "Ford gave nothing and nobody away, although subject to severe physical torture. Ford took all the responsibility on himself, and maintained that no senior officers were involved, thereby saving the lives of General Maltby and Colonel Price of the Royal Rifles of Canada. Ford gave an outstanding example of cheerful and courageous fortitude which was an inspiration to all those who were imprisoned with him and which aroused the respect and admiration even of the Japanese."[6]

The trial was presided over by Major General Ashidate. Evidence was given that Ford, Gray, Ruttledge and Hardy had received in Shamshuipo, over a period of three months, six messages from the British Army Aid Group operating in China, after which they had compiled several reports on conditions in Shamshuipo. The Court was told that Newnham and Haddock had received and sent out 15 messages from Argyle Street. The prosecution did not try to prove that the information was of any military significance.

The Japanese were clearly unaware of our activities, which were much greater than the evidence suggested.

In the evening, after the trial was completed, Commander Craven was "mortified to see Newnham, Gray and Ford put in the condemned cell. The remaining three were fortunate to receive 15 years' imprisonment. Newnham and Gray were very sick, but behaved most gallantly during their 18 days under sentence of death. Ford was fit, and his good spirits were an example we shall never forget."

On the morning set for their execution, Lieutenant H C Dixon, the New Zealander, crept up the prison corridor while ostensibly washing the floor. When he was near their cell, he asked if there were any messages he could take. Newnham requested that his love should be sent to his family; Gray asked that his remains and silver watch should be sent home. A warder then hustled Dixon away. Ford later said that he hoped his remains could be re-buried one day in Edinburgh.

On 18th December the three officers were removed from their cells. Neither Newnham nor Gray could walk unaided. Ford half carried them to a waiting truck. They were shot on the beach at Shek-o.

Notes

1. Reminiscences of Maj. J R Flynn, written for OL.
2. Goodwin, Ralph, *Passport to Eternity*, London: Arthur Barker, 1956, p. 6.
3. Garneau, G S, *Royal Rifles of Canada*, Bishop's University, 1971, p. 297.
4. Interview Bird with OL.
5. Report to Admiralty, 1945, RN Historical Branch.
6. Report by Maj. C R Boxer, 26.8.45.

CHAPTER 20

The British Army Aid Group and Fresh Disasters

In Argyle Street POW Camp a few of us in late 1943 wondered what organisation in China had been responsible for sending us medicines, communications and encouraging us to escape, very much endangering us in the process. To what use had the British officers there put the intelligence we had sent them? We knew we had lost from Argyle Street alone Newnham, Haddock, Boxer, Dixon, Young and Craven, but we did not know what had happened to them. Nor did we appreciate the horrifying slaughter which had occurred in the Stanley Internment Camp. Rumours reached us that Ford and several others had been taken from Shamshuipo, as had an Indian officer named Captain M A Ansari from Mau Tau Chung POW Camp across the road from us. To what extent would they reveal, under torture, details about us? It was not until after the war that I discovered the horrifying answers to these questions: they certainly preyed on my mind.

* * * * *

In January 1942 Lieutenant Colonel L T Ride, who had commanded the Volunteer Field Ambulance so ably during the fighting, had escaped from Shamshuipo. He persuaded Major General L E Dennys, the British Military Attache in China, that an organisation be established to arrange the escape of POWs and internees from Hong Kong. Dennys was sympathetic, but said he could spare no vehicle, weapon or wireless set. As far as manpower was concerned, Ride could only use any escapers who reached him. As a cover, the organisation was to be called 'The British Army Aid Group'; it should claim to be helping

Chinese refugees. General Chiang Kai-shek agreed to the proposals and gave orders that the Chinese should support it.

Ride's first recruit was Captain R D Scriven, Indian Medical Service, who had escaped from Shamshuipo with Captain A G Hewitt. Scriven was an excellent choice for he knew Hong Kong well and spoke Cantonese fluently. "Ride told me I should do anything I could to find out what was happening in the Colony and to contact guerrillas who might be helpful in guiding further escapers," recalls Scriven. "I was able to ingratiate myself with General Cheung who was commanding the forces in Waichow. And so I set off with a good supply of medical stores and a Chinese, Henry Chan, who had been a tour guide in Hong Kong. How long my mission would last, I had no idea. We reached Waichow hidden under sacks after passing Japanese patrols."[1]

At Waichow, Scriven, among the most charismatic and delightful of men, struck up a useful friendship with General Cheung over an alcoholic dinner. Cheung told him that three other escapers from Hong Kong were two days' march away. They were the group led by Captain J D Clague Royal Artillery. Cheung accompanied Scriven back to the Italian Medical Mission for a nightcap. "The drinks finished, I bade a courteous goodnight to the General and fell senseless to the floor, smashing an oil lamp and the table in my descent. An admirable Chinese priest, Father Ma, put me to bed and assured me I had acquired much face."

In June 1942 Clague replaced Scriven because the Indian Medical Service in New Delhi had become restless that one of their officers should be employed in duties other than medical.

Clague, now promoted to Major and, like Hewitt and Scriven, wearing a Military Cross for their daring escape, established his advance post which consisted of five British officers and ten Chinese. "You are appointed M19 representative in China ..." read his directive which told him he had to rescue any Allied POWs; he must confide in the Chinese military authorities; give all the credit for any success to the Chinese and gather intelligence. Permission was not given for him to use ciphers.

The role of the BAAG was made most difficult owing to local politics, personalities, intrigue and the growing unwillingness of the Chinese nationalists and Communists to work together. BAAG never formed an integral part of any Chinese military body. Its existence was usually recognised by both the Americans and Chinese; its presence was tolerated and its help accepted; but officially it was ignored. Ride found that the biggest stumbling block was that Britain's prestige in China had reached an all-time low. "If the defeated British were considered to be a world power, why not the undefeated Chinese?" was an occasional comment.

China's contribution to the total war effort has not been adequately recognised. When the Pacific War began in December 1941, China was engaging 22 Japanese divisions, plus 20 brigades, compared with ten divisions and three brigades which Japan used on its offensives in Malaya, Burma, Hong Kong and the Dutch East Indies. By August 1945 over a million Japanese troops were in China. Almost 400,000 of them were killed there, which belies the later charge that China did not really fight.[2]

"A special reconnaissance for an escape operation on Argyle Street POW camp was carried out in August 1942," read one of the first reports submitted by BAAG to the War Office.[3] "The first step in our plans was to obtain a complete set of maps of the underground drainage system of Kowloon. These were stolen from the Japanese. Three British officers and two Chinese were sent into the New Territories to investigate the possibility of a large-scale rescue of prisoners through the underground drainage system."

According to the report, many interned Chinese soldiers had escaped from Argyle Street before the war through these drains, which passed under our camp into Kowloon Bay.

To the best of my knowledge this part of the report may be misleading. There was certainly no escape from Argyle Street throughout the time we were there. Had we found underground nullahs or drains, there would have been escapes, as there were at Shamshuipo in early 1942.

In September 1942, as already related, BAAG's Chinese agents made contact with the Volunteer POWs from Shamshuipo who were working at Kai Tak, and escape equipment was smuggled to them. By 1st May 1943 BAAG had grown to 13 officers and four men. They were divided between the Headquarters at Kweilin and outposts at Chungking, Waichow, Macao and Dunming. A further 35 British and Chinese staff served at the HQ as clerks, accountants, medical staff and messengers.

Ride's and Clague's plans for the mass breakout of POWs never materialised, but they were very successful in infiltrating BAAG agents into the commercial dockyards in Hong Kong. Allied submarines could be deployed to sink Japanese vessels when they left port, particularly if good intelligence was available. The Allies therefore tried to establish 'coast watchers' near ports in Burma, Singapore, Hong Kong and China. By 1944 the cumulative losses to Japanese merchant shipping were considerable. BAAG was also successful in persuading skilled labour in the Hong Kong dockyards to leave the Colony. They also helped escapers and those evading captivity.

One outstanding success was achieved. The Japanese Governor held a military parade on the cricket field in Victoria near the Law Courts to read out the annual rescript from the Emperor. There was a stand for spectators and a high vertical railing around the cricket field to restrict entry. At 10.00 a.m. I heard the drone of planes. Without warning, through the scattered cloud covering the Peak, American aircraft dived upon the pitch machine-gunning the parade. There was no escape; the death toll must have been very high.

We were kept short of rations for a week. Our undercover work was, I felt, achieving results.

BAAG gained a good reputation with GHQ India for gathering naval intelligence. The organisation accurately tracked the arrival of the *Lisbon Maru* into Hong Kong, "but despite this early warning, one of the worst maritime tragedies of the Pacific war resulted from miscommunication on the part of the Americans after they had received knowledge of the ship's whereabouts and function." Selwyn-Clarke's report to Macao on the *Lisbon Maru*'s POW role had also been tragically mishandled, as we have seen.

Captain Flynn in Argyle Street and Ford in Shamshuipo meanwhile gathered intelligence via the Indian and Chinese Volunteer POWs respectively. The information was embodied into a weekly Waichow intelligence summary which went to the Military Attache in Chunking and the Director of Military Intelligence, India. By 1943 these reports were passed by wireless, taking four days.[4] The Americans received copies of everything worthwhile.

I have described how the spying organisation affecting the POWs collapsed in July 1943 with the arrest of Newnham and others, but not what happened at Stanley Internment Camp. There were resistance groups there, and among British bankers in Victoria who had not been interned because they were still useful to the Japanese.

Dr Talbot, being returned to Stanley after undergoing an operation in Victoria, was thoroughly searched at a police post at the Wong Nei Chong Gap. The Japanese found beneath his bandages 4,000

Yen and messages. Sir Vandeleur Grayburn, head of the Hong Kong and Shanghai Bank Corporation, who had refused to escape when BAAG contacted him earlier, bravely went to the Japanese Chief of the Foreign Affairs Department. Grayburn told him that he had asked Talbot to take the money to Stanley as it was partly for the nursing staff at the camp's hospital. He was arrested two weeks later and died of ill-treatment in prison.

Tragically, many more arrests followed when the Japanese established a link between BAAG and the internees. A radio engineer was forced to dig in a bank where a wireless set was hidden. Another set was voluntarily surrendered. Those arrested were accused of spying or of inciting or assisting espionage, although most messages passed from Stanley concerned trivial matters such as the health of prisoners.

On 19th October 1943 27 British internees were tried by five Japanese officers. In addition, a most courageous Indian Army officer was unexpectedly added to the civilian group.

Captain M A Ansari 5/7 Rajputs had been a POW in the Mau Tau Chung POW camp. He was related to the ruler of a large Indian state and, thanks to his influence, the Japanese were determined to persuade him to support the extensive anti-British movement. Ansari was a strong character; before the war Wallis, then commanding the Rajput Battalion, had to discipline him frequently for fighting Royal Scots officers in the Hong Kong Hotel.[5]

The Japanese had kept him in Stanley Prison between May and September 1942, so starving and ill-treating him that Ansari had become unable to walk. After some time in the camp hospital, he returned to the Indian other ranks POW camp, which contained no British officer. He was involved with BAAG in helping escapers but was entrapped by *agents provocateurs* and arrested again in May 1943 to be starved and brutally tortured for several months.

The trial was presided over by Lieutenant Colonel Fujimoto, a tired, wizened old man. The Japanese regarded J A Fraser, the former Hong Kong Government Defence Secretary, as the ringleader. Major Kozi, the prosecutor, made a speech which lasted most of the morning. The Chinese interpreter translated so infrequently and so badly that the prisoners were scarcely aware of what was being said. Fujimoto at one stage put his arms on the table, rested his head on his arms and for half an hour seemed to be asleep. On awakening, he went to the lavatory to smoke a cigarette while the trial continued. At 2.00 p.m. Kozi mopped his brow, bowed and sat down amidst much Japanese applause. The interpreter, after a confused discussion in Japanese, translated: "In the eyes of the law, you are all guilty of High Treason, and the prosecution has demanded the death penalty." Fujimoto, after fumbling with a book, announced, "All are sentenced to death. The Court is adjourned."

On 29th October, after ten days in solitary confinement, 32 men and one woman were led out to be executed. A group of children from the internment camp who were passing the prison saw the van drive out. As it went by, English voices shouted out, "Goodbye, boys."

"I was in the prison garden when I saw the prisoners leave on their last earthly journey," noted W J Anderson. "I was told that some had asked to be granted the services of a minister, but that this was refused. They were allowed to mix and talk to each other for five minutes before being tied up preparatory to their death march. Captain Ansari, I was told, gave them a 'pep talk' which greatly cheered them.

"Warders who were present at the execution said that it was a cruel and bloody affair. All were decapitated, though the executions in their near final stage were said to be so bad that some lives were ended by shooting."[6] The dead were heaped together in a common grave making later identification impossible.

* * * * *

On 23rd December it was the turn of Boxer, Craven, Dixon and Young to be sentenced, following the finding of the wireless set in Argyle Street. After the execution of Newnham, Ford and Gray, and now Ansari with the 33 others, Boxer did not expect to survive. Moreover, his Japanese guards had three times taken him outside the barracks, telling him he would soon be executed. Boxer met Dixon in the latrine and warned him they were for the 'high jump'. It was therefore to their considerable relief that the four were provisionally sentenced to 15 years' imprisonment. They waited in an anti room for the sentence to be confirmed. Boxer warned them that a heavier penalty might be imposed. He was wrong; the sentence was reduced to five years.

Had Boxer saved himself and the three others because over the last few years the Japanese had "recognised his competence in the language of the *samurai* class; his skill as a kendo fencer; and his extensive scholarly interest in Japanese history? No other British officer in occupied Hong Kong could match those qualifications."[7]

It is unlikely that Boxer's Japanese friends, who made such a fuss of him in Bowen Road Hospital almost a year before, could have helped him. There were no more crates of whisky in the pipeline. This is because within weeks of the Colony's surrender the regiments, despite being seriously weakened from casualties incurred in Hong Kong, were despatched towards Timor, Java and Sumatra.

* * * * *

As Christmas Day 1943 approached we POWs still despaired of our survival. Fortunately the Japanese had resumed allowing POWs to receive food parcels from contacts in Hong Kong because no escape had taken place for many months. Maltby's policy of no individual or small group escapes was paying dividends, although he himself had been sent to Formosa and criticised in some circles for his policy.

The parcels were pooled; most of us had something extra to eat on Christmas Day, although we didn't do so well as some in Shamshuipo, judging by one POW who wrote in his diary: "We really spread ourselves: we had a special meal for the men with Red Cross tins. The orchestra played, and the officers gave each man a packet of fags. Afterwards we had a guitar player and a singsong," wrote Captain G White of the Winnipeg Grenadiers. "A wonderful day – hope we are home next Christmas."

Sergeant A J Alsey, a Musician in the Royal Scots, had a rather different Christmas: "Carol singing lasts for an hour. Three buns and a third of a tin of bully for Xmas dinner. Bed at 8.30 p.m. but up at 2.00 a.m. and made a really good cup of tea at 4.30. My scabies are terrible and I scratch for hours, and my feet are aching like hell."

One source of profit was gold teeth. Most of those with a gold filling had it removed and sold through the wire to buy food.

The Japanese suddenly told us in Argyle Street that we were going to have a sort of psychological proforma to fill up – the names of our relatives, jobs, schooling, ages, our sex, and so on. The last question was, "In what capacity/job will you be willing to serve the Greater East Asia Co-prosperity Sphere? My friend Dudley put down Public Hangman; another put Grave Digger; while a third put Overseas Representative," recalls Captain Flynn.

"On quite a different form, those with musical experience were asked to put their names down for their musical instrument," remembers

Major A R Colquhoun, a former Battery Commander in the Hong Kong and Singapore Royal Artillery. "I put mine down for the saxophone, not because I had ever played one, but it was probably easy to carry and interesting to look at. Months later enough instruments for a complete orchestra arrived. The camp lay back, anticipating long Summer evenings with the limpid strains of the violins. Unfortunately most players couldn't read a note and the Japs wouldn't allow any practice or rehearsal.

"We were ordered to play in the canteen. Twenty of us assembled – army officers, naval ratings, legal and government officials and former schoolmasters – all united under the baton of Lieutenant Commander Stanley Swetland RN who was elderly, caustic, sardonic, morose and completely imperturbable.

"The entire camp including the Japanese guards assembled. We sounded rather professional as we tuned up – so much so that the guards applauded under the impression that this was the first item in our repertoire. Stan Swetland, with fingers like a bunch of sausages, could coax real music out of anything from a tiny mandolin upwards. He tapped twice with his baton for silence, raised his arms and collected us with a baleful glare over the top of his steel-rimmed glasses. 'Black Diamond Overture,' he gravely announced. 'Letter A. Count of three. Come in on the down beat… '

"We did. The resulting discord of sounds was excruciating. Stan Swetland blanched. It was generally agreed that, throughout the war years, this was the only occasion he was ever seen to betray any sign of emotion. We cowered behind our music stands, facing an audience which was convinced it had been conned by a bunch of impostors.

"When the Japanese decided that we should do mass PT before breakfast, the 'Worst Orchestra in the World' was resuscitated to lighten the burden. Stan orchestrated some rousing marches and simple waltzes to which the POWs could jump and wave their arms. The only advantage of being a 'musician' was that we didn't have to join in these capers, which were not popular. Fortunately we had two superb players – Len Corrigan and Noel Bardel, both Canadians."

Occasional concerts in Hong Kong's POW camps were an immense success for they enabled the POWs to forget their miserable surroundings.

"The improvising in the play last night was really amazing," wrote Captain E L Hurd on 21st May 1943. "Wigs were made from the string of rice sacks, evening dresses from mosquito nets and the 'chorus girls" wings from wooden frames." A Portuguese, 'Sonny' Castro, invariably played the leading lady with such success that some POWs to this day are unsure of his sex. More than one ex-POW was rumoured to have a sex-change operation in Singapore long after the war.

The Japanese enjoyed the shows as much as everyone else, and they provided the chalk for makeup. They sat in the front row and roared with laughter, although they had only one interpreter among them and so could have understood very little. The lyrics had to be changed when they were in the audience. Plays produced included *Journey's End, You're No Lady* and *The Merchant of Venice*. John Trapman brought the house down as a 'black Mammy'.

Afternoon lectures were popular. In one month alone they included, 'Scents and Perfumes', 'A Holiday in a Lunatic Asylum', 'Gamekeeping', 'Murder and Armed Robbery in Shanghai', 'Communism', 'Hollywood', 'A Cruise in Swedish Waters', 'Ten Years in Destroyers', 'Training of a Minister of the Church of Scotland' and 'Life of a London Taxi Driver', which I particularly remember. I also recall Lord Merthyr speaking on 'The House of Lords and Democracy'.

The camp magazines were professional and enabled us to amuse ourselves. Godfrey Bird and I took a leading part in producing them.

The camp cobbler's shop was run by an Etonian, Harrovian and Wykehamist which prompted the following:

Though your boots were made by Maxwell
And your shoes designed by Lobb,
Aren't you still a social climber
Aren't you candidly a snob?
Are you suited – we'll go further
Are you booted by Lord Merthyr?
With a coronet on every heel to mark the finished job?
Need we prove our gentle breeding,
Need we show our pedigrees?
Eton, Winchester and Harrow – aren't they always guarantees:
One and all we pull together,
Put the 'polish' into leather,
Won't you let us be your 'sole'-mates, fit you with our
family trees?

I wasn't the Harrovian in question! Instead I had the job of repairing the roof of the huts and such other chores.

Lord Merthyr, who had nearly had me removed from the ship en route to Hong Kong, took a leading role in cobbling, using a last made out of a piece of steel and a log of wood. His aim was to create a pair of shoes for each prisoner. With this in mind he collected nails that had fallen out of shoes around the camp. He wanted everyone in the camp to have shoes in case there was an opportunity to escape. Usually we went barefoot.

Lord Merthyr became a confirmed pessimist and told his friends the war would last ten years. He kept spare tins of food unopened. "When asked why," one POW recalls, "he replied, though in more dignified phraseology, that when the crunch came and we were starving, he would be laughing. He was extraordinarily unselfish, often undertaking the most unpopular jobs in the camp. He was later Chairman of Committees in the House of Lords." One of his great objects in life was to fix a date for Easter.

Despite the magazines, few of us could divert our minds from food for long, as the following poem suggests:

A Prisoner's Prayer

You know, Lord, how one must strive
At Shamshuipo to keep alive.
And how there isn't much to eat –
Just rice and greens at Argyle Street.

It's not much, God, when dinner comes
To find it's just chrysanthemums.
Nor can I stick at any price
Those soft white maggots in the rice.
Nor yet those little, hard black weevils,
The lumps of grit and other evils.

I know, Lord, I shouldn't grumble
And please don't think that I'm not humble
When I most thankfully recall
My luck to be alive at all.

But, Lord, I think that even You
Would soon get tired of ersatz stew.
So what I really want to say
Is: if we soon don't get away
From Shamshuipo and Argyle Street,
Then please, Lord, could we have some meat?

A luscious, fragrant, heaped-up plateful.
And also, Lord, we would be grateful
If you would send a living boon
And send some Red Cross parcels, soon.

"One working party used to steal 'dubbing' for several months from a Japanese cobbler's shop. It made oil to enable us to taste the rice, and for the fat content. (It was horrible.) We could find no way to make chrysanthemum leaves palatable. Sometimes that was the vegetable brought in by the Japs," recalls Captain Flynn. "It was worse than the green seaweed we sometimes got. Many crops were raised in the vegetable garden by seeds sent in. Tomatoes, much enjoyed, enabled the seeds, found thereafter having passed through us, to be replanted successfully.

"Some slops from restaurants were sent in by parcel to us. Amazingly enough, many brothels and prostitutes sent in things to former patrons. Inevitably, 'sharp boys' emerged who traded with the POWs. Possessions, such as rings, watches, pens and jewellery were sold for cigarettes and eggs – choice delicacies. This enabled the traders to amass their own supplies of cigarettes, food and money which they sold at exorbitant prices for post-war IOUs and cheques," continues Flynn "I myself signed away nearly £500 to keep alive. Amusingly enough, 'traders' became identified through having clothing, bedding, cigarettes, and not being skeletons." The film *King Rat* will be familiar to some.

"After the war, I was bugged relentlessly and felt obliged to repay the £500. As a serving officer, I couldn't afford the bad publicity if it went that far. Later I heard of an Australian who agreed to repay in cash what he owed – on the steps of the Sydney Town Hall at an agreed time and date. (Presumably he had alerted the press.) I wish I had been as smart. I still feel cheated; I am sure the 'traders' were anything but straight. You would be shocked by some of the names I could mention."

Once a month we were permitted to print one postcard, not to exceed 50 words. This was later reduced to 25 to make the Japanese censor's job easier. We were not allowed to say anything about sickness. The first batch of letters arrived on Christmas Day 1942. For the last two years of the war, large quantities of mail reached Hong Kong. Colonel Tokunaga let it accumulate and then ordered that those letters containing more than 50 words be burnt. Six wooden trunks containing mail were also destroyed two days before the Japanese surrender. One wife impregnated her letters with scent, hoping the censor might prove sympathetic. One officer, Flynn, was given 23 letters on the same day because his fiancée painted pictures of flowers on the envelope. (Despite this, he didn't marry her in the end.) A Gunner officer received only one letter in three years – it was from his tailor in Saville Row demanding instant payment. My father enabled me to get three letters. One of them came via the International Red Cross thanks to Count Bylandt, who was Foreign Secretary in the Free Dutch Government in London and rented my father's house. I was much relieved that my parents knew I was alive.

Throughout the war, the Japanese attached importance to POWs in the Far East broadcasting messages to their families. The Japanese knew that the faint chance of hearing a loved one would create a large and willing listening audience. These broadcasts gave the Japanese a chance to insert propaganda and lies. The broadcasts from Hong Kong were ineffective because the POWs chose their words with care.

* * * * *

We had all become very cautious of any possible involvement with unknown people trying to pass us messages. In November 1943 Major R A Atkinson Hong Kong and Singapore Royal Artillery was told by an Indian guard in a watchtower that he had a very important letter for him. The Indian dropped a piece of paper, which Atkinson picked up much later. He took it to Captain G V Bird Royal Engineers. It was misspelt and signed '68'. Bird suspected a trap and ordered that no reply be sent.

In December a Chinese threw a message in front of two other POWs. It was also signed '68' and seemed to be genuine. Bird consulted Lieutenant Colonel F D Field DSO MC, Royal Artillery, the senior officer now in Argyle Street. Communications were maintained with the Chinese contact by Bird and T S Simpson walking to the wire talking to each other in a loud voice so that the Chinese contact, strolling beyond the wire on the road, could hear the camp news. It was agreed that contact be renewed, but also that no written messages be sent because there was no proof that BAAG was still involved. Five months later another note was dropped over the fence. By now we were very suspicious and those involved agreed to break off visual contact, and to pick up no more messages.

In early May 1944 the Japanese moved us all from Argyle Street to Shamshuipo, which now had room for us as large numbers of former inmates had been sent to Japan, or had died of disease or ill-treatment.

In June G V Bird, F D Field and T S Simpson were arrested and moved to Military Police Headquarters. The Japanese believed that Bird was the ringleader. He was indeed the last remaining POW who knew the names of the officers in the BAAG. Bird was taken to a back room where he saw in a corner a large concrete washing tub with a tap over it. Also in the room, apart from the guards, was a half-caste British subject, Jerome Lan.

The big, tall interrogator, named Fujihara, told Bird to take off his shirt and get into a coffin-shaped box. His arms and feet were tightly bound so that he could move only his head. "I was then lifted in the coffin onto the washing tub and my head was placed under the tap," he recalled. "A dirty cloth was put over my face, and the tap was slowly turned on to drip, drip, drip onto the cloth. I had no idea what was going to happen and I was very frightened. Soon the cloth became saturated with water and my breathing became very difficult. I was gulping down vast quantities of water through my nose and mouth with every breath I tried to take. I got less and less air, and more and more water in my lungs. Fujihara asked me for the names of the British officers in Waichow. I replied that I knew nothing about any of them.

"Back went the cloth over my face and on went the tap. I was gasping, struggling and fighting for breath until I thought the end had come. I began to say a prayer we Roman Catholics are taught to say on dying. It begins, 'Jesus, Mary, Joseph… '. I had just managed to mutter 'Jesus, Mary' when the cloth was whipped off and the tap stopped. Fujihara thought I was giving the names of the officers. Lan, the interpreter, was a Catholic too and told Fujihara that I was merely praying. I was pushed under the tap again and eventually passed out. Lan later told me that I was unconscious for 40 minutes."[8]

(A black and white film shot in Vietnam shows in the background a Vietcong suspect being similarly treated in the 1960s.)

Bird's interrogation was resumed on the following days, the torture taking various different forms which were equally excruciatingly painful. Six days later the Japanese decided that they could prove nothing against Field, Bird and Simpson. They were told that the interrogation had ceased, and were returned to Shamshuipo. We were overjoyed and most surprised to see them once more.

Torture by water continues to this day. *The International Herald Tribune* reported on 19th March 2005 that Porter Goss, the Director of US Central Intelligence, has said he could not assure Congress that the CIA's methods of interrogating suspected terrorists since 11th September 2001 had been legally permissible under federal laws prohibiting torture. Senator John McCain, who spent years as a prisoner of war in Vietnam, asked Goss about the CIA's previously reported use of a technique known as waterboarding, in which a prisoner is made to believe that he will drown. Goss replied that the approach fell into "an area of what I will call professional interrogation techniques". He vigorously defended "professional interrogation" as an important tool in efforts against terrorism.

I and the others were saved by Godfrey Bird's bravery. I have always felt an everlasting debt to him.

Lan told the three that, had they admitted anything, they would have been shot like Newnham. Fortunately Fujihara had not connected them with Newnham's activities and they had never replied in writing to any of the Chinese messages.

* * * * *

Christmas Day 1944 was not very different to the previous one, but there was a sense of optimism as the following months went by.

The newspaper *The Hong Kong News*, produced in English under Japanese control, and edited in part by a cashiered former Royal Navy officer, continued to tell us of endless Japanese victories and crippling American losses. Nevertheless, with the small atlas I had retained throughout my imprisonment, there was no disguising that the fighting was coming closer and had reached the Philippines in late 1944. We knew nothing of Slim's victories in Burma, of the American supremacy at sea, nor of their bypassing some islands occupied by the enemy – leaving them to starve for the Japanese no longer had control of the air or sea. ('Island hopping' would not be the correct expression.) Crippled by a lack of fuel, their most secret codes broken by the Allies, the Japanese were in desperate straits although the truth continued to be hidden from them.

The increasingly frequent American air raids over Hong Kong gave us every encouragement. We knew they were destroying Japanese shipping, oil depots and docks.

On 6th August 1945, as we were devouring our pitiful breakfasts, two American Superfort aircraft appeared in the sky above Hiroshima. Seventy-five hours later it was Nagasaki's turn.

Two days later, a ration truck pulled into Shamshuipo. One of the POWs found a scrap of paper hidden in a crack in the truck's floor; he hid it in his pocket. A short while later stories were circulating among us that a strange new bomb was devastating Japanese cities. On 9th August *The Hong Kong News* published a Tokyo syndicated report announcing the Vatican's condemnation of the atom bomb.

On Wednesday 15th August Watanabi, the kind Lutheran minister, slyly told a few that the war was over. That same day some Portuguese ladies, seeing some of us marching back to Shamshuipo after a working detail, came close. They were seemingly engaged in conversation and suddenly raised their voices. "It's all over," they exclaimed.

On the following day *The Hong Kong News* announced, "Peace signed: His Imperial Majesty Broadcasts to Nation: Imperial Rescript Issued." Lieutenant Colonel Simon White Royal Scots stepped forward at the morning roll call on the 16th and told the Japanese officer that there would be no count of his men as the war was over. The Japanese replied that he knew nothing of this. White showed him the newspaper. A few hours later a truck delivered toilet rolls to us! Arming themselves with iron bed-legs, a party of POWs drove to the Japanese HQ in the Peninsula Hotel and loaded up with food. Gradually our guards disappeared. Two lorries arrived with three dead oxen. We had never seen so much meat for four and a half years.

We held a victory parade in Shamshuipo on the 18th. A White Ensign was run up the mast; our band played *Abide with me* and we sang *God Save the King*.

"It was the most impressive ceremony I have ever attended," noted the Canadian, Captain H L White. "Hearts were too full for much singing; many tears were in evidence. I couldn't keep them back. We all realized more than ever before the meaning of freedom. We also flew the Stars and Stripes and Russian, Dutch, Chinese and Free French flags, all made from coloured rags. Some Indians came over from their camp, and it was very touching to see them greet their British officers with real big hugs. Some wives with their children arrived from Stanley to meet their husbands. It was so moving I couldn't watch."[9] On Victoria Peak someone had hoisted the Union Flag.

There now began a strange period when we waited with growing impatience for an Allied fleet to appear. Discipline was difficult to maintain. Some ex-POWs crept out at night to seek the company of Chinese girls, one of whom was smuggled into Shamshuipo: there was quite a queue for her.

The few Japanese we saw saluted us and bowed before approaching us. During these weeks the Chinese looted everything worth taking.

Two American Dakota aircraft flew over our camp, dropping large boxes of food which burst when they hit the ground. They were eventually followed by an RAF plane which came very low over our camp. The pilot dropped a brown envelope; it was marked 'OHMS' and contained a letter signed by Admiral C H J Harcourt. It told us that our location was known; and we should remain there. We reluctantly did so.

At 10.00 a.m. on 30th August we saw HMS *Swiftsure* approach the harbour led by minesweepers. Beyond were cruisers, an aircraft carrier and submarines. It was a large fleet.

Several days later I was invited on board HMS *Euryalus* where I had my first pink gin for over three and a half years. I saw on the wardroom table *Country Life* with its pictures of British villages and farmsteads at their best. It brought tears to my eyes.

Notes

1. Interview Scriven with OL.
2. Young, A N, *China and the Helping Hand*, Cambridge MA: Harvard University Press, 1963, p. 418.
3. WO 208 3260 HN 04176, p. 45.
4. Ride, Edwin, *BAAG: Hong Kong Resistance 1941–1945*, Oxford: OUP, 1981.
5. Letter Wallis to OL.
6. Statement by W J Anderson, PRO Archives Hong Kong CR 7676/45.
7. Alden, D, *Charles R Boxer*, Lisbon: Fundação Oriente, 2001, p. 181.
8. Interview Bird with OL, and report dated September 1945.
9. Capt. H L White's diary.

CHAPTER 21

Sinister Developments: Stanley Internment Camp, the Japanese Occupation and the Privileged Nightmare

I gradually heard of the horrors faced by those imprisoned in Stanley Civilian Internment Camp. The internees had been moved there from 21st January 1942 onwards. Rather like our arrival at Shamshuipo, everything was initially chaotic at Stanley.

"Four of us were given a cold, grey cell with no beds or furniture. We huddled together and couldn't sleep, so we talked long into the night about our husbands and wedding days, and how wonderful life would be when we were released. I thought to myself, 'We can't live like this – we will die,'" recalls Mrs Topsy Man, whose husband had so distinguished himself preventing the Japanese breaking into Victoria during the fighting.

"Teamwork counted for most," wrote another internee. "The American community was small enough to function as a single entity and it set the pace, while the British community was initially divided by class, occupation and prejudice." One portly matron, watching a gang building a store, was most impressed and announced, "Isn't it fortunate that the Americans have so many members of the working class in their camp!"

Three autonomous groups quickly formed – 2,325 British, 290 Americans and 60 Dutch. Each group had its own quarters and committees which had control over such matters as billeting, assignment of duties in work details, sanitation, medical clinics and education.

After Hong Kong's surrender the Governor, Sir Mark Young, had been held incommunicado in a place unknown to us. His responsibilities fell on the Colonial Secretary, F C Gimson, who had the misfortune to arrive in the Colony from Ceylon the day before the Japanese invasion.

Gimson believed it imperative to maintain the Government in being, and issued orders to the internees that no official should take instructions from the Japanese except through him. He started by writing "in a language scarcely diplomatic", protesting at the squalid and inhuman conditions in which the internees had to live in the Chinese 'hotels' before the move to Stanley. The letter resulted in his immediate arrest and imprisonment. On being transferred to Stanley three months after the other internees, he was dismayed to find the former Hong Kong Government was regarded most unfavourably for failing to have made better preparation before the Japanese attack and for refusing to surrender once resistance seemed futile.

All schemes for the pooling of cash and personal food supplies were opposed by Sir Atholl MacGregor, the Chief Justice, on the grounds that the whole principle of private property was involved and "endless litigation" would result. The Americans were more sensible and pooled many of their resources.

Fortunately the camp at Stanley lay alongside a pretty bay, and "the green trees, flowers, wide spaces, warm sky and friendly sea were things to feed our souls, if not our bodies," recorded an American. A healthier site for the camp could not have been chosen. The accommodation consisted partly of the residential quarters of the former European, Indian and Chinese prison officers and their families. Other buildings included those used before the war as a sanatorium, hospital and canteen which had all formed part of the Hong Kong prison. A former school, St Stephen's College, and staff bungalows also lay within the camp.

There were sufficient teachers to educate all the children. Many youngsters forgot what 'outside' was like; it seemed to them a kind of fairyland, full of abundance, except for food. One child saw a horse and assumed it was a big dog. Another could not imagine what a river looked like. Yet their education may not have suffered unduly. After liberation, five of the older ones entered British universities.

Men and women were not separated into two camps as happened in some other places occupied by the Japanese. Morale may thus have been enhanced though morals were jeopardised. The cemetery proved to be a popular place for lovers. The Japanese authorities issued an order on the lines of "Sexual intercourse is prohibited except between husband and wife or close friends."

Religion played an important part in camp life. There were 20 different denominations represented. The Anglicans, Roman Catholics and Christian Scientists all held separate services. The thin pages of the prayer books were found to be excellent for cigarette paper: guards had to be posted during services to ensure that the pages were not torn out.

The internees endured a starvation diet which led to malnutrition and discord. As the years dragged by, conditions became harsher and a growing moral and physical deterioration was evident. Welcome parcels were received by some, due to the courageous generosity of some Chinese, Indians and Portuguese still living in Hong Kong and not interned because the Japanese wanted their co-operation.

Very controversially, Gimson did not endorse the principle of repatriation. He felt that the British internees were British subjects on British territory, therefore they had no claim to transfer from one section of the Empire to another. He also believed that repatriation would weaken the case for Britain retaining Hong Kong as a Colony after the war. Much later he admitted that he might have misjudged the situation.

The repatriation of 1,500 people in the Far East, including the British at Stanley, was prevented by General MacArthur, commanding the southwest Pacific area, and by the Australian Government, because they would have been exchanged for 330 Japanese merchant seamen interned in Australia. These Japanese were familiar with the Australian coastline and harbours. Some of them were probably spies before the war.

Yet in June 1942 the American civilians were repatriated in exchange for Japanese interned in America. They subsequently publicised the plight of the British and Dutch left behind.

Dr P S Selwyn-Clarke, the former Director of Medical Services, had still not been interned because the Japanese had confidence in him. He was allowed to visit the camp at least once a week, providing he gave no news and discussed only medical and relief matters. Everyone knew that some improvements in diet and the provision of medicines and clothing were the result of his untiring efforts. His arrest on a charge of treason was a culminating blow: the lifeline of extra foodstuffs was severed. Sixteen months later, he was given the light sentence of three years' imprisonment because there was no evidence against him.

The discovery of the wireless set in the internment camp and the link to the BAAG which led to so many tragic deaths have already been described.

Fourteen internees were killed when they were bombed by the Americans. By resolution the internees stated that, while the incident was most tragic and unfortunate, no bitter feelings were held against the Americans, who were seeking out Japanese anti-aircraft batteries.

Two weeks before Admiral Harcourt reached Hong Kong, Gimson, hearing rumours of the surrender, told Lieutenant Kadowake, the Camp Commandant, that unless there was a formal announcement, serious incidents might arise if the guards continued to adopt their usual attitude of arrogance and violence. Kadowake replied: "His Majesty the Emperor has taken into consideration the terms of the Potsdam Conference and has ordered hostilities to cease." Seeing the bewilderment in Gimson's face, Kadowake added: "In other words you've won; we've lost."

Gimson left Stanley and met the senior British officers at Shamshuipo Camp. He was, in turn, one of the first to meet Admiral Harcourt, who reported to London, "Gimson and his gallant band of ex-POWs and internees had already got going and continued to give very good service until some of them literally cracked up, not yet being fit."[1]

In August 1995 Oliver Lindsay took a large Royal British Legion Pilgrimage to the former Stanley Internment Camp. After a moving service at the Sai Wan cemetery, we had lunch in the prison officers' club, looking forward to the former internees in our party telling us of their reminiscences in the precise buildings in which they had been imprisoned. It would have been an exceptional experience for all of us. Alas! Typhoon warning No. Three had just been hoisted. We had not even finished lunch before we were bussed back to our hotel. Perhaps it was just as well we didn't eat too much for a few of our party fell seriously ill with food poisoning attributable, apparently, to lack of hygiene in the club's kitchens.

* * * * *

The Japanese Occupation of Hong Kong

When I was first interned in Shamshuipo, I saw a steady trickle of Chinese moving north each day, returning to China. As months went by, it became apparent that fewer and fewer were left in the Colony.

It was only after my release that I could gradually piece together what 'Japan's New Order' in Hong Kong had amounted to.

The Japanese administration's first priority had been to reduce the Chinese population to avoid the responsibility of feeding them. In the face of starvation, unemployment, reduced educational and other social services, over one million Chinese fled to China during the occupation, leaving only 650,000 in Hong Kong by 1945. Many unfortunates died on the way, never reaching their destination, thereby doing untold damage to Japanese propaganda.

Several hundred of the more destitute were herded into large junks and abandoned on Lantau Island, which had no water.

Crime rose dramatically in view of the semi-starvation; draconian punishment kept it within bounds. Periodically there were mass executions of thieves, who were first made to dig their own graves. The Chinese whom I had seen executed at the water's edge in 1942 had probably come from the nearby prison, which was overflowing. A Catholic nun who was released from the Internment Camp in July 1943 remembers: "We saw a Chinese man tied up in a cage which was three foot high and three foot square. He was kneeling and begging for mercy from a Japanese soldier who was amusing himself by poking a stick through the bars. We were told that the man was going to have his head cut off."[2] (Just as terrorists in Iraq behead some of those whom they have kidnapped.)

Father Granelli, an Italian priest who fled to Macao, reported that "Colonel Eguchi, the Director General of Medical Services, beheaded his cook at a dinner party. Eguchi was annoyed because the dinner was late and so bullied the cook before cutting off his head with his sword. A Portuguese lady who saw the whole performance had to go to bed for a week."[3]

After the British surrender, nearly all Allied military equipment, ammunition, fuel, medicines, food and other stores were shipped methodically and efficiently to Japan together with any movable booty including trucks and cars. My little Morris was broken up for scrap metal, I fear.

Chinese labour was paid in rice; prices soared. Every commodity was strictly rationed and food queues were evident everywhere.

The Japanese set great store by hygiene. Hands had to be washed in a basin of antiseptic on entering a public building; feet were wiped on a mat saturated in the same liquid. The Japanese language was enforced in the few schools which continued to function.

Despite all these difficulties, life in Hong Kong went on as it did in cities in Europe under German occupation. It was not Japanese policy to antagonise Chinese or Indians for there were vague plans for Hong Kong and India to have an eventual role in Japan's Greater East Asia Co-prosperity Sphere, and this would need the conquered races' co-operation.

The Chinese had no alternative other than to co-operate with the Japanese if they were to survive. Even so, the degree of collaboration would seem to have been no greater than in German-occupied territories in Europe, excluding Guernsey. (Incidentally the British made no attempt to defend Guernsey, choosing an 'open city' policy there. Hong Kong internees would have liked to have seen a similar policy in the Colony.)

Much has been written about Chinese collaboration; people such as Sir Robert Kotewall Keung, a former member of the Hong Kong Legislative Council, and Sir Shousan Chow were vilified after the war for allegedly co-operating with the enemy. It was suggested that they should be stripped of their knighthoods, just as Professor Anthony Blunt, the Russian spy, had his removed by the Queen in 1979.

The key point, however, is that both Sir Robert and Sir Shousan had been formally requested to work with the Japanese by the leading members of the former Hong Kong Government. Within a week of our surrender, R A C North, Secretary for Chinese Affairs, J A Fraser, Defence Secretary, and C G Alabaster, Attorney-General, had called on them and specifically asked them to promote friendly relations between Chinese and Japanese, and to do their best to restore public order and preserve internal security since the British were powerless. Moreover, some wealthy Chinese were secretly passing funds to Dr Selwyn-Clarke, and others after his arrest, for the POWs and internees.

Racing at Happy Valley was restarted, but the horses frequently collapsed during the races due to starvation; eventually the course was turned into a vegetable patch.

The Anglican St John's Cathedral was used by the Japanese as a stable. Dr Charles Harth, a German Jewish refugee, enabled services to continue in the Anglican Bishop's House. He was a tower of strength, although before the war some British thought he was a German spy.

Valtorta, the Italian Roman Catholic Bishop of Hong Kong, was given $50,000 by the Pope to buy food and clothing for the internees. He spent it as best he could to help us all.

As Allied submarines sank more Japanese ships, Hong Kong became increasingly destitute and isolated. "Fear lay upon the town like an impenetrable fog, hope seemed dead and deliverance far away. At intervals a few tramcars rumbled along Victoria, Hong Kong's capital. They were continually halted by American air raids," recalls one eyewitness.

The Japanese Governor of Hong Kong was Lieutenant General Rensuke Isogai. He had an undeserved reputation for good living and geisha parties, whereas he preferred to be studying calligraphy and walking in his garden in his slippers listening to the croaking of bullfrogs. He was quite ineffective; it was the Military Police who wielded the power. Government House had been badly damaged before the war when air raid tunnels had been dug in the rock beneath its foundations. It was gradually rebuilt as a tiered and turreted east-west hybrid vaguely reminiscent of Japanese palaces and the Imperial Hotel in Tokyo. Its completion coincided with the Japanese surrender.

Within one month of the Japanese capitulation, trains, ferries, telephones, electric power, lighting, docks and wharves were all working once more, albeit on a reduced scale. The corpses found rotting in the streets were buried; the filthy hospitals cleaned up; rice, fuel, wood and vegetables were imported. Trade rapidly resumed. Over the next five months 250,000 Chinese flocked back into the Colony which had staged such a remarkable recovery. Hong Kong's Chinese, encouraged by this restoration, expressed no wish to be part of China.

Chiang Kai-shek wanted his representative to take the Japanese surrender in Hong Kong, just as he asked for all the Japanese war material found there. Prime Minister Attlee appealed to President Truman for help; he promptly gave it. Chiang Kai-shek had never made formal claim to Hong Kong and appeared satisfied that he could use the Colony's port to redeploy his troops prior to his unsuccessful campaign against the Communists. Japanese ships and transport captured by the British in the Colony were given to him. The deadlock was therefore broken and the formal surrender took place in Government House on 16th September.

The British fleet took so long to reach us because Attlee, the War Office and indeed all the Allies did not anticipate the relatively quick surrender after the atom bombs were dropped.

* * * * *

The Privileged Nightmare

During these weeks, following the news reaching us in Shamshuipo POW Camp that the war was over, I wondered what had happened to General Maltby. I had considerable admiration for him; he had stood up to the bullying enemy so well on our behalf in the camp. It is not for me to judge some of the events in Hong Kong, but I did have an insight into General Maltby's problems over the captive years. He was indeed a great man.

I discovered subsequently that he and the other senior officers from Hong Kong had been sent to Shirakawa in Formosa. Lieutenant General S J M Wainwright, together with A E Percival and Sir Lewis Heath from Malaya, were already there.

Sir Mark Young was also in Formosa. Following his surrender of the Colony on Christmas Day 1941, he had been treated with humiliation despite the fact that, or perhaps because, he was the King's representative and former Commander in Chief. In February 1942 Private J Waller of the Middlesex Regiment was sent to the Peninsula Hotel to become his batman. "He called me John. To my mortification, when he wanted us to start doing press-ups together, he could do ten more than me. The following day, we were flown to Formosa. I had never flown before," recalls Waller, "and Sir Mark seemed mildly surprised when I asked him where the parachutes were. We sat between two Japs who vomited continuously into their hats as the weather was bad." [4] As usual Sir Mark was quite imperturbable just as, throughout the shelling, mortaring and machine-gun fire, he had been found by Maltby's ADC inspiring people to keep going, when the Japanese were closing in on Victoria.

The former Governor was moved on to Shanghai where Waller managed to smuggle meat to him. It was given to them by British awaiting internment there. But Sir Mark refused to eat the meat as it was not available to other prisoners. In September 1942 they were flown to Formosa to be joined by Maltby, Wallis and other senior officers from Hong Kong and Singapore.

They were shocked to hear of the final days in the battle for Singapore. Armed deserters forced their way onto ships which were evacuating women and children. Two Commanding Officers of units which melted away had claimed that during the battle they could scarcely lay their hands on 100 men. Yet each unit possessed almost 800 men in captivity, having suffered few casualties.[5]

In October 1944 the Governors of Hong Kong, Malaya, the Netherlands East Indies and Sumatra, with the most senior officers, were moved to Japan and marched to Bappu. They saw three aircraft carriers at anchor in the bay.

The prisoners spent several delightful days in a small tourist hotel there. "Another boon," recalls Brigadier T Massy Beresford who had been captured in Singapore, "was that we were able to indulge in hot sulphur baths which were 20 feet wide and five feet deep. We were startled when the hotel girls jumped in and rubbed us down."

They were sent to South Korea and then on to the bleak Manchurian village of Sheng Tai Tun, close to the Gobi Desert. It was freezing cold and the prisoners' teeth clattered like castanets. Morale soared when Red Cross parcels arrived. Moreover, news reached them that the Allies had advanced to the Rhine and Japan was being heavily bombed.

On 20th May 1945 the Governors and senior officers were next moved to Mukden in Manchuria to work in a factory. Life was hard there; 200 Americans had died in the camp during the first Winter.

In early August 1945 the POWs were seriously alarmed to hear that haversack rations were being prepared for them. "This meant an imminent move to some remote encampment," recalled Brigadier Wallis. "None of us could have marched more than a mile, and we knew that thousands of Americans had perished on Japanese forced marches in the Philippines. Intense uncertainty descended upon us."[6]

* * * * *

That week I was still in Shamshuipo Camp. A rumour was spread to us by some of the guards that if there was a surrender or an American attack, all of us would be put in the specially prepared basements in tall buildings which would then be blown up; the Japanese, we were told, would then claim that we had been killed by American bombs.

Many of us believed by early August 1945 that the Allies would triumph, but we were far from certain that we would live to see the liberation. Major Charles Boxer, Commander J N Craven RN, Lieutenant H C Dixon RNZNVR and Commander R S Young RN, now imprisoned in Canton, were surreptitiously warned by one well-meaning Indian guard that the Japanese were preparing to kill all their prisoners. This may well have been true. But on 6th August the atomic bomb was dropped on Hiroshima as already related. Three days later Russia attacked the Japanese in Manchuria and elsewhere. The second atom bomb was also dropped on Nagasaki. The Japanese military prevaricated and seemed determined to fight on. The Supreme War Council and Cabinet remained divided, incapable of recognising the inevitability of Japan's defeat.

On 15th August Emperor Hirohito announced that "the war did not turn in our favour... the new outrageous bombs used by the enemy caused incessant bloodshed of innocent people and havoc which cannot be stopped." Just as relevant to us, he ordered all military forces to lay down their arms forthwith to "endure the unendurable and bear the unbearable". His orders were obeyed to the letter. He dispatched members of his family to different battle zones to ensure that was the case.

All the lives of the POWs and internees in the Far East were immediately saved, just as the lives of the many thousands preparing to invade Japan were not endangered.

Many years later in Bath Abbey, Oliver Lindsay heard a Bishop in the pulpit announce that it would have been better if the atom bombs had been dropped on green fields in Japan. "Anyone with dissenting views can discuss them with me afterwards over coffee," he graciously added, not anticipating the strong views Oliver expressed to him after the service! It took two atom bombs and the Russian invasion to bring Hirohito, if not the others, to his senses. A vast explosion amidst "green fields" would not have proved effective to save our lives!

Notes

1. The Colonial Office files CO 980 59 HN 00493, CO 980/53 and 129 590/18 HN 00152 have details on the Stanley Internment Camp. Gimson's story is recorded in his *Personal Impressions*. See also CO 129 590/18 HN 00152. All the above are in the Public Record Office (National Archives). See also *At the Going Down of the Sun*, Chapter 4.
2. *South China Morning Post*, 4.6.50.
3. CO 129 591/4 HN 00035.
4. Letter Waller to OL.
5. Interview Brig. T Massy Beresford with OL. The Brigadier's lengthy reminiscences, read by Oliver Lindsay beforehand, are in RHQ The Royal Green Jackets, with a time embargo preventing their being read for many years.
6. Interview Brig. C Wallis with OL in Aldershot in 1978.

CHAPTER 22

The Calm after Thunder: Returning Home

On 10th September 1945 I boarded *The Empress of Australia* bound for Manila after almost precisely five years in Hong Kong.

I arrived there and spent three weeks in a US transit camp, where some 25,000 American Servicemen had been getting ready to invade Japan. The American camp was something I had never imagined. There were four films to choose from every night showing on open-air screens, and almost every kind of facility. We were issued with Australian blankets, one of which I still possess.

The approach to Manila up the 50-mile Gulf was dramatic since there was line after line of American ships, all loaded to the gunwales, all carefully placed for the coming invasion of Japan. It was the largest assembly of shipping I have ever seen or am likely to see.

When we arrived at the head of the sound after some six hours, we were given a berth adjoining one of the few undamaged quays. Around us were masts and funnels of ships projecting above the water. These were Japanese ships which had been sunk in the capture of Manila.

The Americans had provided some 40 ambulances for those seriously ill. But before the ambulances arrived on the quay the American Marine Musicians struck up *God Save the King*. All cheered, and the American national anthem was then played. Very few of the ambulances were needed as the Royal Navy had earlier brought the hospital ship *Oxfordshire* to Hong Kong and she had collected those who were in a serious condition.

After about two weeks I boarded a P37 American transport, a 6,000-ton landing ship designed with many others to capture the Pacific islands one by one. On board were 2,000 Americans and 40 British and Canadians. We all had mattresses. There were no complaints. We were all going home. I need hardly say the food was excellent; the galleys never stopped serving us. It was the first time I had seen food being served on a tray with indentations for all the different courses. After a three-week voyage on the P37 we arrived off Honolulu. At the entrance to what had become one of the world's greatest naval bases was anchored a British aircraft carrier with the White Ensign flying at her stern – a most moving sight.

We spent the day on board the P37 as the Admiral at Pearl Harbor had prohibited our landing. Our Captain made amends for our disappointment by asking the ship's company to gather round the main hatch at 2.00 p.m. Right on time he posted 40 Marines around the hatch; a few minutes later Hawaiian dancers in grass skirts arrived to everybody's delight.

Just before arriving in Seattle a message came through to the Captain that we would be diverted to Esquimault (the Canadian naval base in the Pacific), near Vancouver. The reason was that America had withdrawn lease lend and there was no money to send us home across the States!

On arrival in Esquimault the names of the first POWs to arrive were read out in turn before each of us went down the gangway. It was dark, but floodlights were on and we were being televised. We saw a large group on the quay below and were greeted individually with cheers and clapping.

That night we were taken to a transit camp on the outskirts of Victoria, where we stayed for about ten days. The camp was still there 35 years later when I visited it, being used as part of the University of Victoria. We then took the Canadian Pacific train from Vancouver to Halifax, the first POW train to make the four-day journey; the Canadian Government had given the officers first-class accommodation. The next day we climbed up and over the Rockies; the scenery was beautiful. In the evening we steamed into Edmonton for a half hour stop. We had gone to sleep wearing pyjamas for the first time for many years. Suddenly a band struck up outside the carriage, *God Save the King*. The station and the town were lit up because everybody was celebrating. A number of girls came into our carriage and pulled us out on the platform in our pyjamas, and started to dance with us. If you have not seen or been with a girl for four years, when something like that happens, you have an extraordinary feeling. The Mayor of Edmonton was there with his gold chain of office while the ladies served tea and cakes. It was an amazing experience.

The next day we crossed the prairies to Winnipeg, deciding to be well prepared and remaining dressed, ready for the reception which we saw as the train drew in. The people of Winnipeg had turned out with the Mayor and a band. Whenever we stopped, whatever the hour, however isolated the outpost, local residents were waiting on the station to give us chocolates, hot coffee, buns and fruit. On the third day we arrived at Montreal, where some Servicemen made a good profit selling their worthless Hong Kong military yen notes to the Canadians as mementos.

Going across Canada we met trains going in the opposite direction, bringing Canadian Servicemen back from Europe. They shouted, "Don't go back. They are watering the beer. England is finished."

Finally we arrived at Halifax. I was able to telephone my mother and asked what I should bring her. "We would love a tin of butter," was her reply.

We waited two weeks to fill the *Ile de France*, a large French ocean liner. Great was the excitement when it was announced that a Royal Army Pay Corps team was about to pay us. Equally great was the disappointment when the 'team' turned out to be a bespectacled Lance Corporal with sufficient funds to pay only 25 men, let alone a couple of thousand of us. Notices were everywhere on the ship telling us not to steal the towels. The POWs retaliated by numbering in Japanese during the ship's boat drills, and released several men from the ship's cells.

On arrival at Southampton on 31st October there was no reception and no Mayor, as there had been at Manila, Esquimault, Edmonton and Winnipeg. There was no Garden Party for us: it had to wait 50 years to be put right by The Queen on VJ Day 1995.

I had taken five and a half years to circumnavigate the globe, leaving from Platform 2 at Woking station and returning to Platform 2 from Southampton. My expenses had been met by the British Government, the Government of Hong Kong, the Emperor of Japan, the President of the United States of America, the Prime Minister of Canada and finally the British Government once again!

"It was misty and a very moving sight when this great ship came in," wrote my father. "Freda and I had been lucky to secure a pass for the quayside. We spotted John at the aft rail and he spotted us. As she tied up, gangways went down, a band struck up welcoming music and John was quickly down the gangway to us at last, after five years. Praise and thanksgiving welled up in our hearts as we welcomed him, and then had to release him for formalities to be gone through."

After spending several days in a hut in Southampton, I received a railway ticket for Woking, the station nearest to my home. And that was my discharge!

* * * * *

The healthier Canadian POWs were embarked on HMCS *Prince Robert*, the same merchant cruiser which had escorted them to Hong Kong 45 months earlier. Thirty-one who were seriously ill were carried aboard the *Oxfordshire*. The remainder paraded to board the *Empress of Australia*. Captain S M Banfill of the Royal Rifles remembers how "the Senior Medical Officer shouted 'Attention! Right turn.' Then he looked at the emaciated, ragged men and said quietly, 'I won't say, 'Quick march' but toddle on the best you can'." [1]

At Manila, the Canadian Shamshuipo survivors were reunited with their comrades who had been imprisoned in Japan. "Nearly every man who came home had physical and psychological problems of one kind or another, and many of them would suffer the effects for the rest of their lives," concluded Brereton Greenhous in National Defence HQ, Ottawa.[2]

Many of the Canadian veterans "had returned with undetected dysentery, and as there was only one doctor in Canada with experience in diagnosing the disease, these cases were neither identified nor treated. One of the more unfortunate results of this was the contraction of dysentery by wives and medical personnel."[3] After considerable political pressure, by 1976 the Canadian Government "generously gave Hong Kong veterans with assessed disabilities an additional 30% pension. Each man therefore collected a minimum 80% pension." The British who were imprisoned in Hong Kong receive no special pension unless they can prove disability. Health in the three camps was governed by the gradual weakening of the prisoners. The doctors who were with us said that if the war had lasted another six months many prisoners would have died. The rations were of course inadequate for health, comprising rice twice a day, a watery vegetable soup and occasionally some unexpected addition.

In my case, and it was probably fairly common, I developed beriberi towards the end of our imprisonment and from then on found myself considerably weaker when walking round the camp. In the Autumn of 1943 beriberi affected my sight. I understand that without a healthy diet eyes become weaker after some months, and this happened to me. Francis Rossini, a POW with us who was an eye specialist from Harley Street in London, collected a small party and each afternoon read to us some pages from a book.

Beriberi is a deficiency disease resulting from sub-standard nutrition, including vitamin deficiencies. The usual symptom was burning pain in the feet. Beriberi also caused my legs to blow up like balloons, and my joints began to ache. I had one injection of thiamine, which was all that could be spared. Was the drug smuggled into the camp by BAAG? I never discovered. I needed thiamine injections for 20 years after the war.

I expect that many British POWs were suffering in the same way as me and the Canadians. Gradually they joined me before we all sailed on the *Ile de France*. It was interesting hearing of their experiences.

Corporal H F Linge of the Royal Army Ordnance Corps, who had ended up as a POW in Japan, was astonished by the American hospitality in Manila: "We were issued with 40 cigarettes, five cigars and two cans of beer a day. When an American Sergeant discovered we were queuing up for a second free chocolate bar, he issued each man a whole box of them. We eventually embarked on HMS *Implacable* where everything was done to help us."[4]

For Staff Sergeant J Winspear and other ex-POWs, the highlight was witnessing the Japanese surrender on USS *Missouri*. They were then assembled on the flight deck of the carrier which steamed slowly round the great battleships, cruisers and destroyers of the Pacific Fleet, every space being manned by sailors who cheered the POWs enthusiastically.

Major A R Colquhoun, a Gunner, also remembers Esquimault well. "The scenery was lovely; we were accommodated in what had been the local golf club over which a Union Jack flew; there was a waiter in a white jacket with a tray under his arm. We were penniless and sat in the sunshine while nice Canadian ladies plied us with tea and amiable conversation, and sewed on our campaign medals. It had never occurred to me that I was entitled to any medal, let alone three."[5]

While I had been dispatched to Woking, others went to Waterloo Station. A uniformed chauffeur employed by the Duke of Grafton's son drove Winspear through devastated, bombed-out East London where disillusionment set in: "We had been given a ration card which entitled us to double rations for six weeks, and we had to apply for them on the same form as a pregnant woman. One of the form's questions was:

'How long were you confined?' I put down 1,324 days. I got the double ration, but a sour note crept in when the manager of the local Co-op would not accept my coupons."

Lieutenant Commander Young, who had been imprisoned in shocking conditions with Major Boxer in Canton, also arrived at Waterloo Station and "saw a taxi draw up which I tried to enter, but a gruff policeman said 'can't you see there's a queue? These people have been waiting an hour or more. Go to the bottom end.' Quite exhausted, I sat on my suitcase and replied: 'I have been waiting five years.' The couple who had just got into the taxi must have realised who the thin, forlorn creature was, and they invited me in, and fed me on the way with biscuits and tea from a thermos. I was a little surprised to find out how bitter the feeling was against the Japanese; to my mind everything that had happened was a clash of Western and Eastern civilisation and culture."

Major Colquhoun was sent to a Rehabilitation Centre which was in a stately home in Kent. "After changing for dinner, we saw a roaring fire, waiters with silver trays and a pompous full colonel in scarlet mess-kit, medals and spurs. The whole idea was to re-create the atmosphere of a pre-war Regimental Guest Night. After dinner and the Loyal Toast, the Colonel announced that he was in a position to guarantee us an appropriate posting of our choice and we should give our name to a waiter if we had any psychological problems.

"All this high-grade flannel induced me to see the Colonel's highly qualified psychoanalyst. I was ushered into a cosy room where I expected to be questioned on a couch and encouraged to think about sex. Instead, over a decanter of Cockburn 1898 port and a brace of Churchillian cigars, an elderly man listened to my story and said, 'My advice to you, old boy, is that you should go to Ireland for a holiday; their steaks are excellent and their Guinness is good, too. You do the paying, but I could probably wangle you a couple of weeks' leave.' So much for the psychoanalysis. Next day I told the qualified career planner that I would like to be posted to a Field Artillery unit in the south of England. 'Excellent, old boy,' he replied. 'Would Southampton suit you? Good! Consider it done.' We shook hands warmly. A week later a War Office letter arrived, posting me to an anti-aircraft battery in the far north of England."

Private Waller, the former batman to Sir Mark Young, had also been on the *Ile de France* with me. He reached an Infantry Depot at Amersham where he was told he must remain until he had been "processed". "I had already been processed at Okinawa, Manila and

Halifax and I had had enough. And so I went absent without leave," he remembers. Eventually he returned to the Depot where "Everyone thought us prisoners of the Japs were all a bit bonkers and so we were given plenty of understanding. I was quickly discharged; a Major drove me to the station."

Sir Mark Young and Major General Maltby had been flown back to England much earlier, on 5th September. Sir Mark had immediately visited Waller's son at school and given him a mouth organ. During the war, Mrs Waller, who never knew for certain that her husband was still alive, received food parcels from Lady Young. Sir Mark never fully recovered his health, as was the case with some regular soldiers who, to their bitter disappointment, were too ill to continue with their Service careers. Then there were the oldest ex-POWs who were told that, after four years and nine months as a POW, there was no future employment for them in the Services. To his great dismay, Major General Maltby fell into this category.

* * * * *

Much is known about the British and Canadians, but virtually nothing has appeared in print about the repatriation of the loyal Rajputs and Punjabis who fought in Hong Kong with us.

The Indian survivors from the POW camp sailed in SS *Takliwa* from Kowloon after the British and Canadian POWs had departed. They were commanded by Major Kampla Prasad and were accompanied by Captain B A Hurd, the Adjutant, and Captain J L Flynn, the ship's Quartermaster. Both were British officers serving in the Indian Army. The other British officers had been sent to Britain independently, not that many of them had survived the war.

After calling at Singapore for supplies, "SS *Takliwa* took a short cut through the Andaman and Nicobar Islands. She tore her bottom out on a reef at about 11.00 p.m. and caught fire," recalls Flynn. "Some life-boats were panic-launched and sank; others caught fire. It was a really dangerous situation. The Indians were badly frightened. Fortunately HMS *Sainfoin* arrived and rescued everyone. But we lost all our possessions. The Royal Navy were marvellous, found space for us, giving us their clothing and cigarettes. They took us through a bad hurricane to Madras and cleared up after the Indians were very sick. On arrival there, we were given an advance of pay and Red Cross amenities. A 'Released

Prisoner of War and Internees Unit' warned us for psychological testing and for retraining for the post-POW changed world." It would appear that they had a better reception than the POWs reaching England!

"I would estimate," continues Flynn, "that of the 2/14 Punjabis only about six or seven Indians were recommended for dishonourable discipline for cooperating with the Japanese, while maybe 20 helped them under duress. In any event, all courts martial were later quashed for political reasons."

Most of the Japanese POWs after the war were moved to Shamshuipo Barracks, which we had just vacated. It is estimated that there were between 7,000 and 10,000 of them. Like some of us in 1942, they were put to work improving Kai Tak airfield, under robust Commando guards. They also swept the streets and removed rubble, "a very suitable job for the Japanese who were responsible in the main for the damage done." After some months they were shipped home, along with their Korean and Taiwanese auxiliaries. The hard core of suspected perpetrators of war crimes had already been rounded up, as will be discussed in the penultimate chapter.

Thus it was that the former internees and the British, Canadian, Indian and Japanese ex-POWs returned home, some to uncertain futures.

We had bid good-bye in Hong Kong to the brave Chinese civilians, some ex-internees and the gallant men of the Hong Kong Volunteer Defence Corps who had truly been fighting as Volunteers for their homes in the Crown Colony in 1941. It is to those we left there that our gratitude should be expressed. They made the Colony such a prosperous, cheerful, vibrant and safe place to live for so many post-war years and thereafter, when wars were raging in turn in China, Korea, Malaya, Indonesia and Vietnam. By comparison, Hong Kong became a haven of peace and a "vision of delight" once more, as those who lived in the Colony will agree.

Notes

1. Greenhous, B, *"C" Force to Hong Kong: A Canadian Catastrophe 1941–1945*, Canadian War Museum Historical Publication No. 30, 1997, p. 316.
2. Ibid. p. 148
3. Vincent, C, *No Reason Why*, Ontario: Canada's Wings, 1981, p. 238.
4. Letter Linge to OL.
5. Interview Colquoun with OL.

CHAPTER 23

New Worlds to Find: An Architect At Last

"He looked a skeleton," my father wrote about me when I arrived home at Chobham in early November 1945. "Diphtheria, beriberi and captivity had taken a heavy toll, but after his discharge from the Army we took him to our local GP and Sir Geoffrey Marshall, the chest specialist."

My sister Rosina had, when she left school in 1940, joined the American Ambulance service rather than accept the place already offered to her at St Hilda's College, Oxford. She took up her law studies there after the war. My parents were proud of her when they saw her drive off with her large Ford ambulance, in company with some dozen others, from Sussex Square in London en route to Reading. She was based there for some 18 months, evacuating the wounded after bombing raids in London, Southampton and other cities. From 1943 to 1945 she was based in London during the V1 and V2 attacks.

My wife Jill remembers one incident when she dived under her drawing board as the sirens sounded for a likely V2 rocket attack. The Architectural Association School had returned to London after being evacuated to Barnet and Jill joined Unit One, in the attic of a house in Bedford Square. The drawing boards lay on old wooden trestle tables. The students automatically dived for cover when the sirens went off, for most had had experience of 'doodlebugs' (V1s). These were different from V2s as they were fuel driven and when their engines 'cut out' everyone knew it would be seconds before they reached the ground with the consequential explosion. The V2s arrived silently and exploded. Luckily for Jill, on this occasion the explosion was heard some way off and the students resumed their 'yellow ochre washes'.

After gradually getting fit, I began again my diploma course at the Architectural Association and there met Jill Rowe, whom I married in June 1950. I owe so much to her.

In the following year we opened our first office in George Street in London's Marylebone district. It was one half of one room, heated by an oil stove; tea was made with an electric kettle on the floor. The telephone was shared. There was a shortage of almost everything and Building Licensing was required for any development over £500. No restaurant could charge more than five shillings for dinner (including the Savoy).

Winning a major competition was one of the best ways of founding a practice. In 1952 there were two major Royal Institute of British Architects' open competitions – one for the rebuilding of Coventry Cathedral and the other for the design of the new State Hospital, Doha. We won the latter.

My interest in health-care buildings dates back to 1935 when I went on a study tour of Scandinavian hospitals with my father, who had just been appointed as surveyor for the rebuilding of Westminster Hospital. In entering the Doha competition I had two advantages. First, I had developed a feel for climate, having experienced those five years in Hong Kong. Secondly, I had already visited the Arabian Gulf in 1951 as the architect for the Building Research Laboratories in Kuwait. I felt that the planning and elevation detailing of the State Hospital design would largely be determined by the inter-related requirements of solar control and natural ventilation. We were very fortunate to be awarded first prize and appointed architects, out of 74 entries from all over the world.

At the invitation of the State Engineer, who had flown to London for the adjudication, I flew out to Doha four days later. His Highness Sheikh Ali KBE, the Ruler of Qatar, was curious to know why I wanted more time to complete the working drawings for his new hospital. His new palace, he told me, had been marked out on the sand and work had started as soon as he had given his authority. I produced an acceptable answer whereby a separate foundation contract (the hospital being designed on a standard grid) would enable work to start on site immediately, although full working drawings took another nine months to complete. The hospital was opened in 1957 by Sheikh Ali who was presented by me with a gold key, and a national holiday was announced.

In the 1980s the office in Doha was commissioned to design and construct the new Women's Hospital and the new National Tennis and Squash complex which placed Doha on the world circuit. In 1997 the firm undertook the 3,000-seat Conference Centre on the direct instruction of the Emir, to be built in time for the MENA (Middle East and North Africa) Summit attended by the US Secretary of State, Madeleine Albright. This Conference Centre was designed and completed in eight and a half months – a record time.

On completion of the Doha State Hospital, I was invited to visit Dubai by the Ruler, HH Sheikh Rashid bin Saeed Al-Maktoum. He wanted me to prepare a town plan for Dubai. This was initiated in 1960 and revised in 1977.

My first building commission in Dubai was for the Al-Maktoum Hospital. We extended the previous single shed-like structure from 18 beds to 125. Some funds were contributed by the British Government. After undertaking a number of small projects in Dubai, I happened to be in the Majlis (the Ruler's court) in August 1966 when an oil company representative rushed in to break the news that oil had been found. He had with him a jam jar full of oil, which he presented to Sheikh Rashid. The Ruler got up and embraced everyone present. It was a marvellous experience to be there at that very moment.

Sheikh Rashid then declared to me that we could now go ahead with the development plan and hospital programme which he had long waited to put in hand. The Rashid Hospital was the first, followed by other hospitals, educational and commercial buildings. The Rashid Hospital was commenced on a loan so I had to detail every cost, right down to the cutlery and linen. When the job was finished I presented Sheikh Rashid with the final account and told him we had saved £18. He said to me in a loud voice, "Keep it!" and the whole Majlis roared with laughter.

Following a visit by HM The Queen to Dubai in 1972, HH Sheikh Rashid was inspired to give the order for a World Trade and Exhibition Centre to be constructed, and he sought my advice. At that time the New York Trade Center was only half built, and the idea of such a building was little understood outside America. I explained to Sheikh Rashid that I needed four months to research into current advances and design solutions by visiting Trade Centres then under construction around the world. Sheikh Rashid said, "Come back and see me when you are ready." This I did. When I finally presented my scheme,

Sheikh Rashid remarked, "That is not tall enough! The tower should be higher." Many people in the Majlis thought that the proposed scheme was too ambitious; few buildings in Dubai were more than three storeys high at that time. However, the tower was raised to its present height and constructed in reinforced concrete (not steel as were the Trade Center towers in New York).

In 1979 the Trade Centre was opened by HM The Queen at HH Sheikh Rashid's invitation. It was the tallest building in the Arab world from Morocco to Bombay for 20 years.

In 1984 we were successful in the design competition for HH the Ruler of Dubai's new Diwan on a prominent site on the Creek. A principal government building, this was one of the first modern buildings in the region to respect the historical tradition of the windtower/courtyard structures.

* * * * *

Our links with the Middle East grew over time. It was from Kuwait in 1955 that I became one of the first Britons to return to the great oil refinery at Abadan after its takeover by Iran three years earlier. Secretly through the reeds in a small boat, I crossed the Shatt al Arab river, an area of conflict between the British and Iraqis in the Second Gulf War. In 1957 we opened an office in Tehran which flourished until the 1977 revolution.

Once established in the Gulf I then became involved in neighbouring Oman. In 1966 I was invited to meet His Majesty Sultan Said bin Taimur at his palace in Salalah, Oman. From this initial meeting a development programme for the country emerged. The first girls' school and the foundation of a hospital was put in hand. The Ottoman Bank, located just outside the town walls of Muscat, was the first commercial building in reinforced concrete to be constructed in Oman apart from oil company buildings. My partner at this time prepared designs for the first Christian church in Oman.

I visited the Sultan regularly, both of us squatting on the floor with plans or maps spread out on the carpet in front of us. Outside the room was an armed guard. On one occasion, when the time came for us to rise, the Sultan stumbled and I instinctively put my arms around him to stop him from falling. Thinking the Sultan was being attacked, the guard rushed in with his rifle. Fortunately for me the Sultan shouted to him in Arabic to hold his fire. He then turned to me and said, "I am so sorry. My foot went to sleep."

After this I suggested it might be more convenient if we worked together at a table, and arranged for one to be sent out from London in time for our next meeting.

A regional office was established which undertook many projects over 24 years. Under His Majesty Sultan Qaboos bin Said, the pace of development in Oman increased and we were appointed to prepare a development plan for Muscat and Mutrah, and designs ranging from small tribal centres to large defence bases and commercial projects.

Expanding eastwards from Arabia, I was approached to be the architectural consultant for the 1,200-bed Kuala Lumpur General Hospital.

In 1976 we were invited to prepare a development scheme for the Royal Brunei Polo Club, which became a substantial project. This involved clearing jungle and preparing the polo fields. Buildings included grandstands, air conditioned stables and accommodation for staff and visiting teams.

While our architectural practice expanded its regional overseas offices, the UK-based firm secured a number of important projects in Britain and Europe. There followed exciting years when new projects included the complete refurbishment of the Dorchester Hotel and major work on Strangeways Prison after the riots.

In the late 1980s the practice had prepared plans and secured the commission for a comprehensive redevelopment of a 2.84-acre site in Kensington above Gloucester Road underground station which incorporated the historic Brunel railway arches of the District Line. The development comprised luxury serviced apartments, an office building, and a retail arcade with landscaped areas. Throughout the contract the District, Circle and Piccadilly tube lines remained in use. Major structural work, including 18.5-metre long beams over the railway, had to be undertaken at night. Access roads were closed to bring in the beams. Gloucester Park was officially opened by HRH the Duke of Gloucester GCVO on 29th November 1991.

During my career much has changed to produce the 'global village' and instant communications of today. In the early years I spent several days travelling to the Gulf on unreliable piston-engined planes with frequent night stops, often unexpected. Nowadays one can fly direct in a matter of hours. When I first travelled to the Arabian Gulf there were few telephones; cables, which had to be sent from cable stations by radio, were the main means of communication. Every word and punctuation mark was chargeable. Over all these years, London remained my base and I travelled laden with rolls of drawings tied up with brown paper and string, and detailed architectural models in wooden boxes which had to be placed in the aircraft hold. The reputation of the practice grew through the nurturing of personal contacts and the building of trust and confidence with clients. Promotion was principally by word of mouth. Cost control and quick responses were essential.

Jill and teams of architects and technicians undertook most of the design work in London. The hardworking professional teams and key personnel who ran the regional offices were no less essential to the success of the practice.

The full story of our architectural practice over more than 50 years, and which still continues, must be told elsewhere.[1] There were many projects and locations – and inevitably there were disappointments.

One project in particular held special significance for me. This was the 1,600-bed Tuen Mun Hospital in Hong Kong. We had won against international competition the commission for one of the largest hospitals in the world to be built in one phase in the 1980s. After 36 years I was back in Hong Kong.

Other hospitals followed in Hong Kong, some in association with Leigh & Orange: United Christian, Caritas and a technical design consultancy for one of the largest hospitals of all – the Pamela Youde with almost 2,000 beds. We were invited to enter the People's Republic of China to plan the Zhuhai Special Economic Zone near the former Portuguese colony of Macau. This was an urban development plan proposal for a new city of over 200,000 people. It incorporated a large resort complex, a city centre and commercial and industrial areas. The initial survey was carried out with my son Mark from the deck of a Chinese warship.

We should remember that the Chinese were our brave allies during the war years.

Mark had returned from the United States in 1981 with a Master's degree in architecture and urban design from Harvard University, after which he had worked for the well-known architect developer, John Portman, who was based in Atlanta, Georgia. Mark introduced Computer Aided Design, then a new and rapidly developing field, into the practice. The first practical use of the system was for the design and working drawings of Tuen Mun Hospital. The Public Works Department in Hong Kong was impressed and subsequently installed a similar system.

The Tuen Mun Hospital was the first building services contract to be awarded in Hong Kong to a Japanese contractor since 1945. Before that, the Japanese were prohibited from tendering for Government contracts in Hong Kong.

* * * * *

Having endured the grim experience of being a POW in Hong Kong and seen at first hand the cruelty to which some of the Japanese descended, I was once asked by Oliver Lindsay, "What are your feelings today about *yesterday's* Japanese?" After some thought I replied in two words: "Very mixed."

As far as *today's* Japanese are concerned, Oliver has seen another side to them. After 35 years as a regular soldier, he worked for six years at the Treloar Trust which looks after 300 very seriously disabled youngsters. Many have severe cerebral palsy, which prevents them having any speech.

A Japanese firm, a household name, visited the charity at Oliver's invitation. After much bowing and inscrutable 'smiles', they departed. Oliver hoped they would pay for several appropriately named 'Liberators', each of which rests on the front of the child's wheelchair, providing synthetic 'speech'. They cost £4,000 each. Without them, the youngsters in question could not communicate.

Oliver heard from the Japanese the following day: they wanted to fund and equip the entire Communication Centre! There was only one condition: the Japanese wanted no publicity – it was the children they wanted to help, not their firm or its reputation.

* * * * *

Our London office has remained in Marylebone. We moved from George Street to Queen Anne Street and then to Devonshire Place in 1963.

In 2000 Jill and I celebrated our golden wedding anniversary with our family and friends; the reception was held on the River Thames on HMS *Belfast*. My life therefore came full circle. HMS *Belfast* was the sister ship of HMS *Euryalus*, the ship on which, within days of my liberation from the prison camp in Hong Kong, I had so enjoyed my first pink gin and the glimpse of *Country Life* once more.

Note

1. The 120-page account of *John R Harris Architects* was published by the Hurtwood Press in 1984.

CHAPTER 24

Retribution

Following Japan's surrender in August 1945, all former members of the Hong Kong Japanese military police (the Kempeitai) were arrested. Colonel Noma who had commanded them was traced to Japan and flown back to Hong Kong. Added to them were some officers of the Japanese 38th Division. They were placed in the cells at Stanley prison, vacated a few weeks earlier by some of our men!

The trials started in Hong Kong in March 1946. All the cases were meticulously investigated. British Army officers represented the accused; four months later a team of Japanese lawyers arrived to defend them, too.

The three most senior officers were tried by the Nationalists in China. Lieutenant General Takashi Sakai, who had been captured in China, had invaded Hong Kong in December 1941 when shocking atrocities were committed against Servicemen and civilians alike. He was found guilty and shot in Nanking.

The two former Hong Kong Governors, Rensuke Isogai and Hisokazu Tanaka, both Lieutenant Generals, had fled to China and Tokyo respectively. Tanaka was shot by a firing squad in Canton. He was heard to grunt defiantly on the eve of his execution, "Let's see who is calling the shots in East Asia in ten years' time." Isogai, who preferred beautiful handwriting to military matters, was given a life sentence for the forced evacuation of the Chinese which led to so many of them dying. He ended up serving only five years.

Colonels Noma and Kanazawa, the two successive chiefs of the military police, had been responsible for many callous murders during interrogations. Much of the testimony against them was provided by Chinese, Eurasians and Indians who had suffered in their cells. Both were hanged along with 19 other high-ranking military police officers.

Two other Japanese who faced the death penalty were Colonel Tokunaga Isao, the overall commander of all Hong Kong's camps, and Saito Shunkichi, the camps' medical officer. Lieutenant Colonel J N Crawford, the senior Canadian medical officer, told the Court during their two months' trial that of 128 Canadian deaths from diphtheria, 101 would have survived if the Japanese had provided the serum.[1] Warrant Officer F W J Lewis said that £30,000 worth of British medicines and surgical instruments were in the Colony when it was captured, but were deliberately withheld. "The death of every man who died of diphtheria because of failure to ensure segregation, or the lack of serum, was directly Saito's responsibility, no less than if he had grasped the man by the throat and choked him to death," declared Major Puddicombe KC for the prosecution.

Major C R Boxer called Lewis's evidence about a beating of Saito "a tissue of lies", while Major S Smith of the Volunteers wrote to the Court about Tokunaga's kindness to him. There is no doubt that Tokunaga stole Red Cross parcels. G White, formerly employed by the Municipal Electricity Company, saw stacks of them when shown over the house by Tokunaga's mistress. "They were given to me by POWs through Major Cecil Boon as an act of affectionate gesture," claimed Tokunaga.

Saito told the Court that there were only three cases of cholera among the POWs due to his efforts, whereas 1,700 Chinese died of it. He blamed the high proportion of Canadian diphtheria deaths on inevitable overcrowding, poor sanitary discipline, Canadians sharing lit cigarettes and the ignorant POW doctors.

In short, they blamed everyone but themselves.

The evidence against them was overwhelming, but their death sentences were commuted to life and 20 years' imprisonment. It is not known if Boxer's evidence enabled them to escape the hangman's noose. "Unlike many former POWs, he did not approach post-war Japan with hostility or with the spirit of revenge," writes his biographer. "He considered that, given the nature of war, he warranted the punishment for disseminating war news in his camp."[2] Laurens van der Post, an ex-POW from Java and since discredited by his biographer, strongly opposed the war crimes trials and refused to testify against his former captors.

Major General Tanaka Kyozaburo received only 20 years' imprisonment although the Court was satisfied that "the whole route of this man's battalion was littered with the corpses of murdered men who had been bayoneted and shot". Lieutenant General Ito received 12 years and Major General Shoji was acquitted. Captain Kyoda Shigeru, who had commanded the *Lisbon Maru,* received seven years. The sentences seem extraordinarily light. The British are not great 'haters'.

By March 1948, when the trials against the Japanese were completed, those facing imprisonment were dispatched to the Sagamo war crimes prison in Tokyo.

By December 1945 over 50 suspected collaborators were charged with specific offences under English law (while the Japanese had been charged with crimes against humanity and the accepted usage of war). Six of them were accused of treason: one was hanged in Stanley Gaol. After the restoration of civil rule on 1st May 1946, 28 Indians, Europeans and Eurasians were found guilty. Five were executed; the remainder received imprisonment with hard labour. Inouye Kanao, the Japanese interpreter at Shamshuipo, a Canadian, was found guilty of treason and hanged.

According to Captain J L Flynn, "after the Japanese surrender it was quite common to see naked, head-shaven women being chased, stoned and beaten by Chinese crowds. Such women were said to have been prostitutes for the Japanese."

About 400 Indian soldiers captured in Hong Kong are believed to have joined the pro-Japanese Indian National Army. Up to 40,000 Indians from all theatres may have done so, many of them in order to obtain better food and conditions than that which the miserable POW camps had to offer. There is strong evidence that their fighting amounted to no more than a token gesture. The Japanese must have found transporting, arming, provisioning and relying on the 40,000 Indians a considerable burden and let-down; their own Japanese forces were increasingly starving when Slim was advancing south of the Irrawaddy upon Rangoon in 1945. "On the way the 1st Division of the Indian National Army was encountered," wrote Field Marshal Viscount Slim. "It surrendered en masse with its commander, 150 officers and more than 3,000 men. They were just in time to begin work on the captured airfields."[3] It can be seen that they were ineffective, as opposed to those French, Dutch, Belgians and others who did fight for the Nazis, largely on the Eastern front.

* * * * *

It came as no surprise to the POWs from Shamshuipo that Major C Boon Royal Army Service Corps faced a general court martial on 11 charges, one of which was assisting the enemy. He had been a staff officer in Fortress Headquarters. Aged 45, he had served in the First World War and had once been a professional ballroom dancing champion. Boon had been in close arrest for 11 months before his trial in London in August 1946. "Boon had never commanded troops in the whole of his career, having always held administrative jobs. The Japs probably spotted him as pliable material because of his subservient attitude and general obsequiousness," noted Major A R Colquhoun.[4] Boon had occasionally attended parties with the Japanese, as he recorded, in Russian, in his diary. "After roll-call had bananas, fruit and roll with Japanese officers... we went to dine with Japanese Commander, plenty of beer."

The Japanese had given him the unenviable job of being in charge of the Other Ranks in Shamshuipo. In 1942 BAAG had addressed a message to him about escapes; fortunately it was intercepted before he received it.

Evidence was given by former POWs that he informed on them and helped the enemy find wireless sets and tunnels for escape. Boon was alleged to have said to other POWs. "We must do as the Japanese tell us. We are officers of the Japanese Army now. I don't regard myself as a British officer, but as part of the Japanese staff. I owe no allegiance to the King." The prosecution called 40 witnesses; there was no ex-POW to give evidence for the defence.

Major Boon was not at his best during the trial and his conviction seemed probable. However it soon became evident that the desperate years of imprisonment had made the witnesses' memories unreliable. Some of their testimony was contradictory; a few broke under formidable cross-examination. "I think," wrote one of the defending counsel, "that it does great credit to the court martial system that after appalling initial prejudice against him, the Major was acquitted." Boon appeared half-stunned by the proceedings and was scarcely able to enjoy the celebrations at the Savoy Grill afterwards. In the absence of legal aid, he had to pay his entire defence costs, a considerable sum.

* * * * *

In conclusion it might be said that the returning British authorities in 1945 "did not launch a policy of vengeance or recrimination... With the passing of the years into the new, more prosperous Hong Kong, the public memory of any shame or humiliation suffered at the hands of the Japanese has faded."[5]

Notes

1. Interview Crawford with OL.
2. Alden, D, *Charles R Boxer: An Uncommon Life*, Lisbon: Fundação Oriente, 2001, p. 29.
3. Slim, FM Viscount, *Defeat into Victory*, London: Cassell, 1961, p. 412.
4. Interview Colquhoun with OL.
5. Endacott, G B, *Hong Kong Eclipse*, Hong Kong: OUP, 1978, p. 250.

CHAPTER 25

"Good and Gallant Leadership"

In the months after the defeat in Hong Kong, Major General C M Maltby was so despondent that he was indifferent to honours and awards being conferred on his Servicemen. Fortunately he changed his mind.

In April 1946 the appropriate recognition was given to the outstanding gallantry of Company Sergeant Major John Robert Osborn of the Winnipeg Grenadiers. On 19th December 1941, having enabled part of his Company to capture Mount Butler at the point of the bayonet and held it for three hours against a much larger number of enemy, he covered his men's withdrawal. Later that afternoon, several grenades were thrown at his Company; he picked them up and threw them back. Suddenly a grenade dropped between him and his men. He rolled on it to protect them and was killed. The citation for the Victoria Cross which was awarded to this most courageous Warrant Officer is best endorsed in the language of a private soldier: "This man sacrificed his life for the boys that might have been crippled or maimed for life. I say he was a real soldier and one of the best I've known." The British named a large barracks in Hong Kong after him. (Although all recent books on the Victoria Cross and Canadian accounts agree that Osborn's action took place on Mount Butler, the precise location is not known.)

Until relatively recently, only the Victoria Cross, the George Cross and a Mention in Despatches have been awarded posthumously. Yet an exception was made in the case of Lieutenant Colonel H W M Stewart whose 1st Battalion The Middlesex Regiment fought so gallantly on the approaches to Victoria and on the peninsula at Stanley. He may best be remembered for his fine leadership on the sinking of the *Lisbon Maru*. Stewart was awarded the Distinguished Service Order, as was Captain (later Major General) C M M Man whose prolonged and heartening defence of Leighton Hill by the 'odds and sods' was so successful. A DSO also went to Major C R Templer who had rolled grenades down the corridors of the Repulse Bay Hotel at approaching Japanese. Two Canadians also won the DSO. They were Majors W A Bishop and E Hodkinson. The former prevented the Japanese breaking through to the Tytam Gap on 18th December 1941, while Hodkinson undertook a daring attack on the 19th; it led to him being seriously wounded.

Padre Uriah Laite, the Regimental Chaplain to the Winnipeg Grenadiers, won the Military Cross when D Company held out for three days until 22nd December. He tended the wounded day and night with no medical backup, as well as giving spiritual and moral comfort. Due to his efforts in interceding with the Japanese, the wounded were not murdered on the spot as elsewhere. Another thoroughly deserved Military Cross went to Captain C Otway Royal Engineers whose gallantry at Lei Mun was remarkable.

Subedar Major Haider R Khan of the 2/14 Punjabis was another proud wearer of the Military Cross. He spent much time in solitary confinement for his adamant loyalty to the Crown.

Three Royal Scots deserve special mention. Captain D Pinkerton, although wounded earlier, stormed through the Wong Nei Chong Gap reaching the objective, the Police Station there, in a frontal assault before being wounded again. 2nd Lieutenant J A Ford, who had earlier held up the Japanese on Golden Hill on the Mainland, carried him back to safety. Both won Military Crosses. There were innumerable Other Ranks who received recognition. Among them was Private J Gallacher who received his Distinguished Conduct Medal from Princess Mary, the Royal Scots Colonel in Chief, in 1944, following his escape from Shamshuipo. Tragically, having survived so much, Pinkerton was killed in action at Port Said in 1956 and Gallacher in Korea in 1951.

The courage of Godfrey Bird, the Royal Engineer who endured the water torture for three weeks in June 1944, was recognised by the award of the George Medal.

A number were appointed Officers of the Most Excellent Order of the British Empire (OBE) including Donald C Bowie, the captive surgeon who ran the British Military Hospital for five years, saving so many lives. Another was the New Zealander, Lieutenant Commander R B Goodwin. He was one of those who smuggled the British Army Aid Group's secret messages into and out of Argyle Street. (John Harris was the first to do so.) Goodwin had been one of the radio operators before he escaped from Hong Kong in July 1944, the only one to get away successfully in the last 22 months of the war. (He wrote two books entitled *Hong Kong Escape* and *Passport to Eternity* in 1953 and 1956 respectively.)

The number of Honours and Awards mentioned above are, literally, only a fraction of the total.

Major Charles Boxer was appointed a Member of the Order of the British Empire (MBE) because of his role in preparing and disseminating news bulletins at the Argyle Street POW Camp and for his conduct during his subsequent imprisonment. Before announcements are made in the *London Gazette*, the Servicemen concerned are not consulted. Boxer responded by asking that the award be cancelled; he said he was merely doing his duty. Moreover, he added that he and others had recommended for honours two members of the Hong Kong Volunteer Defence Corps "who were deeply involved in all underground work in the POW camps... neither of whom have received any official recognition". Boxer announced, "I have neither the wish nor the intention to receive any decoration whatsoever whilst the far greater services of these and others whom I could name have gone unrewarded."

Boxer had a good point: Honours and Awards, particularly in wartime, are strictly limited. A poorly written or mishandled citation, or an act of extreme gallantry witnessed by practically nobody, is unlikely to lead to recognition. Boxer, who died aged 96 in 2000, was not referring to Major H R Forsyth whose "fine leadership, courage and devotion to duty... " led to Brigadier C Wallis writing a citation for a Victoria Cross for this mortally wounded Volunteer who refused to leave his post. Forsyth received nothing. (Oliver Lindsay, however, was able to send a photostat copy of the citation to his son.)

The Military Secretary at the War Office ignored Boxer's plea that others be given honours and told him that "refusing an award which has been approved would constitute an act of grave discourtesy to His Majesty The King". Nevertheless Boxer did not back down: a subsequent edition of the *London Gazette* cancelled the MBE. When asked, an official at St James's Palace was unaware of any other Serviceman who refused an Honour after it had been gazetted.

There is no evidence whatsoever that Boxer helped the Japanese during the war, as has been alleged. He became the leading foreign historian of the Portuguese Empire and of Dutch exploits overseas. In 1984 it was twice suggested to Sir Keith Joseph, the Minister of Education, that Boxer be placed on the New Years Honours List, but this proposal was met with stony silence because of earlier negative responses. A knighthood was also considered appropriate later, but was not pursued.

Paradoxically, while Boxer declined his MBE, it was widely felt that one name *was* missing from the awards. "After the war, when the Hong Kong Despatches came out, I found out that either Maltby or the pundits at the War Office had watered all my recommendations down," remembers Wallis. "But I noticed that Maltby had been given no recognition. I felt that this was a slur on the whole force which had by and large fought with great gallantry, and also I had observed that, as our chief POW, Maltby had stood up well to the Japs." Wallis was unaware that, with Colonel L A Newnham and Captain D Ford, Maltby had played the pivotal role in dealing with the British Army Aid Group's spying organisation. Its vital contribution in smuggling medicines into the POW camps saved many lives and it provided military intelligence of considerable value to the Allies.

"Seeing that Maltby's name was not to be found in the UK awards, I at once contacted all the senior survivors I could reach and I wrote to the War Office to complain," wrote Wallis. "I pointed out forcibly that General Maltby had inherited a hopeless assignment and had done his best." As another survivor of the campaign put it: "Maltby did not have a hope in hell of undoing the lethargy and blindness of the past, nor of trying to remedy and reorganise the Defence Scheme in a few months."

At last the appropriate recognition was given: Major General C M Maltby received the award of the Companion of the Bath, which was not given to many Second World War Generals.

Wallis ended the war in Manchuria and was moved to Manila. He displeased the authorities there by refusing to be flown home, insisting instead that he must return via India as he was determined to see the survivors of his old Battalion, the 5/7 Rajputs, who had fought so bravely in Hong Kong, endeavouring to hold the waterfront against three regiments of Japanese troops. Wallis rejoined them briefly near

Lucknow where he was given a great welcome. He addressed the battalion; a special Guest Night and sports events were held in his honour. Wallis received a Mention in Despatches after returning to England. He later emigrated to Canada and became a prosperous Business Consultant. Oliver Lindsay was able to discuss the campaign with him over two years when they were in Canada together.

Due recognition was also given to those who had played a very different part in the war against Japan.

Lindsay Ride had held the post of Dean of the Medical Faculty in Hong Kong Hospital before the war. He was the first to escape from Shamshuipo after commanding the Volunteer Field Ambulance during the fighting. For over three years, when organising the BAAG, he had endeavoured to maintain Britain's prestige in South China. He was an outstanding person: his subsequent extremely successful career culminated in a knighthood.

With spectacular timing, F C Gimson, the Colonial Secretary, arrived in Hong Kong the day before the Japanese invasion. He laboured far-sightedly throughout the internment at Stanley to form a shadow administration and was able to put it into effect immediately the Japanese surrendered. The British Government recognised that Gimson had done extraordinarily well. He was rewarded with a knighthood and later became Governor of Singapore.

Throughout the Japanese occupation, until his arrest on trumped-up charges, Doctor P S Selwyn-Clarke, the former Director of Medical Services, had been deeply committed to the welfare of Hong Kong's Chinese citizens of all classes, and also to the POWs and internees. He then survived 20 months of intense interrogation in the utmost squalor. Frail and crippled as a result of Japanese tortures, he thought he would never survive. Nevertheless, after the war he re-established medical and health control in the Colony. In 1947 he became Governor of the Seychelles – an unparalleled honour for a doctor and a tribute to his surreptitious relief work. He, too, was knighted. As with the military honours, the number of the names recorded here are only a fraction of those civilians who were recognised for their outstanding endeavours in terrible circumstances.

On 30th April 1946, Sir Mark Young, the first post-war Governor of Hong Kong, returned to the Colony. The King had re-appointed him as he had shown such outstanding leadership during the battle and as a prisoner of war, despite being subjected to every humiliation by the Japanese; during one period he was tending goats. Sir Mark's return to Hong Kong gave great pleasure to many.

One other person received an unexpected reception. He was the Japanese guard Kyoshi Watanabe, who had risked his life smuggling medicines and money to the POWs, doctors and internees. Through him, some POWs were able to keep in touch with their families in Stanley Camp; he was a Lutheran Minister and put Christian charity ahead of his own survival. Tragically, his entire family was killed in Hiroshima. According to several reports, he appeared in the programme *This is Your Life* in London, receiving considerable applause.

Some Chinese in the New Territories and beyond had very bravely helped the POWs and internees who had escaped. They received the appropriate thanks and financial rewards after the war. This applied also to those Chinese who had hidden the three survivors from the *Lisbon Maru* and later taken them to Free China, thereby enabling everyone to know the truth of the terrible atrocity when the Japanese did their best to drown and shoot the POWs.

* * * * *

The military lessons learned in Hong Kong were not lost on the new generations of British, Gurkha and Chinese Servicemen in the Colony. Just as Staff College Camberley students studied the 1944 Normandy battles, so two-day battlefield tours in Hong Kong were occasionally run by Oliver Lindsay until 1995. Colonel A G Hewitt MC MBE, who had escaped from Shamshuipo and died in 2004, was the principal speaker for the Island battle, while J A Ford CB MC was among those who covered the battles for the Mainland and the Wong Nei Chong Gap. John Harris spoke on the smuggling of messages to and from the British Army Aid Group. Gurkhas played the part of the Japanese; they were dressed appropriately and quoted the precise reminiscences of the surviving Japanese regimental commanders who had been brought back to Hong Kong in 1946 to be charged with the atrocities. Thanks to the Commander British Forces in Hong Kong in 1990, Lieutenant General Sir Peter Duffell, steps were cut up to the Shingmun Redoubt for the veterans and their wives; coloured smoke, blank machine-gun fire and charging Gurkhas re-enacted the Japanese attack at the redoubt. The splendid lunch in glorious sunshine which followed was a more gentle affair, with a Regimental band serenading us. The battlefield tours usually finished with a Canadian playing the part of Brigadier Lawson staggering in, riddled with 'gunshot wounds', to tell the spectators that criticism was ludicrous when there was no air cover, inadequate ships, communications, transport, mortars, mobile artillery and so on.

Some of the guest speakers were members of the Argyle Street POW Association, which has met for lunch or dinner in London every year since the war. Major General Maltby regularly attended until his death. Derek Bird, the son of Godfrey Bird GM TD, took over as Chairman of the Association from John Harris TD in 2004. In November 2005 members of the Association and other Hong Kong veterans plan to participate in the Remembrance Day Service and Parade at the Cenotaph in Whitehall for the first time. The High Commissioners of Canada and India have been asked to publicise this participation in the hope that some of their veterans and descendants will join us.

* * * * *

Many of the battles in Hong Kong deserve to be legendary. The gallantry of the Canadians has already been described. Their last desperate charge was at Stanley Peninsula on the orders of a thoroughly controversial, newly promoted Indian Army Brigadier who was totally out of touch with reality, contemplating shooting those Canadian officers who wanted to surrender, complaining about a "bloodless mutiny" and considering blowing up Stanley Fort where the wounded were sheltering! The Canadian Battalions had earlier been considered in Ottawa as "not recommended for operational consideration".

Then there were the two Indian Battalions who fought gallantly; many of them remained loyal, despite horrific conditions in the POW camp and relentless pressure to join anti-British organisations.

The men of the Royal Hong Kong Volunteer Defence Corps deserve special mention. Their motto was 'Second to None'. Their fighting was certainly consistent with such a motto. The truly epic defence of the Volunteers at the North Point power station and their participation in some of the fiercest fighting, particularly at Stanley, reflected their extraordinary gallantry throughout the battle for Hong Kong. The Regiment received 37 decorations. The Corps was created 'Royal' after the war in recognition of its achievements.

The Middlesex Regiment owed their enviable nickname, 'the Diehards', to the encouragement of a former Commanding Officer who lay mortally wounded on the battlefield of Albuhera in 1811, during the Peninsular War. "Die hard, my men, die hard," he was heard to shout. Their courage was such that Wellington exclaimed: "Cockneys make the best Troopers." They lived up to this reputation in Hong Kong.

Finally, we come to The Royal Scots (the Royal Regiment), the First of Foot; the Regiment which enjoys the prestige and privilege of being the oldest and senior British Infantry Regiment of the Line, tracing its unbroken service to the Charter given to it by King Charles I in 1633.

The reputation of the Royal Scots was needlessly maligned by Brigadier C Wallis. On no occasion did he or Major General Maltby ever visit or witness the Battalion in action throughout the entire battle. They relied instead on telephone calls to assess the Battalion's progress. These calls were logged in battle diaries which were then destroyed to prevent the Japanese capturing them.

The two Colours of the Middlesex Regiment, presented by The Prince of Wales in 1930, were hastily and secretly buried in boxes in the grounds of Flagstaff House by Captain I MacGregor, the General's ADC. Exhaustive and unsuccessful efforts were made to find the Colours after the war. It was assumed that ants must have eaten them. The brass parts of the pike and staff were recovered and are now in the Regimental Museum. Field Marshal Sir John Harding presented new Colours to the 1st Battalion in Austria in 1953. They bear the battle honour 'Hong Kong'. The Middlesex amalgamated to form The Queen's Regiment in 1966, which in turn amalgamated in 1992 with The Royal Hampshires to form The Princess of Wales's Royal Regiment. In each case the new Regiment proudly continued to have Hong Kong emblazoned upon its Colours.

In 1940 the Colours of 2nd Battalion the Royal Scots had been sent to the vaults of the Hong Kong and Shanghai Bank in Singapore for safekeeping; they vanished when the Japanese captured the Island. Four years and eight months later, Captain A S Carr Royal Electrical and Mechanical Engineers was "going along a street just behind the waterfront when we were attracted by colourful embroidery", he reported. "We found on closer examination that it was a Regimental Colour. It was lying amongst a pile of old clothing on a wayside vendor's barrow; I bought it for one dollar." The Royal Scots Regimental Colour is now in the Regimental Museum in Edinburgh Castle.

When Princess Mary, the Princess Royal, presented the new Colours to the Battalion in 1948, there was no Battle Honour 'Hong Kong' upon it because the War Office said the Royal Scots did not deserve it. (The Regiment also fought in Burma 1943–1945 for which Battle Honours were received, but that is a different matter.)

There is no doubt that the Royal Scots, however belatedly, deserve the same recognition as the Middlesex Regiment. The Royal Scots had a much higher number of officer casualties than any other unit – no fewer than 27 officers out of 35 were killed or seriously wounded – brave men who really were leading from the front.[1] While virtually no 'outsiders' witnessed the Royal Scots' gallantry when three highly trained Japanese battalions launched their ferocious Mainland attacks upon only them, there were those who saw the repeated assaults, led by Pinkerton and others who tried to clear the Japanese from the Wong Nei Chong Gap, the vital ground. The Japanese battalions on the high ground overlooking the Gap were thrown into confusion, and "suffered heavy losses in a fierce battle with the Royal Scots", according to Colonel Shoji Toshishige.[2]

A campaign should be launched in Scotland to obtain the Battle Honour. True, it is too late for most of the veterans. However, their descendants, the few survivors still alive and the Regiment today, would be well satisfied if this injustice was addressed.

Five days before the last shot was fired in Hong Kong, Winston Churchill had signalled Sir Mark Young on 21st December 1941: "The enemy should be compelled to expend the utmost life and equipment… Every day that you are able to maintain your resistance you and your men can win the lasting honour which we are sure will be your due."[3] He later wrote in his history of the war: "These orders were obeyed in spirit and to the letter… the Colony had fought a good fight. They had won indeed 'the lasting honour'."

"There was," as the Official History has it, "no lack of good and gallant leadership."[4]

That, then, almost brings this account to an end – the final curtain, the ultimate accolade, the end of the book. But not quite.

In April 1946 King George VI approved the posthumous award of no fewer than four George Crosses. It was an unprecedented number

for one small theatre of war. They were in recognition of the most conspicuous gallantry of four men who were tortured most cruelly in Hong Kong's cells for many months.
The recipients were

Colonel Lanceray A Newnham MC	The Middlesex Regiment
Captain Douglas Ford	The Royal Scots
Captain Mateen A Ansari	7th Rajput Regiment
Flight Lieutenant Hector B Gray AFM	Royal Air Force

"I had recommended Gray for the Victoria Cross," recalls Wing Commander H G Sullivan. "The Air Ministry reminded me that this was awarded for bravery in the face of the enemy, to which I replied that many VCs were won in the heat of battle surrounded by one's comrades. Gray, Newnham, Ansari and Ford had deserved theirs in the cold of the torture chamber."

Colonel Newnham had been starved and tortured for five months. In spite of his acute suffering, both physical and mental, he refused to implicate any of his brother officers or connections, thus undoubtedly saving their lives. (Had he named John Harris, this book would never have been written!)

Captain Ford, like Colonel Newnham, had been in touch with the BAAG agents. He received the same treatment. "Throughout his terrible ordeal his behaviour 'was superb'", reads his citation. "He refused to implicate any of the others. He maintained his spirits and those of his fellow prisoners until the end."

Captain Ansari, Indian Army, "steadfastly continued to counteract all traitorous propaganda and resolutely opposed all attempts at undermining the loyalty of his compatriots. In May 1942 he was thrown into Stanley Gaol, where he remained until September 1942, by which time, owing to starvation and brutal ill-treatment which is alleged to have included mutilation, he had become unable to walk." On return to the POW camp, he not only resumed his previous efforts, but also organised a system for aiding escapers, before he was betrayed. Ansari and over 30 other British, Indian and Chinese were executed in horrifying circumstances by beheading on 20th October 1943.

Flight Lieutenant Gray was planning a mass break-out from Shamshuipo and had been much involved in smuggling secret messages and medicines. He was the first officer to be arrested and so bore the brunt of the torture inflicted by the Japanese. "In spite of this, and the fact that he was suffering from illness during the five months of his imprisonment, he steadfastly refused to implicate anyone," reads his citation.

Newnham, Gray and Ford had all been condemned to death on 1st December 1943. Throughout the proceedings, Ford continued to accept full responsibility for everything. They lay for 18 days with no hope of reprieve and the certain knowledge that they would not get even one adequate meal before their deaths; but they never lost their courage.

When the three officers were removed from their cells, neither Newnham nor Gray could walk unaided. Ford half carried them to the waiting truck. "As the junior of the three, he took up his position on the left. The Japanese officer in charge, recognising his gallantry, insisted upon Ford standing on the right," concludes the history of the Royal Scots.[5] Their cold, calculating courage, steadfast behaviour and conduct were beyond all praise.

In October 1946 King George VI approved a fifth posthumous George Cross. The recipient was John A Fraser MC and bar. When questioned by the Japanese about the wireless news received by Stanley Internment Camp he replied, boldly and clearly, his voice ringing resonantly throughout the courtroom, that he alone was responsible and that he had the right to act as he thought fit in the best interests of the British interned in Stanley. His citation which appeared in the *London Gazette* on 25 October 1946 read as follows: "John Alexander Fraser was interned by the Japanese in the Civilian Internment Camp at Stanley. Fully aware of the risks that he ran he engaged continuously in most dangerous activities. He organised escape plans and a clandestine wireless service and succeeded not only in obtaining news from outside but also in getting important information out of the camp. Subjected by the Japanese to prolonged and most severe torture he steadfastly refused to give any information, and was finally executed. His fortitude was such that it was commented upon by the prison guards, and was a very real source of inspiration to others. His magnificent conduct undoubtedly saved the lives of those others whom the Japanese sought to implicate."

Newnham, Ford, Ansari and Gray are all buried close together in the peaceful, beautiful cemetery at Stanley. Royal British Pilgrimages to Hong Kong invariably say prayers among their graves.

The words on the British memorial in Burma to those who lost their lives in the Far East come to mind: "When you go home, tell them of us and say 'for your tomorrow, we gave our today'."

Thousands had fought and died in Hong Kong to restore freedom to mankind. Their name liveth for evermore. Remember them with pride.

Notes

1. The figures are taken from Appendix B to *The London Gazette*, dated 27.1.48.
2. Shoji's statement to Capt. E C Watson in November 1946 (NDHQ).
3. Churchill, W S, *The Grand Alliance*, London: Cassell & Co, 1950, p. 634.
4. Kirby, W S, *The War Against Japan*, Vol. I, London: HM Stationery Office, 1957, p. 150.
5. Paterson, R H, *Pontius Pilate's Bodyguard*, The Royal Scots History Committee, vol. 2, 2000, p. 132.

Bibliography

The detailed source notes at the end of each chapter name the publishers of the books quoted from most frequently and give additional details on other sources.

Adams, G P *Destination Japan,* 1980
Alanbrooke, Field Marshal Lord, *War Diaries,* 2001
Alden, D *Charles R Boxer*, 2001
Allister, W *When Life and Death Held Hands*, 1989

Barrett D F *S.S.* Lisbon Maru, 2004
Bennett, D *18 Days* ,1976
Best, B (ed.) *Secret Letters from the Railway*, 2004
Bosanquet, D *Escape Through China*, 1982
Bowie, D C *Captive Surgeon in Hong Kong,* 1975
Brown, W *Hong Kong Aftermath,*1943
Bush, Lewis *The Road to Inamura,*1961

Cambon, K *Guest of Hirohito,* 1990
Carew, T *The Fall of Hong Kong,* 1960
Churchill, W S *The Second World War* Vols. I to III, 1948-1950
Crew, F A E *The Army Medical Services,* Vol. 2 *Hong Kong*,1957

Dew, G *Prisoner of the Japs*,1943
Douglas, W A B & Greenhous, B *Out of the Shadows*,1977
Duff, L P *Report on the Canadian Expeditionary Force to the Crown Colony of Hong Kong,* 1942

Elphick, P *Far Eastern File: The Intelligence War in the Far East,* 1999
Endecott, G B *Hong Kong Eclipse*. 1978

Field, E *Twilight in Hong Kong,* 1960
Ford, J A *The Brave White Flag*. 1961

Garneau, G S *Royal Rifles of Canada,* 1971
Ghosh, K K *The Indian National Army,* 1969
Goodwin, R B *Hong Kong Escape,* 1953
Goodwin, R B *Passport to Eternity,* 1956
Greenhous, B *'C' Force to Hong Kong: A Canadian Catastrophe 1941-1945,* 1997
Guest, P E *Escape from the Bloodied Sun,* 1956

Hahn, E *China to Me,* 1943
Hamilton, G C *The Sinking of the* Lisbon Maru, 1966
Harrop, P *The Hong Kong Incident*,1945
Hewitt, A *Bridge With Three Men,* 1986
Hewit, A *Corridors of Time*. 1993

Hong Kong Volunteer Defence Corps *Record of the actions of the HKVDC in the battle for Hong Kong,* 1953

James, D H *The Rise and Fall of the Japanese Empire.* 1951

Kawai, T *The God of Japanese Expansion,* 1938
Kemp, P K *The History of the Middlesex Regiment*
Keung, K T & Wordie, J *Ruins of War,* 1996
Kirby, W S *Singapore the Chain of Disaster,* 1971
Kirby, W S *The War Against Japan* Vol. I, 1958

Lindsay, O J M *At the Going Down of the Sun,* 1981
Lindsay, O J M *The Lasting Honour* , 1978
Luff, J *The Hidden Years,* 1967

Manchester, W *American Caesar,* 1978
Marsman, J H *I Escaped from Hong Kong,* 1942
Ministry of Defence (Navy) *War with Japan,* 1995
Montefiore, S Sebag *The Court of the Red Tsar*
Morris, A E J *John R Harris Architects,* 1984
Muir, A *The First of Foot,* 1961

Paterson, R H *Pontius Pilate's Bodyguard,* 2001
Penny, A G *Royal Rifles of Canada,* 1962
Prasad, B *Official History of the Indian Armed Forces in World War II,* 1960
Priestwood, G *Through Japanese Barbed Wire,* 1943
Proulx, B A *Underground from Hong Kong.* 1943

Ride, E *BAAG,* 1981
Rollo, D *The Guns and Gunners of Hong Kong,* 1991
Russell of Liverpool, Lord, *Knights of Bushido,* 1958
Ryan, T F *Jesuits under Fire,* 1951

Selwyn Clarke, Sir S *Footprints.* 1975
Shennan, M *Out in the Midday Sun,* 2004
Snow, P *The Fall of Hong Kong,* 2003
Stacey, C P *Official History of the Canadian Army in the Second World War* Vol. I, *Six Years of War,* 1957

Starling, P H *Army Medical Services in Hong Kong,* 1994

Thorne, C *Allies of a Kind,* 1978

Vincent, C *No Reason Why,* 1981

Wiseman, E P *Hong Kong,* 2001
Wright, R J *I Was a Hell Camp Prisoner,* 1963

Young, A N *China and the Helping Hand 1937-1945,* 1963

* * * * *

The poem at the beginning of Part 3 is from *The Memory of the Dead* by John Kells Ingram (from page 277 of *An Eton Poetry Book* published by Macmillan, 1938

Despatches

1 Despatch by Air Chief Marshal Sir Robert Brooke-Popham, Commander-in-Chief in the Far East, on Operations in the Far East from 17 Oct. 1940-27 Dec. 1941. (Published in the supplement to the *London Gazette*, 20 Jan. 1948.)
2 Despatch by Major General C M Maltby, GOC British Troops in China, on Operations in Hong Kong from 8 to 25 Dec. 1941. (Published in the supplement to the *London Gazette*, 27 Jan. 1948.)

War Diaries

1st HK Regiment Hong Kong Singapore Royal Artillery (HKSRA) *Chief Signal Officer, China Command* (1941) compiled by Lt Col. M E F Truscott.

East Infantry Brigade in the Defence and Fall of Hong Kong (133 pages). Compiled in Argyle Street POW Camp between 1 June 1942 and 15 Aug. 1942 taking account of war diaries of 1 HK Regt HKSRA East Group RA; B and D Coys 1 Mx; 5/7 Rajput; No. 1, 2 Coys HKVDC. The other war diaries had probably been destroyed or not written.

Mainland Infantry Brigade and Attached Troops (90 pages). Compiled as above.

Preliminary Summary compiled in 1942, based on Fortress HQ messages to and from Brigade HQs and units.

Reports and Notes (in author's possession)

1945 Report on Indian POWs HKSRA (29 pages) unsigned
Australian War Crimes Commission Questionnaires compiled by some POWs
Building Reconstruction. Appointed by C.-in-C. HK 1946.
Christmas Day 1941 at Stanley by J A Lomax
Conditions in Hong Kong of POWs by Lt Col. R J E Cadogan-Rawlinson
Far Eastern POW Bulletin August 1945
Hong Kong 1941 by Rex Young
Hong Kong 1941–1945 by Mrs G Man
My Time as a POW by the Bishop of Mashonoland
Officers' POW Camp Argyle Street by Captain G V Bird RE
Original Notes (184 pages) largely concerning debriefing RN and RNVR in POW camps. Compiled 1942–1945
POWs: New Zealand in the Second World War by W W Mason
Recollections by C B J Stewart
Record of Service by Surgeon Lieutenant C A Jackson
Reminiscences by H F Linge
Report on Fraternisation with Japanese by M C Tugby
Reports of General MacArthur in Japan Vol. I Supplement

Selected Articles

Adams, I Macleans, Jul. 1968
Bowie, D C 'Captive Surgeon in Hong Kong', *Journal of the Hong Kong Branch of the Royal Asiatic Society*, Mar. 1977, Vol. 15
Burd, F 'Canloan', *The Guards Magazine*, 1996
Canadian Veterans News Magazine, Spring 1977
Crawford, J N *The Canadian Medical Association*, 1947
Crawford, J N *Manitoba Medical Review*, Feb. 1946
Dobbs, K *Star Weekly*, Aug. 1965
Hong Kong Volunteer Defence Corps – various articles
Journal of Imperial and Commonwealth History, Oct. 1973, Vol. I
Morrison, W K 'Malaria in Hong Kong', *Journal Royal Army Medical Corps*, Vol. 114, No. 4, 1968
Muir, A *The Scotsman*, 14 Nov. 1960
Penfold, R J L 'The Defence of Hong Kong', *The Gunner*, Dec. 1946
Penny, A G *A Short History of the Royal Rifles of Canada*
Pinkerton, D *The Thistle*, Oct. 1946, Jan. 1947
Stacey, C P 'The Defence of Hong Kong', *Canadian Army Journal*, Dec. 1950

Diaries

Author	**Location**
Anslow, B C (née Redwood)	Imperial War Museum
Fenn, C H	author's possession
Joyce, D	Imperial War Museum
Lawson, J K	Wolsey Barracks, London, Ontario
Levett, E	Royal and Gurkha Signals Squadron
McEwan, M C	author's possession
Newnham, L A	Imperial War Museum
Newton, L	Imperial War Museum
Otway, C E	author's possession
Redwood, M	Imperial War Museum
Skelton, S	National Defence Headquarters, Ottawa
Strachan, T	author's possession
Templer, C R	author's possession

Files

1.The principal documents at the National Archives, Ruskin Row, Kew are:

Admiralty (ADM)	199 series	Colonial Office (CO)	129,519,980 series
Foreign Office (FO)	916 series	War Office (WO)	203,208,3260 series

2.Numerous relevant files are in National Defence Headquarters, Ottawa. Some are also in Hong Kong, Washington and Tokyo.

Websites

1.National Archives, Kew (formerly Public Record Office)
www.nationalarchives.gov.uk (Telephone 020 8392 5202)

2.Imperial War Museum
www.iwm.org.uk (Telephone 020 16 5320)

3.National Army Museum, Chelsea
www.national-army-museum.ac.uk (Telephone 020 7881 2455)

The Confusion of Events

Colonel C P Stacey, Canada's most distinguished military historian, stated in his memoirs that Hong Kong gave him "the most difficult problem I had ever encountered." One of his military researchers wrote "From whatever sources they come, reports all emphasise the confusion of events." Battles throughout the Second World War, and in Hong Kong in particular in 1941, often descend into "Chaotic affairs… " As Brereton Greenhous puts it "Throughout these various historical minefields, the hopeful chronicler can only step with caution." In short, the most thoroughly researched accounts often contradict each other despite authors' best efforts. Almost 65 years later, precisely what happened in some events in Hong Kong may never be established or agreed upon.

Index

Abadan 238
Abyssinia 22
Afghanistan 18
Alabaster, C G 222
Alanbrooke, Field Marshal Lord 6, 9, 22, 39, 62, 64, 136,143
Albright, M 237
Ali, Sheikh 236
Alsey, A J 207
American Air Force 181,188, 194, 204, 215, 216, 220, 223
American Ambulance Service 235
American Pacific Fleet 3, 70, 87, 214, 227
Anderson, W J 206
Ansari, M A 197, 205-206, 258
appeasement 18, 21, 23, 53, 64
Architectural Association 236
Architectural Association School 235
Argyle Street POW Camp 13, 160-224, 255
'armchair critics' 51, 112
Arundell, D 25, 29, 37, 38, 65, 158
Ashidate 199
Atkinson, R A 212
Attlee, C 223
atom bombs 188, 215, 223, 226
Australia 7, 25, 31-32, 92, 148, 178, 184, 186, 211, 219
Austria 19, 21
Awatea 41, 89

Banfill, S M 230
Bardell, N 208
Barnett, K M A 179
Bath Abbey 226
Bartholomew, Major General A W 49, 52
Battle Honours controversy 67, 83, 146, 151-152, 257
Battle of Britain 27
Beevor, A 133
Belfast, HMS 242
Belgium 26, 93, 245
Belgrano 148
Bennett, H T 57-58, 166
Bennett, Padre 163
Berlin 127
Bird, D 255
Bird, G V 189-190, 195-196, 209, 212-214, 250, 255
Birkett, S A 105
Bishop, W A 111, 250
Blair, Prime Minister Tony 58
'bloodless mutiny' 138, 255
Blunt, A 222
bolt, used for passing messages 193
Bond, Corporal 193
Boon, C, trial of 241, 246
Boorman, Major General D 52-53
Borneo 4
Bosanquet, D I 167-169
Bowen Road Hospital 141, 172-176
Bowie, D C 176, 250
Boxer, C R 8, 56-58, 63-66, 86, 122, 145, 172, 175, 196-199, 206-207, 225, 244, 251-252
British Ambassador's staff in Tokyo 56-58
British Army Aid Group 199-213, 220, 231, 246, 252-253, 258
British Army of the Rhine 51
British Expeditionary Force 24, 25-27, 70
British military weakness 6, 18, 22
British spying in Hong Kong 203-204
broadcasts made by POWs 212
Brooke, General Sir A *see* Alanbrooke
Brooke-Popham, Air Chief Marshal Sir R 40-41, 60, 71, 83
Brown, W 101
Browne, H W 29
Brunei 239
Burd, F 66
Burma 7, 83, 85, 245, 257, 260
Bush, H 123
Bush, President 58

Cambon, K 42
Campbell, K J 113
Canada 73, 175, 180, 228-231, 255
Canadian contribution to victory in Europe 62
Canadian Forces 7, 25, 41, 51, 55, 62, 69, 85-187, 230
  brief before they departed 61
  lack of training 51, 89-93,100, 112, 152
  reputation maligned 67, 150-152, 255
Carr, A S 256

Carroll, D 28
Castro, S 209
casualties, overall 159
  Canadian 102
  Japanese 87, 100, 151, 159
  Royal Scots 83, 257
Ceramic 32
Ceylon 63, 85
Challoner, R H 141
Chamberlain, N 22
Chan Chak 164
Chan, H 202
Chaplin, C 22
Chennault, C L 181
Cheung 202
Chiang Kai-shek, Generalissimo 48, 54-55, 87, 197, 202, 223
China 25, 41, 48, 86, 193, 202, 220-223, 240, 254
China's contribution in Second World War 203
Chinese involvement in smuggling secret information 189-199
Chinese Servicemen 51, 82, 87-89, 107, 254
Chow, Sir S 222
Churchill, Sir Winston 6, 7, 15, 17, 23, 31, 55, 69, 85-87, 124, 152, 257
CIA 151, 214
Cicala, HMS 77
Clague, Sir Douglas 167-169, 202-204
Clark, M 15
Clarkson, W 65
Clifford, E H 157
Coldstream Guards 16
collaboration 222, 234, 245
Colours, lost in Far East 256
Colquhoun, A R 208, 231-232, 246
Colvin, R B R 139
communications in Hong Kong 79, 127, 132
conscription in Hong Kong 69
Cooper, A D 7
Cooper, Lady Diana 7
Corrigan, L 208
Country Life 216, 242
Craigie, Sir Robert 56
Craven, D H S 197-199, 206, 225
Crawford, J N 165, 244
Crerar, Major General H D G 54, 62
Crewe, Q 28
Cripps, Sir Stafford 64
Crossley, D 165
Cuthbertson, H 185
Czechoslovakia 21-22

D'Almada, C 191
Dawson, G 21
decapitation of internees 206
Deloughery, F J 100
Dennys, L E 197
Detroit News 85
Dew, G 85, 97
Dill, Field Marshal Sir John 64
diphtheria in POW camps 13, 175-177, 180, 244
discipline in POW camps 161-162
Dixon, H C 197-199, 206, 225
Doha 13, 236-237
Doi Teihichi 9, 72-83, 99, 102-132
Dorchester Hotel 239
Dubai 237-238
Duff, Sir Lyman 58
Duffell, Lieutenant General Sir Peter 51-53, 254
Duke of York's HQ 19
Dutch East Indies 4, 48, 85, 203

East Brigade HQ 88, 95, 112
Eden, A 26
Edward, Prince of Wales 22
Egal, R 179
Egle, E 178-180
Eguchi 221
Elizabeth II, Queen 229, 237-238
Empress of Asia 40
Empress of Australia 29, 227, 230
escape controversy 163-169, 174, 194-195, 203, 207, 251
Esquimault 228, 231
Eton College 27, 63, 209
Eucliffe, massacre at 120
Euryalus, HMS 216, 242
Evans, A J W 186

Fairclough, C H 160
Falklands War 93-94, 148
Fallace, J C 186
Fanshawe, D V 51, 112
Ferguson, G P 191
Field, F D 212-214
Fifth Columnists 63, 96, 105, 115
First World War 14, 27
Flynn, J R 181, 191-195, 204, 207, 211, 233, 245
Ford, D 79, 113, 193, 196-199, 252, 258-260
Ford, J A 78-83, 95, 114, 250, 254
Formosa 177, 224
Forsyth, H R 140, 150, 251
Foulkes, Lieutenant General C 92
France 22, 24, 30, 93, 245
Fraser, J A 205, 222, 259-260
Frederick, E C 118
Freedom of Information Act 147
French Indo China 8, 47, 214
Fujihara 213
Fujimoto 205-206

Gallacher, J 166, 250
Garneau, G 120
Geneva Convention 168, 173
Genichiro, N 177
George Crosses 257-260
George VI, King 18, 175, 246, 251, 257, 259
German POW camps in UK 194
German-Soviet Pact 22
Germany 6, 19, 168, 187, 194
Gibraltar 31, 148
Giffard, Sir S 57
Gimson, F C 218-220, 253
Gin Drinkers' Line 7, 47, 52, 56, 59, 71-83
Gloucester, Duke of 239
Goodwin, R B 168, 191, 193, 251
Gordon, V R 114
Gort, Field Marshal Lord, VC 25
Grayburn, Sir V 205
Grafton, Duke of 231
Granelli 221
Grassett, Major General A E 39, 54-55
Gray, H B 166, 193, 196, 199, 258-260
Greater East Asia Co-prosperity Sphere 207, 222
Greenhous, B 62, 73, 108, 148, 151, 230
Grenadier Guards 50, 139, 147
Gresham, A B 105
Grew, J C 4
Grey, G E 6, 68-71, 191-193
Gross, D C E 36
Guards Armoured Division 93
Guernsey 222
Guest, F 122
Gurkhas 254

Haddock, J R 191, 195
Hahn, E 8, 57, 172, 175
Hall, W A 106
Hamlon, CSM 120
Happy Valley racecourse 3, 8, 96, 222
Harcourt, C H J 216, 220
Harding, Field Marshal Sir John 256
Hardy, R J 193, 196, 199
Harland, H 143
Harriman, A 6, 69
Harris, A 14, 26, 27, 39, 157, 229, 236
Harris, F 14, 27, 229
Harris, Jill 13, 235-236, 240-241
Harris J R
  youth 13-19
  as an architect 13, 16, 18, 233-240
  joins TA 19, 23
  illness 15, 32, 175-177, 230, 235
  in Hong Kong 35-42, 65, 68, 102, 115-119, 122-123, 225-232
  as POW 157-224, 258
  smuggling secret information 189-194, 251, 254
Harris, M 18, 240
Harris, R 235
Harrison, G C F 176
Harrow School 15-18, 27, 209
Harth, C 222
Harvard University 240
Heath, Sir L 224
Hennesey, F 166
Hewitt, A G 39, 42, 71, 165, 202, 254
Hill, D S 191
Hindenburg, President, von 17
Hirohito, Emperor 4, 6, 220, 226
Hisokazu, T 242
Hitler, A 17, 18, 22, 48, 85, 127
Hodges, D 166
Hodkinson, E 250
Holland 4, 26, 217, 245
Holliday, M 25, 29, 36, 37, 158
Home Guard 26
Home, W J 89, 127-143, 196
Hong Kong and Shanghai Bank 205, 256
Hong Kong Club 36
Hong Kong defence plans 3, 49, 50, 52, 54-56, 59-70, 88
Hong Kong Hotel 205
Hong Kong, negotiations for handover in 1997 52
Hong Kong News 214-215
Hong Kong, reasons for defeat 68, 75-76, 82, 87, 137
Hong Kong reinforcements 50, 54-55, 61
Hong Kong, relative strengths 59, 68, 70, 99
Hong Kong reservoirs 35, 124, 137
Hong Kong, threat facing Colony 40, 47, 52, 54
Hong Kong Volunteer Defence Corps 7, 36, 69, 80, 88-143, 150, 164, 167, 179, 234, 251, 255
Hong Kong's importance 48, 50, 53
honours and awards 150, 196-197, 245-260
Howell, W M 185
Hughesiliers 106, 113, 255
Hull, C 62
Hunter, T D 178
Hurd, B A 233
Hurd, E L 208
Hyland, Lieutenant 182

Ile de France 229-231
Imperial Defence College 54
Implacable, HMS 231
Indian collaboration 234, 245
Indian Medical Service 202
Indian POWs 191, 204, 216, 233-234

Indian Servicemen 25, 51, 88-138, 255
Indians involved in smuggling secret information 191-193
Inouye Kanao 177
Intelligence (British) 26, 41, 47, 54, 56-58, 66, 203-204
Inukai 57
IRA 148
Iran 238
Iraq 18, 51, 58, 60, 94, 221, 238
Italy 30, 194
Ito 245

Japanese Air Force 9, 41, 95, 97, 130
Japanese atrocities 41, 120, 131, 142, 164-165, 185-187, 198, 221, 243-247
Japanese generosity 166, 241
Japanese Intelligence 47-50, 69
Japanese Navy 3, 6, 64, 77
Japanese occupation of Hong Kong 220-223
Japanese Regiments 9, 99
Japanese threat 6, 54-55, 87, 99
Japanese war preparations 4, 49
Jardine Matheson 107
Jews, persecution of 21, 222
Jockey Club 96, 107
Johnstone, W C 186
Jones, C R 74-75
Jones, M 148
Joseph, Sir K 252

Kadowake 220
Kai Tak Airport 36, 56, 68, 79, 197
Kanazawa 243
Katayama 177
Kendall, F W 74
Kennedy, J N 136, 143
Kenya 40
Kershaw, I 18, 19
Keung, Sir R K 222
Khan, R 192, 250
Kidd, G R 113
Kimura 108
King's Regiment 50
King's School Canterbury 38
Kissinger, H A 53
Kiszely, Lieutenant General Sir John 94
Korea 225, 234, 250
Kozi 205
Kuala Lumpur 239
Kure 184
Kuwait 18, 236, 238
Kyoda Shigeru 185, 245

Laird 75
Laite, U 123-124, 250
Lamb, R G 107, 142
Lamble, R 176
Lan, J 213
'Lasting Honour' 257
Lawson, Brigadier J K 60, 89-95, 97, 100, 105-108, 123, 255
Lee, C R 85
letters sent by POWs 212
Lewis, F W J 244
Liddell, I, VC 16
Lincolnshire Regiment 8, 56
Linge, H F 188, 231
Lisbon Maru 13, 183-187, 204, 245, 250, 254
Lomax, J A 191
Lyndon, C A 108

M19 202
MacArthur, General D 3, 4, 7, 70, 219
Macauley, T G 128-130
MacDonald, Mrs 85
MacDonell, G S 141
McDouall, J C 191
McDougall, D J 82
MacGregor, I 7, 59, 96, 135, 256
MacGregor, Sir A 218
McGregor, R R 184
MacKenzie, A K 114
Macmillan, H (*later* Lord Stockton) 147
MacMillan, P 96
Macpherson, R A P 119
Macao 3, 48, 184
Malaya 4, 29, 48, 55, 67, 85-87, 93, 143, 166, 203, 224, 234
Maltby, Major General C M 7, 56-64, 71, 87, 104, 111-138, 148-149, 162-169, 191-198, 224, 233, 245, 252, 255-256
  character 59, 173, 224
Malzuno 48
Man, C M M 94, 125, 137, 151, 250
Man, Topsy 125, 217
Manchester, R 108
Manchester, W 9
Manchuria 225, 226, 252
Manners, C M 137
Marshall, General G 6
Marsman, J H 42, 43, 130
Mary, Princess 250, 257
Masaichi Mimi, Admiral 97
Masanobu Tsuji 67
mass escape plans 167, 194-195
Massy Beresford, T 225-226
Matsuda 196
Mau Tau Chung POW Camp 171, 191, 197
Merthyr, Lord 30, 32, 209-210
Middlesex Regiment 149, 151, 256, 258
  1st Battalion 3, 7, 39, 59, 88-140, 183-187, 245

Military Language Officers in Japan 56-57
Millar, H A W 178
Ministry of Defence, clearance of articles 146-147
Missouri, USS 231
Mizuno 86
Montevideo Maru 184
Montgomery, Field Marshal Viscount 67, 145
Moore, Flying Officer 166
Morgan, B 158
Mosey, Miss 131
Mosley, L 22
Muir, A 120, 147
Munro, J H 166
Muscat 239
music in POW camps 163, 208
Mussolini, B 18, 21

NAAFI 101
NATO 17
Naylor, Major General D M 94
Newnham, L A 122, 128, 148-149, 162-168, 173, 189-199, 214, 252, 258-260
Newton, H R 74-76
Newton, I 81
Neve, G E 122
New Zealand 25, 31, 148, 165, 197
Noma 242
Northcote, Sir Geoffrey 63
Northern Ireland 51
North Point POW Camp 161, 168, 179
North, R A C 222
nurses in Hong Kong 40, 95, 115, 125, 131, 140, 158, 173, 178, 205

Okada Yoshimasa 48, 108
Oman 238-239
'Open City' scenario for Hong Kong 49, 52-53, 222
Osama bin Laden 18
Osborn, J R 106, 245
Othsu 86
Otway, C 162, 250
Oxfordshire 227, 230
Oyadomani 77

Parachute Regiment 94
Pardoe, T M 122
Parsons, W W 36, 118
Paterson, J J 107
Pearce, J L C 167
Pearce, Tam 107
Pearl Harbor 3, 69-70, 85, 87, 228
Peffers, A 121
Peninsula Hotel 3, 8, 39, 49, 65, 215, 224
People's Liberation Army 50-53
Percival, Lieutenant General A E 87, 224
Philippines 4, 70, 214
Phillips, Admiral Sir Tom 4, 86
Pinkerton, D 78-83, 113-114, 250, 257
Poland 22
Porter, J 174
Portugal 69, 215, 219, 252
Potter, Lieutenant 185
Potts, A H 119
POWs in Japan 187-188
Prasad, H 191
Prasad, K 233
President Coolidge 40
Price, J N 138, 193, 196-198
Priestwood, G 101
Prince of Wales, HMS 4, 86
Prince Robert, HMCS 230
Princess of Wales's Royal Regiment 256
Prior, J T 142
Proes, G E S 117
Prophet, D L 193
prostitutes 49, 95, 211, 216, 245
Proulx, B A 181
Puddicombe, Major 244
Pugsley, W J 106
Punjabis, 2/14 6, 7, 59, 68, 88-138, 171, 255

Qaboos bin Said, HM Sultan 239
QAs 29, 32
Qatar 13, 236
Queen magazine 21
Queen Mary Hospital 68
Queen's Regiment 256
Quetta 24, 59

Rajputs, 5/7 7, 59, 74, 80-83, 88-138, 171, 252, 255, 258
Rashid bin Saeed Al-Maktoum, HH Sheikh 237-238
Rashid Hospital 237
Rawlinson, R C 82
Red Cross 40, 166, 175, 178-180, 212
Red Cross parcels 181, 225, 244
Redman, J 191
Redwood, M 43, 95
Reeve, Brigadier 82
Regimental Histories 146-148
rehabilitation, lack of 232, 234
relative strength 93, 203
religious influence 100, 163, 219, 222
Rensuke Isogai 223, 243
repatriation 219, 228-229, 234
Repulse Bay Hotel 39, 88, 122, 128-141
Repulse, HMS 4, 86
Richardson, F S 79
Ride, Sir Lindsay 164-165, 171, 197, 203, 253

Ridge, battle for 118-120
Rifle Brigade 63
Robb 75
Rollo, D 120
Rommel, Field Marshal 87
Roosevelt, President F D 6, 47
Rose, H B 123-124
Rose, W R T 79
Rossini, F 231
Royal Air Force 6, 22, 40, 68, 81, 86, 88, 166, 216, 258
Royal Army Dental Corps 176
Royal Army Medical Corps 176
Royal Army Ordnance Corps 188, 231
Royal Army Service Corps 38, 118, 145
Royal Artillery (*and* the Hong Kong and Singapore RA) 36, 74, 100, 112, 116-117
  arcs of fire 31, 36
  mentioned 29, 30, 77, 80, 96, 101, 140, 159-160, 163, 167, 183-187, 208, 212, 232
Royal British Legion 102, 220, 259
Royal Engineers 19, 23-42, 54, 68, 80, 107, 117, 124, 158, 168, 250
Royal Hampshire Regiment 256
Royal Horse Guards 60
Royal Marines 94, 124
Royal Navy (*including* HKRNVR) 30-31, 65, 68, 77-83, 88, 100, 117, 119, 164-165, 183-187, 214, 227, 233
Royal Rifles of Canada 42, 65, 88-143, 152
  demands to surrender 131-133, 138, 151, 255
Royal Scots 7, 59-83, 88-138, 166, 178, 183-187, 250, 256, 258
  reputation maligned 83, 150-151, 256
  should have Battle Honour of Hong Kong 152, 257
Royal Scots Regimental History 147
Royal Signals 127
Russia 6, 25, 64, 127
Rutledge, R J 196, 199

sacking senior officers in battle 133, 138-139
Saddam Hussein 18, 152
Said bin Taimur, HM Sultan 238
Sainfoin, HMS 233
St John's Cathedral 64
St Stephen's College 140, 218
St Swithuns 32
St Theresa Hospital 178
Saito Shunkichi 175, 244
Sakai 85-88, 97-99, 243
Sakata Seisho 48
Sandhurst, Royal Military College 56, 191
Sano, Major General 99
Scandinavia 236
Scots Guards 93-94
Scott, M I E 94
Scriven, D 165, 202
Sedana 30
Sejima Ryuzo 47
Selwyn-Clarke, P S 175, 176, 184, 219, 222, 253
Shamshuipo Barracks 7, 39, 42, 68, 234
Shamshuipo POW Camp 13, 56, 160-224
Shanghai 50, 186, 224
Sherwood Foresters 60
Shields, A L 137
Shingmun Redoubt, battle for 47, 61-76
Shirer, W L 28
Shoji Toshishige 99-132, 245
Siam 6, 48
Silesian Mission murders 131
Simpson, T S 213-214
Sing Pan Islands 186
Singapore 4, 6, 25, 30-31, 40, 47, 48, 58, 171, 253, 256
  battle for 70, 224
Skelton, S 101-102
Slater-Brown, A M S 114
slave labour in Japan 187
Slim, Field Marshal Viscount 214, 245
Smith, S 244
Soden, E J 186-187
Somerville, Admiral of the Fleet Sir James 30
South China Athletic Club 3
South China Morning Post 71, 136
Special Air Service 148
Speight, Private 185
spies in UK 194
Staff College, Camberley 54, 254
Stalin, Generalissimo 64
Stanley Fort, plan to blow up 142, 255
Stanley Internment Camp 49, 175, 177, 186, 197, 204-206, 216-220
Stanley Prison 174, 198, 258
Stewart, C B J 159
Stewart, H W M 138, 165, 183-187, 245
Strangeways Prison 239
Strellet, Captain 119
Sudetenland 21
Sullivan, Wing Commander H G 6, 166, 258
surrender discussion 86, 97, 132, 136-138, 223
Sutcliffe, J L R 92, 108, 121, 131, 172-173
Suzuki 49
Swetland, S 208
Swiftsure, HMS 216

Takliwa, SS 233
Tala, Colonel 86
Talbot, Dr 204
Tamworth, I 191

Tanaka, K 99-132, 244
Tanaka Hitoshi 182
Taylor, A J 183, 185
Templer, C R 128-130, 250
Territorial Army 93
terrorism 18
Thailand *see* Siam
The Times 21, 42, 179
Thomas, O 131
Thomson, J S R 74
Thracian, HMS 88, 122
Tokunaga, I 172, 174, 177, 212, 244
torture of POWs 213-214, 258
Tosaka 48, 100
training soldiers for war 51
traitors in POW camp 182
Trapman, J 209
treason trials 245
Treloar Trust 241
Trevor, I B 166
Triads 47, 48
trials of Japanese 243-245
Truman, President H S 223
Tuen Mun Hospital, Hong Kong 240-241

United States of America 17, 19, 48, 53, 70, 214, 217-219, 225, 227
USS *Grouper* 184
USS *Sturgeon* 184

V1s, V2s 235
Valentine, R K 193
Valtorta, Bishop 222
van der Post, L 244
Viceroy of India 27-32, 38
Victoria Cross 16, 150, 245, 251, 258
Vincent, C 150-151
Volunteers *see* Hong Kong Volunteer Defence Corps

Wada 184
Wainwright, S J M 224
Wakefield, J 65
Waller, J 224, 232-233
Wallis, Brigadier C 60, 72-83, 105-143, 149, 152, 161, 172-173, 182, 192, 205, 224, 251-252, 255-256
considers shooting Canadians 138, 150, 255
War Diaries 149
Wards, G T 58
Watanabe, K 215, 254
Wavell, Field Marshal Earl 31
Weedon, Captain 132, 140
Wellington College 27, 56
Welsh Guards 93
West Brigade HQ 89, 95, 112
West, Captain 158
White, G 181, 207
White, H L 215
White, L S 167
White, S E H E 72-83, 114, 215
Wilcox, L C 74-75
Wilson, B 42
Wilson, G S 65
Wilson, T B 8
Winchester College 209
Winnipeg Grenadiers 65, 71-73, 79-83, 88-138, 147, 168, 245
Winspear, J 231-232
Wiseman, E P 38, 42, 145, 172
wives, evacuated from Hong Kong 7, 40
Wong Nei Chong Gap, battle for 88, 95
Wordie, J 169
Wright, R J 158, 161
Wyllie 74, 147

Yamamoto, Admiral I 3
Young, C A 119, 129
Young, Sir M 3, 7, 63-65, 85-86, 131, 135, 143, 162, 217, 224, 233, 253, 257
Young, R S 39, 95, 197-199, 206, 225, 232
Yugoslavia 17

Z Force 74
Zau, S 8, 175
Zempei Masushima 94, 97
Zindel, R 178-180